Interpersonal Skills and Health Professional Issues

Cynthia H. Adams, Ph.D.
Associate Professor
School of Allied Health Professions
University of Connecticut
Storrs, CT 06268

Peter D. Jones, M.D.
Internist in Private Practice
Willimantic, CT 06226

Glencoe Publishing Company

Send all inquiries to:
Glencoe Publishing Company
15319 Chatsworth Street
Mission Hills, California 91345

Printed in the United States of America
ISBN 0-02-685482-1

1 2 3 4 5   92 91 90 89 88

Design by Carol Tornatore
Cover photo by Grant Heilman Photography
Charcoal Drawings by Elizabeth Purcell
Cartoons by Llyn Hunter

Foreword

As health care becomes more technically advanced, it also requires greater communication skills. This book is designed to enhance the ability of health care students to be **helping** professionals. It is a book about communications, contemporary concerns, the health care delivery system, professionalism, and basic interpersonal skills. No longer can health professionals rely upon their scientific and technical knowledge and skills to meet the needs of their patients/clients, but rather they must communicate with them and include them in their plan of care. Helping means providing an environment in which the client is comfortable, understands the problem, and participates actively in getting and staying well.

Today's health care provider must focus on helping relationships. Such relationships are characterized by mutuality; each person contributes to the process while maintaining the appropriate professional association. This type of helping should be reliable and valid based upon a thorough understanding of the factors that influence the health care delivery system and the skills necessary for competent practice within that system.

This book assumes that the reader has been introduced to the health care system and psychological theory. However, an indepth knowledge of personality theory, developmental psychology, and sociology is not necessary to use the text profitably. Additional knowledge of the health care system is not necessary for the reader to benefit from this text. The text is rooted in theory yet written from a practical orientation.

Discussion of the topic, examples where appropriate, and summary questions in each chapter allow the book to be used either for independent study or classroom instruction. The subjects are appropriate for all health occupation and allied health students at all stages; community college students through graduate education and practicing professionals. While there is an overall coherence to the text, individual topics can be considered according to the interests or needs of the reader.

This book has been written for those who need to learn about and practice those skills required for the helping process. Helping is an art and like other arts it is improved by performance. The fundamental communications and interpersonal skills contained here are essential to that performance.

As health care moves from the acute care setting to multiple community environments, from an illness to a wellness focus, and from a hierarchial to a cooperative interactive process, the health care provider faces greater challenges than ever before. The knowledge of, and abilities in, a specific health discipline will no longer be sufficient in and of themselves. The skills taught and issues raised in this text will aid the helper in furthering competence as a health professional.

Glenda D. Price, Ph.D.
Dean, School of Allied Health Sciences
University of Connecticut

Preface

There is a need for a text such as this one. It introduces the health care student to the need to build skills for interpersonal relations/communications and it addresses some of the most demanding issues in health care today. Issues such as ethics, funding of care, and prevention or wellness programs must be thought about, discussed, and analyzed by current and future practitioners. Our leaders of tomorrow must be taught how to communicate better. They must be taught to explore difficult issues. Only then can we as educators and health professionals have faith that we have done right by them and by society.

The health care arena is complex and enormous. Traditional health care delivery patterns and roles of health care providers are rapidly evolving. Ethical issues such as those surrounding a definition of death and those of surrogate motherhood frequently grab our attention and tear at our hearts. As we write, the nation is faced with a crisis due to the shortage of certain key health care providers, most critically, nurses. Some describe this crisis as one of financial compensation. Others believe the problem is more complex and will only be resolved through changes in communication channels and institutional management structures.

No text written at a given time will be able to provide answers for generations of health care workers to depend upon. But this text offers the foundation materials for exploring problems, examining issues, and delving into true human understanding. When we value ourselves, our patients, and our co-workers, we can appropriately use the skills described in this text to ease and perhaps to solve many of the problems of health care. As part of this, we must look squarely at the critical and dynamic issues facing our nation and, indeed, our planet.

Chapters one, two, and three look at how we observe and listen to others, how we can focus our energies to receive and send accurate messages, and various theories that serve as a foundation for human understanding.

Specific issues dealing with grief and loss, understanding human developmental milestones, and the impact of addictions are dealt with in the following three chapters. Here the reader gains further insight into human needs when faced with health problems, with loss, and simply with growth stages.

The next two chapters in this section broaden our scope of the role counseling must play in maintaining a well society. Emphasis is given to the role of the health educator. This person must prepare and motivate the patient for wellness and prepare and educate society for a more aggressive role in their own health care.

Finally, this section ends with a view of how our role within the health care system influences how we are treated and how we may treat others. Issues of role ambiguity and role sharing are discussed.

Section II of the text takes the focus off the individual somewhat and aims at professional issues. In this part of the book controversies in ethics and the law are explored. Further emphasis is placed on relevant health-related issues of abuse and discrimination. The text closes with a description of the role and importance of our professional organizations. This perspective looks both at the needs of the health care provider and the system itself.

It must be noted that, while the material covered herein is serious, the total mood of the book is dramatic. Issues, both professional and interpersonal, come to life through the real life experiences of all the authors and their patients. This book brings to life the critical dilemmas facing health care workers today.

We wish to acknowledge and offer special thanks to L. Luan Corrigan, our editor and discoverer. She talked us through the bad times and led us to believe that so broad a task could be committed to paper.

Our secretarial assistants were also superb. A special thanks to Judith de la Torre who was both dedicated and interested.

Our contributing authors, Glenda D. Price, Priscilla D. Douglas, and Pamela Roberts, were knowledgeable, cooperative, and above all made deadlines! Without their help we could not have succeeded. There would have been too much information to handle. They are each experts.

We also need to thank our families who uncomplainingly offered us the space to get the work done. They took on not only more of the domestic burden but, in the case of Roger Adams, even edited and delivered copy.

Thank you all.

Contents

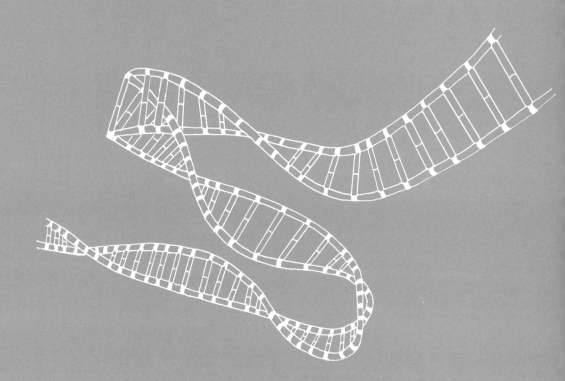

Developing Communication Skills

Chapter

1

After reading this chapter, you should be able:
- To define nonverbal behaviors.
- To recognize which of these behaviors may carry significant meaning.
- To check your perceptions of these behaviors with the patient/client.
- To use these observational skills in communicating with patients/clients who are unwilling to talk.
- To check your own nonverbal behaviors.
- To improve the professional message you send nonverbally.
- To create an appropriate atmosphere for communicating.

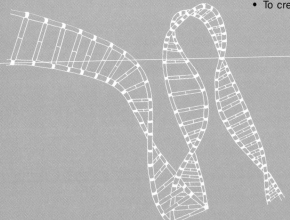

Body Language and Nonverbal Communication

Throughout the day we all witness many behaviors. But few of us put our observations to use. Have you ever noticed that Yoko Ono wears dark glasses all the time? What might we learn from this observation?

Observing and Reflecting Nonverbal Behavior

When someone wears dark glasses whether or not they are in sunlight, we can safely assume that the explanation is out of the ordinary. Perhaps the person has an eye condition or a headache problem that is triggered by light. Perhaps the person is self-conscious about how their eyes look. The sunglass wearer might have red, infected looking eyes, severely disfigured eyes, or even very baggy eyes. Some famous people wear dark glasses to help hide their identity. Others may wear sunglasses as a neurotic attempt to hide from the world and hide their feelings from the world.

In Yoko Ono's case we know the answer. She has told reporters that she feels more at peace and gains privacy with her grief when

*Many of the ideas and principles in this chapter are based on the writings of Robert Carkoff, Steven J. Danish, Fritz Perls, and Carl Rogers. For more communication exercises, we recommend **Helping Skills: A Basic Training Program,** by S. J. Danish, A. R. D'Angelli, and A. L. Hauer (Human Sciences Press, New York, 1980).*

wearing sunglasses. She has made a habit of wearing them only since John Lennon's death. This explanation makes sense to us. But, if she had not answered the question, or if we hadn't connected her new habit with John Lennon's death, we might easily have misinterpreted the meaning these glasses hold for Yoko Ono.

Wearing dark glasses habitually is just one example of **nonverbal behaviors.** As health care providers we must be careful in our interpretations. We must learn to recognize universal neutral behaviors and to use this information to better understand our patients. (A neutral position or behavior is the body's *natural* position. Hands at sides is a neutral position; other positions would be purposeful and have non-neutral meaning.)

In a classroom or hospital setting, you can learn a great deal about others simply by observing them. You will note that some people sit with their backs straight whereas others sit with their feet up on the chair in front of them; some sit close together whereas others seem to place themselves apart.

Many people reveal much through their facial expressions. They may sit alone and frown at what appears to be nothing at all; others may exhibit a faint pleasant smile or offer a nearly vacant blank stare. Just by these observations we can begin to formulate opinions about others and react according to our impressions.

Imagine that you are a newcomer to a clinical setting and describe the person you would most wish to sit next to. Now describe the person you would least wish to sit near. (Remember, no words have been exchanged.) As an exercise with your classmates, write down all the nonverbal observations you might see during a class. Your list should include facial expressions, body posture, and proximity. (See summary of this chapter.)

Once individuals begin to interact, verbal behaviors, mannerisms such as nail biting or pen flicking, and eye contact enter the picture. For example, a person who holds your gaze and speaks to you in a pleasant, expressive tone makes a better impression than does the individual who speaks in a quivering voice while staring at the floor.

While the use of eye contact may differ among cultures, we focus here on what is most appropriate for most Americans. Certainly all body cues need to be interpreted with a view toward the sender's ethnic background.

Unfortunately, you cannot always be sure of what certain behaviors indicate. For example, if you observe patient X sitting with her arms folded across her chest, you must take care not to misinterpret her position. Perhaps she is wanting to protect herself from others, is hugging herself as a form of comfort, is self-conscious about her figure, or is simply cold and trying to warm up. Just as with Yoko Ono there are many possible interpretations.

What is your immediate response to this patient with her arms folded? Can you think of several other explanations?

If you are working with someone and wish to understand what they are communicating nonverbally, you must make your observation known. Then you must follow your observation up with a question about what this behavior means to the individual. For example: "I see you've turned away from me and your arms are folded across your chest.

1. I'm wondering what that means to you."

or

2. "I guess you're feeling a little alone and frightened."

Either of these responses may be correct. The second, however, would be recommended only if you had already established rapport with the client. Otherwise you risk losing them by labeling their feeling too quickly or inappropriately. Remember, first you make a strictly behavioral observation (nonjudgmental) such as "I see your arms are folded across your chest." Then you want to identify accurately what this non-neutral behavior means to the client.

Another benefit to making these observations in communication work relates to conflicting messages. Often a patient will verbalize one message while indicating the opposite with his body. For example, a person may smile broadly while telling you how afraid he is of returning to work following a heart attack. By reflecting this obvious conflict back to the patient you will be better able to appreciate what he is feeling.

1. "What does it mean to you when you are smiling while talking about your heart attack?"
2. "I wonder if you are smiling because that helps mask how frightened you really are?"

Behavioral observation may also be the only tool we have for communicating with patients who are speech impaired or are unwilling to speak with us. If the patient can hear and speaks a language we know, we can respond to them simply by reflecting what we see. For example, an adolescent may sit grimly and silently in the health professional's office after being dragged in by a parent. The health professional may find that the adolescent meets most verbal approaches with more silent resistance. But, if the following approach is used, the patient may decide to talk simply because someone has conveyed understanding.

1. "You've been sitting on my couch for nearly 20 minutes now without saying a word. You've kept your eyes on your hands and your whole body is leaning forward. I'm getting the message that you don't want to speak with me."

or

2. "You haven't spoken in 20 minutes and you won't even look at me. Perhaps you are angry with your mother for bringing you here. If I were you I'd probably feel the same way."

Again, the second approach involves some risk because it brings in more feelings. You should use feeling words with patients only when you are confident that you understand the emotional issues involved. How and when to use feelings is discussed in more detail in the section on empathy in Chapter 2.

Now that we have begun to see the value of body langauge in understanding others, we will look at the messages we ourselves may be sending.

Sending Nonverbal Messages Ourselves

Perhaps the most obvious nonverbal message we send is our appearance. Good hygiene — a clean body and neat, clean clothing — coupled with a pleasant or benign odor is ideal. Heavy perfumes or aftershaves are inappropriate in a work setting. If oral disease or spicy foods make others back away from you, you will suffer for it professionally.

A less obvious consideration is your facial expression. Few of us realize how we look in random or candid moments. Generally, we prepare our face subconsciously for a moment before we look into a mirror. We are usually shocked by a photograph taken during an unexpected moment. Try to observe objectively what you see in such candid shots of yourself.

Sometimes, due to chronic pain or worry, an individual carries a sad or sour face into the world even long after those difficulties have been resolved. Others may look tough and unapproachable even though they are warm and friendly. Your colleagues and patients will observe you beyond the time you spend directly with them. They may form an opinion of you simply by observing how you walk down a hallway. Try to get an objective analysis of your candid, off-guard expression and train your face to change slightly if a problem is evident. Videotaping can be especially valuable, particularly if you record yourself interviewing another person.

Professional apparel is also part of the nonverbal message you send. If you begin clinical training looking like Madonna your patients probably won't feel a great deal of confidence in you. You may feel comfortable yourself, but you may make your patients uncomfortable. Begin by playing the role of the health professional complete with costume. If professionals in your field generally wear white lab coats, uniforms, or tailored suits, you would do well to dress as they do, at least until you have established yourself professionally.

The kind of body language that makes us comfortable with others makes others comfortable with us. If you want to encourage your patients to talk openly, then you must offer them open, approachable nonverbal as well as verbal cues. The rushed and tense health practitioner does not stimulate dialogue nor does she or he escape detection. Recognizing the patient's nonverbal messages isn't enough; we must send the right nonverbal messages ourselves.

Creating an Environment for Communicating

So far, we have noted that health care providers must take responsibility for sending out appropriate messages regarding their desire to interact with the patient. Through their behavior, they convey to patients a sense of friendliness, confidence, and professionalism.

Nonverbal Communication

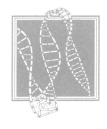

Further, health professionals must develop highly attuned observational skills and learn by observing the patient. They use their observations to better establish rapport and to better understand patient problems and conflicts by appropriately reflecting them back to the patient.

The final aspect of nonverbal communication training entails creating the best atmosphere for communication to take place. Health practitioners and patients should not be separated by great distances or large barriers such as desks or machines. An arm's length apart is culturally acceptable in the United States. This distance is close enough for intimate conversations without making most Americans feel that their personal space is being violated.

Hospital settings can pose barriers or distractions that are less than ideal. The lack of privacy in most hospital rooms may necessitate some creative rearranging when professionals need to deal with sensitive questions. The patient's right and need for privacy can become a major stumbling block to communication progress if the health professional does not take it into account.

Patients may *need* to be touched. Some studies have found an increased rate of healing in those who receive stroking or massaging as part of their treatment compared to those who are not intentionally touched. This may be especially true among elderly patients. Certainly we want to be close enough to our patients to hold a hand, pat a shoulder, or offer a tissue if emotions are strongly expressed.

Establishing the **ideal** communication model with respect to nonverbal skills and settings would involve the following:

- A professionally attired health practitioner would be sitting approximately an arm's length from the patient.
- The room would be privately occupied for at least the duration of their interaction.
- The health professional would be relaxed but in an attentive posture.
- The health professional's facial expressions and vocal tone would be friendly and interested; eye contact would be held throughout most of the interaction.
- The health professional would focus attention on the body language of the patient, reflecting out loud any aspects that didn't agree with what was being said.

The health professional also would reflect back to the patient and analyze any body language that appeared to carry a message of its own (such as tightly crossed legs or clenched fists).

Chapter Summary

Nonverbal communication skills serve us well as we learn to observe and interpret the behavior of others. When nonverbal behavior contradicts verbal behavior, we are cued to focus our attention there. Nonverbal interpretations also help us in establishing communication with those who cannot or will not talk.

As a health provider, you must cultivate the message you wish to send nonverbally. The right attire, good hygiene, and attention to body language are essential to success. You want to appear open, interested, and approachable. Facial expressions and proximity are significant, as is vocal usage. How you use your voice can significantly alter the way your message is received.

Focusing on specific behaviors in a nonjudgmental way can be a primary communication tool for the health professional.

Ideal Communication Style

Facing patient/client, holding gaze
Arms at sides or gently folded
Legs upright or gently crossed
Posture erect but not rigid
Distance of approximately one arm's length between professional and patient/client
No barriers between health practitioner and patient/client
Professional attire
Good hygiene
Facial expression relaxed or matching that of patient/client
Vocal tone moderate and clear
Providing privacy whenever possible

Communication Pitfalls

Poor hygiene
Inappropriate attire
Too relaxed or rigid posture
Failure to make eye contact or too intense contact
Sitting too close or too far from patient/client
Sitting behind a desk or large equipment when not necessary
Creating a barrier with folded arms or legs
Maintaining inappropriate behavior such as hair twirling or gum snapping throughout an interview
Lack of privacy

Behavioral: based on specific actions or behaviors, visibly observable
Benign: favorable, not harmful
Empathy: feeling for another person's emotions, a projection of how the other must feel which allows for better understanding
Neutral: giving no message, not one thing or another
Proximity: nearness, distance, or position from another
Rapport: an established agreeable/trusting relationship

1. How do behavioral observations differ from judgments?
2. What value may establishing rapport with a patient/client have for the client's physical well-being.
3. How may issues of proximity be effected by gender? By culture?
4. How might a careful observer of nonverbal behaviors know when they are *not* being told the truth?
5. Bring a candid photo of yourself to class. Discuss how you *wish* you looked versus how you do look in this photo.
6. Observe two or more strangers from a distance. Jot down the behaviors you see. Guess at what may be communicated between or among them. Discuss their behaviors and your guesses with the class.

Chapter

2

After reading this chapter, you should be able:
- To describe the value of good listening skills.
- To demonstrate paraphrasing.
- To understand the value of paraphrasing.
- To define and appropriately demonstrate empathizing.
- To describe the value of empathy versus judgmentalness.
- To demonstrate open-ended questions appropriately.
- To understand the limited role of closed questions.
- To avoid the communication hazards common in social comment.
- To examine the problems of overinvolvement with patients.
- To value taking responsibility for your personal problems.
- To demonstrate skill at giving and receiving feedback.

Basic Skills in Verbal Communication

We all want to be competent practitioners within our chosen fields. Most of us equate competency with building professional skills based on new information. But, although knowledge may be the cornerstone of the health professional's repertoire, knowledge alone is not enough.

Not too many years ago, many medical schools chose their students purely on the basis of grades. These schools produced physicians who had a great deal of scientific knowledge but who often had weak interpersonal skills. They were excellent diagnosticians — when they could get a patient to come to them. Knowledge without the skill to impart or transfer it is like a fancy automobile without someone who knows how to drive: it looks good, but you aren't going to go very far.

Think about the patient contact you are likely to have. Although people see health professionals for a variety of reasons, fear or con-

Listening and Paraphrasing

Many of the ideas and principles reviewed in Chapters 1 and 2 are based on the writings of Robert Carkoff, Steven J. Danish, Fritz Perls, and Carl Rogers. For more communications exercises, we recommend **Helping Skills: A Basic Training Program,** *S. J. Danish, A. R. D'Angelli, and A. L. Hauer (Human Sciences Press, New York, 1980).*

cern over their own health or actual treatment is almost always involved. These feelings may be accompanied by pain, loss, and worry.

Many of us have chosen to become health care providers because we want to help people. Knowing how to take an X-ray may contribute a good deal to a patient's well-being, but we have to be prepared to hear a patient's fears and objections before we may be allowed to help.

Perhaps you can remember a situation in which you held back information because no one seemed to care or listen to you. This often happens during social conversation. You may begin to introduce a difficult or sensitive topic only to have the conversation abruptly turned to another topic. The person with whom you were talking did not really hear what you were saying. What you wanted was a good listener; what you got was a good talker. Thus an opportunity for sharing and intimacy was lost.

Good listening skills require training and **practice**. We have undoubtedly all been guilty of not hearing the true message in a conversation, but when we fail to hear our patient's true message it affects our competency.

The foundation for developing listening skills is **paraphrasing**. To paraphrase, you simply listen to a speaker and then repeat what they have said. Although you can repeat exactly what they say, it is most helpful to rephrase the information in your own words; in other words, to paraphrase it.

Example 1

Speaker: "I am so tired of working with Sandra. Every time I think she understands the importance of not skipping meals or taking laxatives she turns around and gets herself into trouble."

Listener: "It sounds as though Sandra persistently ignores your helpful advice and therefore creates dangerous situations for herself."

Example 2

Speaker: "I work so hard all year long it doesn't seem that I'd be out of line to expect decent accommodations and good weather for two crummy weeks!"

Listener: "When you finally have a vacation you want things to go well!"

Of course, the listeners could have used other words as well. These examples are intended to convey the gist of paraphrasing: repeating concisely in your own words the relevant points you have heard.

Remember how easy it is not to hear what others are saying. What if we lived in a world where every speaker had to be paraphrased before the listener could make an original response? Your first thought might be that it would be a tedious world, but we would undoubtedly cut down on misunderstanding, hurt feelings, and errors. Certainly it is a necessary part of verbal communication training to begin each patient session (simulated or real) with paraphrasing. There are five important reasons for paraphrasing.

1. Paraphrasing is a check for the listener. Paraphrasing allows the listener to immediately check out his or her understanding of what has been said. Let us re-examine Example 2 above. What if the speaker had instead been trying to convey this thought: "I work so hard all year long I can't believe my only reward is a two-week vacation where anything could go wrong." By paraphrasing, the listener would then have been able to refocus on what the speaker really wanted to say: "Then what you are really saying is work takes so much out of you, you want more than two weeks off as compensation." The speaker's point would not have been lost or misunderstood.

2. Paraphrasing is a check for the speaker. Paraphrasing allows the speaker to hear what her or his words sound like. People often do not mean things exactly as they come out. Hearing your own words reflected back by a listener helps you to clarify what you really meant to say. Look at Example 1 again. A possible response to the listener's paraphrase might be: "It's not so much that I mind her ignoring my advice as it is that I can never relax and trust that she is safe." This change in focus may help both the speaker and the listener more quickly and accurately understand what is really troubling the speaker.

3. Paraphrasing builds rapport. Paraphrasing shows the speaker that he or she is actually being listened to, which effectively builds rapport. Remember how hard it can be to be heard. What a unique and warm experience it is to find someone who actually listens to you. What if the listener in Example 2 had said: "Your vacation couldn't have been as bad as mine. Not only did it rain every day, but a tornado took the roof off our cottage." With such a response, the speaker would not have felt very listened to.

4. Paraphrasing focuses on the patient. As we can see from the paragraph above, the listener can easily end up talking about herself or himself. (This type of response may be acceptable in a social setting, but it is usually unacceptable with our patients.) Listening and paraphrasing would eliminate this danger. Sticking with what the patient wants to convey prevents the health practitioner from missing vital information or possibly offering impossible solutions. Until you have established firm rapport with your patient and followed his or her lead in exploring all the dimensions of a problem, it is best to limit your responses to paraphrasing for the reason explained in Point 5.

5. Paraphrasing keeps the patient talking. Paraphrasing enhances a speaker's willingness to continue talking. If we are to get as much objective information as possible, we want the speaker to keep talking, at least in the first few encounters. Once we begin asking questions we take the lead. See what happens with Example 2 if the listener starts asking questions right away.

Speaker: "I work so hard all year long it doesn't seem that I'd be out of line to expect decent accommodations and good weather for two crummy weeks!"

Listener: "Don't you enjoy any part of your work?"
"What kind of work do you do?"
"How long have you been living this way?"

Can you see how potentially distracting and off-center these questions may be? Although the speaker may eventually want to explore some of the issues these questions raise, the timing is clearly off. Asking questions too early in a session **prevents** rather than enhances good communication.

Listening and paraphrasing skills are the essential ingredients of good communication skills training. One cannot be overtrained. All of us must refresh ourselves on these skills if we wish to remain client/patient-focused. If, out of all the communication skills, a knowledgeable health care provider were to master only listening skills, she or he could be a successful practitioner. That is how valuable listening skills are.

Empathizing

To empathize is to convey understanding of another person's feelings. Empathizing is a skill you should learn only after you have mastered paraphrasing. It is a listening skill that relies on the proper use of paraphrasing before it can be introduced successfully. Whereas paraphrasing involves rewording a speaker's message, empathizing involves both the basic message and the emotion involved with the message. Thus the listener not only rewords the content of the message but also brings out and labels the speaker's underlying feelings. Empathizing is based on feelings rather than on thoughts. Empathizing may dramatically expand the meaning beyond paraphrasing while still keeping the focus on the patient. Consider two examples.

Speaker: "I am so tired of working with Sandra. Every time I think she understands the importance of not skipping meals or taking laxatives she turns around and gets herself into trouble."

Paraphrasing Listener: "It sounds as though Sandra persistently ignores your helpful advice and therefore creates dangerous situations for herself."

Empathizing "It sounds like you've tried very hard to help Sandra
Listener: and you're feeling exhausted and frustrated."

Example 2

Speaker: "I went in to draw blood from Mrs. Morgan this morn-
             ing and she told me flat out to get out. She said she'd
             have nothing to do with anymore of us 'damn vam-
             pires.' Now what do I tell my supervisor when they
             can't run the tests?"

Paraphrasing "A patient stopped you from doing your job and you
Listener: are on the spot to explain this to your supervisor."

Empathizing "You're feeling shaken by a patient's flat refusal to
Listener: cooperate and afraid that you'll be seen as a failure by
             your supervisor."

THE PATIENT'S VIEW

YOUR PERCEPTION

What body language do you imagine the persons in these examples would exhibit? Explore your answer with your classmates.
Perhaps someone will volunteer to act out the speaker's role without
words. Empathizing in real life is easier than empathizing based on
reading because in real life we have the advantage of nonverbal cues.

Before reading any further review the responses of the empathizing listener in Examples 1 and 2 above. List the **feeling** words contained within these responses. The use of feelings is the key difference between paraphrasing and empathizing. After you have identified these feeling words, try to make an empathic response to the speaker in the following example: "I worked so hard all year long it doesn't seem that I'd be out of line to expect decent accommodations and good weather for two crummy weeks." (One empathic response would be: "You seem to be angry about having a lousy vacation." **Angry** appears to be the essential feeling label for this example.)

What feeling words did you list when reviewing Examples 1 and 2 in this section? If you came up with *exhausted* and *frustrated* for Example 1 and *shaken* and *afraid* for Example 2, you are understanding empathy. If you are having trouble picking out feelings words or labeling and understanding human emotions, work on improving your skills as we continue.

Understanding Feelings

We live in a world biased toward the cognitive (what can be reduced to factual knowledge). Being a thinking person is thought of as superior to being an emotional person. Although we may find some merit in this view, it also has limitations. Many individuals fail to develop their emotional antenna as they seek to feel less and think more. Males especially may believe it is unbecoming or unmanly to show emotions. Even in the face of acute sorrow and grief there are those who will not shed a tear.

It is little wonder that many of us who have been raised in this "big boys and girls don't cry" culture have to learn how to get in touch with our feelings. As an introduction, turn to the accompanying list of feelings. This list contains the words most commonly used to describe feelings. Becoming familiar with these words will make it easier for you to recognize them when you are listening to others. But familiarity with this list alone is not sufficient.

Just as we may have difficulty picking up on feelings, our patients often have trouble clearly conveying what they feel. Even the feeling words on our list can be used in such a way that they are not truly feelings. For example: You can "feel down" and we understand a sense of depression or despair; that is a feeling use of a feeling word. But what does the speaker **feel** who says: "I feel that he was putting me down."

Partial List of Feeling Words to Help
Improve Your Empathic Responses

Abandoned	Doomed	Insecure	Responsible
Adequate	Dreadful	Insulted	Ridiculed
Affectionate	Eager	Intimidated	Rotten
Agreeable	Ecstatic	Irate	Sad
Amused	Elated	Jealous	Satisfied
Angry	Embarrassed	Joyful	Savage
Annoyed	Empty	Jumpy	Secure
Anxious	Enraged	Justified	Selfish
Apprehensive	Enthusiastic	Kind	Sensitive
Badgered	Exasperated	Lame	Sick
Baffled	Excluded	Lonely	Stable
Beaten	Fantastic	Lost	Strong
Betrayed	Fearless	Loving	Stupid
Bitter	Flattered	Lucky	Sweet
Bored	Foolish	Mad	Tender
Brotherly	Fortunate	Majestic	Terrible
Bruised	Friendly	Malicious	Thrilled
Calm	Frightened	Maligned	Tight
Carefree	Frustrated	Mean	Tired
Caring	Furious	Miserable	Torn
Cast off	Generous	Misunderstood	Tremendous
Cautious	Giddy	Mocked	Triumphant
Cheated	Glad	Moody	Uncomfortable
Cheerful	Good	Nervous	Unhappy
Cold	Greedy	Nice	Unloved
Comfortable	Grief stricken	Numb	Unsatisfied
Confident	Grouchy	Obsessed	Unstable
Confused	Happy	Offended	Unsure
Content	Hardy	Open	Valuable
Cranky	Hated	Optimistic	Virile
Crushed	Helpless	Panicky	Vivacious
Curious	High	Patient	Vulnerable
Cut	Hopeful	Peaceful	Warm
Daring	Hostile	Powerful	Weak
Delighted	Humiliated	Proud	Well
Desperate	Hurt	Puzzled	Withdrawn
Dirty	Ignored	Quiet	Witty
Discouraged	Impatient	Rejected	Worried
Disgusted	Inadequate	Relaxed	Wounded
Dissatisfied	Inept	Resentful	Zonked
Disturbed	Inferior		

The use of **that** after the word **feel** tells us that we are about to hear a thought, not a feeling. If we rewrite the above message to read: I **think** that he was putting me down," it makes more sense. The word *feel* is often used instead of the word *think* when the speaker is confused about or blocking her or his feelings. Probably the speaker in this example was feeling **angry** that someone was putting him or her down.

Besides the difficulty many of us have in recognizing and expressing feelings, we also may be reluctant to deal with certain feelings. We may even consider some feelings taboo. The group of feelings that people may consider taboo encompasses emotions that can be seen as harsh or negative. Of these, **anger** is probably the most significant. Every human being experiences varying levels of anger on a relatively frequent basis. Those who are constantly angry, hostile, and negative are certainly not well and are not pleasant to be around. But human beings who never express anger have their own set of emotional problems. Obviously there are degrees of difficulty between these two extremes. A typical patient may feel angry but not know how to show it appropriately. When you are the empathic listener, keep in mind that many people have difficulty expressing anger, and may need your help to focus. Also be certain to look for a deeper, perhaps hidden, feeling when the speaker starts with "I feel that . . ."

The Timing and Power of Empathy

What do you think would happen if your first words to a client focused on feelings? Although your response might be well-received, chances are that it would be too threatening for your client to accept. It is important that you listen first and analyze later. You must establish rapport before you shift the focus to your patient's feelings. Remember that labeling feelings accurately is not an easy task.

One of the key values of paraphrasing is that it allows the patient to realize that you are with him or her. You must build trust through paraphrasing before you attempt to label feelings. If you mislabel a feeling without first developing rapport, your patient might well feel hurt, misunderstood, and angry — a reaction that will make it difficult for you to establish trust. Patients will often retreat with their feelings if they are frustrated by an early mistake on the part of the health care provider.

Another advantage to timing empathy correctly is that you reduce your chances for making errors. Remember that an essential purpose of paraphrasing is to find out if you actually understand what the patient is saying. If you label feelings without being certain that you have clarified the message, the outcome is likely to be disastrous.

An example of how you might reach the wrong conclusion follows:

Patient: "My daughter cannot make up her mind whether she wants to live with me or her father."

Health
Care "Sounds like you are feeling rejected by your daughter's
Worker: ambivalence."

Patient: "I'm not worriedd about rejection — I'm scared to death she'll ruin my life by moving back in — don't you see how destructive that would be?"

A well-labeled empathic response can be a powerful tool. It can further establish you as a caring, understanding health care provider, and can assist in rapidly helping your patient. Poorly timed, however, an attempt at empathy can frighten your patient into putting up a defensive roadblock. The key to success is timing. An empathic response is well-timed if you established rapport and clarified your interpretation of the patient's issues. Both are accomplished through paraphrasing.

One further caution regarding the appropriate use of empathy: Be careful not to use judgmental comments when responding to patients. If your response indicates criticism or a negative value for the patient's position, you will shut off communication. How would you react if you were the patient in the following situation?

Patient: "I hate my brother. He has everything. Good looks, good grades, and he is a great athlete. Meantime, I'm an ugly duckling crippled kid."

Response: "Now you don't mean that about your brother. You're just having a bad day and feeling sorry for yourself. That doesn't give you the right to hate anybody else."

Can you see how insensitive such a response would be? Even though the patient is exhibiting some self-pity, reflecting his words back to him with such judgments is not going to help him work out these feelings. **Remind yourself that you are on the patient's side.** Your job is to assist him in understanding himself and helping you to help him. **It is not your job to judge** what you hear, at least not in the sense of this example. Strong judgments on the part of the health practitioner only inhibit true understanding.

The Role of Open-Ended Questions

Once you have established rapport and a clear understanding of the patient's issues through paraphrasing, you can proceed to empathic responses. These responses permit you to communicate your understanding of the patient's feelings and to expand on the content of what the patient has said. While you remain focused on the patient, you want to expand the patient's understanding of the issues in which she or he is involved. The only kind of question that lends itself to paraphrasing and empathizing is the open-ended question (a question that can't be answered simply, but encourages further discussion). It is the only kind of question you should use during the beginning of your interactions with a patient. Perhaps you have been using open-ended questions already in your practice work. Such a question sounds something like the response in the following example.

Speaker: "If you ask me to do any more of those leg lifting exercises I'm never coming back."

Response: "So you're pretty bothered by the leg lifts and you want me to understand how hard they are for you?"

Such a response relates directly to what the patient has said. It does not lead the patient away from discussing his or her needs or problems. Once you have established rapport and understand the patient's issues, you may have to ask a limited number of questions. Again, you would begin asking only after you are certain that you understand the patient's needs and are not leading the patient away from further explaining those needs.

Even at this stage, you should ask only open-ended questions. Remember that open-ended questions encourage the patient to discuss issues further. Can you distinguish the open-ended questions from the closed questions listed below?

1. Can you tell me how you feel?
2. How did it feel to be on a strict diet when you were only nine years old?
3. What can you describe as contributing to your problem?
4. Have your parents been divorced long?
5. Did anyone else in your family have high blood pressure?

If you said 2 and 3 were open-ended you were correct. The other questions could be answered with a single word (especially yes or no). Closed questions do not allow us to learn any substantiating information. Also, the way we ask closed questions can determine the answers we receive. Remember that many people, especially when ill, feel emotionally frail and overwhelmed by the health care system. They may respond to questions as they believe they are expected to respond. If you ask a question that threatens them in any way, you will get the easiest answer they can come up with. Something as simple as "Did you eat breakfast this morning?" may cause them to feel defensive and cover the truth.

A key to enhancing your ability with open-ended questions is to remember two little words: *how* and *what*. Ninety-five percent of all how and what questions are open-ended. Use these two words whenever you are struggling to ask an open-ended question. You can use other words to introduce an open-ended question. But your questions must be carefully thought out to avoid closing off discussion. Here is one example:

1. Would you describe for me the situations in which you begin to experience pain?
2. Can you tell me how often you feel pain?

Sentence 1 might elicit an open-ended response because the word *describe* opens the question. Sentence 2 might elicit a response with some depth, but note that it could be answered with a word or two, leaving an information gap. What do you think about using one of the following two questions?

1. How would you describe your pain?
2. What can you tell me about this pain?

These sentences flow easily and invite the patient to share information. It is important to keep in mind that there are times when you may need to get very specific information from the patient and closed questions may be more appropriate.

In general, you shouldn't ask *why* questions. Gestalt therapy (see Chapter 3) teaches us that in truth there may be no real answer to a why question. Further, many why questions come across as threatening and confrontive:

"Why did you do that?"
"Why didn't you call for help?"
"Why don't you take your medicine?"

Questions that sound threatening generally go unanswered or are answered dishonestly.

The Role of Closed Questions

As a health professional, much of your contact with patients will still consist of closed questions. A closed question is one that is designed to elicit a short, focused answer like "yes," "no," "5 years," or "sometimes."

It is important that you can judge when to ask open-ended and when to ask closed questions. For example, a nurse could start a patient history with a question such as "Tell me about yourself" or "Why are you here?" But, if the nurse has a four-page questionnaire to fill out in 15 minutes, she or he will not have much time for such open-ended questions.

As a general rule, health practitioners ask too many closed and not enough open-ended questions. Interestingly, more information can often be elicited faster by using open-ended questions, perhaps because patients feel less on the spot. On first meeting a patient, even if you only have 15 minutes with him or her, it is often advisable to allow the patient to ramble for at least a couple of minutes. This rambling may contain the seeds of the person's problems, which two hours of direct questioning might not elicit. According to one old rule, if you listen, the patient will tell you the diagnosis.

Of course, some questions — "Which knee is it?" or "Are you single or married?" for example — have to be closed questions. The point is that it is more productive to start with general questions before zeroing in on specifics. For instance, "What can I do to help you?" would be better than "What are your symptoms?" and "What is bothering you?" is better than "Which tooth hurts?"

Merging Your Empathic and Questioning Skills

We begin a session with a new patient by offering paraphrasing responses until we fully understand the individual's situation and have established rapport. We may then focus in on the underlying feelings related to the message we are hearing by using empathic responses. When the patient begins to flounder or needs help in continuing the discussion of her or his situation, we can ask open-ended questions. These questions should be well thought out and should be based on an understanding of the patient's problems. As a health care provider, never ask a question simply to satisfy your own curiosity. A question you may wish to ask yourself is: What question does the patient want me to ask?

Paraphrasing → empathic responses → open-ended questions

Such a line of questioning will often help the patient to come up with solutions for his or her own problems. For example, if a patient were to say to you: "I only experience this pain after a fight with my husband," she is clearly asking whether she can talk about her husband, and you must respond. She may well begin to see what really needs to be worked on further. Solutions always work better if they come from the patient.

Learning the art of helping patients to help themselves is the purpose of acquiring the skills described thus far in this chapter. When you stick to the patient's issues long enough and develop an understanding of his or her feelings, you may be able to assist in focusing on meaningful discovery. Just remember that questions asked without an empathic understanding are likely to be wasted.

Early Communication Issues

If you have ever felt inadequate or insecure about your skills, you are not alone. Beginners in every field experience the fear that they will not be good enough to perform the work for which they are training. Feeling confident about developing communication skills is no exception. Repeated practice and experience are the keys to security and success. The issues addressed in this section are included as preventive medicine in the hope that they will help avoid some of the most common mistakes beginners make. When you do make errors, it is important that you recognize them and then continue your practice work.

Social Comments

The most common communication errors entail what we have called social comments: giving advice, talking about yourself, and saying, in effect, that you know how the other person feels. Each of these responses has its own drawbacks.

Giving Advice.   Listen to someone explaining their problems to a friend. Usually the friend has begun to "solve" the problem before the speaker has even stopped talking. Offering such rapid advice generally serves to close off discussion before the listener really even hears what is being said. Remember that it takes concentration on paraphrasing to actively understand most problems. By giving advice, you offer solutions that might work for you but are rarely helpful to the speaker. Your goal is to clarify the problem. When you help someone to better understand their own problem, solutions often emerge. The natural emergence of a solution without the need for outside advice is ideal; giving advice may be totally unnecessary.

Talking About Yourself.   Students often ask whether they shouldn't say they have had the same problem when that is so. What we would ask is what would be gained?

The paramedic on the scene of an accident is best advised to listen and *not* to report the circumstances surrounding her own auto crash.

Although wanting your patient to feel at ease is kind and admirable, telling her or him something about you may not be the best way to do it. If you respond to a patient by describing trouble in your own life, what have you done? You've switched the focus from the patient to you. An occasional patient may be interested in your common experiences, but generally patients are not interested. They want to be heard! They want to be listened to. Remember that a therapeutic dialogue should be one-sided. Your job is to focus on the patient and understand his or her problem. Discuss yourself with your friends.

Saying You Know How the Other Person Feels.   This common mistake overlaps with talking about yourself. By saying "I know how you feel," you may be hoping to empathize, but most likely you will be talking about yourself. You then lose the patient focus. In general, you should avoid self-disclosure. The few occasions on which it may be appropriate are discussed later in this chapter.

You also are making a false claim when you say you know how someone else feels, for we have no way of knowing if we truly know how someone else is feeling. Even when we have had the same experience as another, our innermost reactions may not mesh with theirs. A very good and caring counselor we know once had the following disastrous experience.

The counselor was working with a man who had ceased to function at his high level job following the sudden death of his son. Years before, the counselor herself had tragically lost a 10-year-old daughter. When her patient began to review the agony of the grieving, she replied, "I know how you feel, I lost a daughter."

His response was totally unexpected as he exclaimed, "How could you know how I feel — I lost a son!"

His response was not an arrogant or sexist comment; it was a measure of inappropriate timing and empathizing on the part of the counselor. This patient was unable to hear that his pain was like anyone else'es. Grief is lonely and private. If often dissolves the world around the griever. The counselor wanted to break through this barrier of grief and show that she too had been there and survived, but her client was not ready. His pain was greater, more exquisite than anything he could imagine sharing with another human being.

Although it may have become appropriate for the counselor to mention her own loss to this patient, this was not the time. She should have empathized without self-disclosure. If she had realized how angry he was, she might have timed her disclosure better. We will study the emotional stages involved with grieving in Chapter 4.

The safest time to disclose something about yourself is never. When you understand a patient's problems well, it may be okay to reveal something about yourself if the disclosure is worded to be supportive. Never use yourself to show the patient how to be, however. Holding yourself up as an example usually invites a hostile reaction or a sense of dependency. You don't want the patient to feel that she or he can only do well by doing it your way. The patient will then depend on you for all major decision making.

Occasionally a troubled patient may ask for your help by saying something such as, "What would you do if it were your mother?" You might wish to answer this question cautiously in a way that supports the speaker. It is best for everyone, however, if the answer does not come from you. Some honest sharing may be appropriate in situations where a stigma may be involved; for example, for an ostomy therapist or for someone working with a woman postmastectomy.

Overinvolvement

The subject of dependency opens another major topic: overinvolvement. Involvement and identification with the patient are important, but overinvolvement drains you and leaves you ineffective.

We lose effectiveness when we become overinvolved!

You have invested time, money, and energy in becoming a health practitioner. Chances are you are very committed to the goal of helping others. Until now you have probably not been in a position to assist people in need. Now that you are entering the health field you may be filled with energy and enthusiasm. Such zeal is welcome in any setting provided that it is well-directed.

We know of a young social worker who wanted to help every kid he came into contact with. If a client needed shoes or a place to stay for a few days or couldn't deal with a parent, this social worker tried to meet the need. His caring was boundless. He worked day and night for his clients. He lost sleep over them as well. The sadness in their lives touched him deeply. Instead of assisting a child's parents to develop resources for a needed pair of shoes, for example, this social worker bought the shoes himself. But what is going to happen next year when the child again needs shoes? And how many feet can the salary of one social worker cover?

Overinvolvement means that we are doing more for our patients than is necessary or really helpful in the long run. We lose effectiveness when we become overinvolved.

Although our social worker friend had the best intentions — helping his clients to have better lives — his actions actually prevented them from finding their own solutions. Not only did he foster their dependency on him by being the sole source of their solutions, but also he overworked himself. If your job has no limits, then you have no breaks, no places to rest, no joy outside the work.

Health care providers who become too involved with their patients usually burn out early and leave their profession. The work becomes too sad, too demanding, too overwhelming. A balance between personal life and professional obligations is essential. Depression and anxiety are often signals that burnout has begun.

Yet you want to help people, and the idea of being cold and objective in the face of human suffering is abhorrent to you. So how do you strike a balance between being too involved and too callous? Practice and experience will be your best teachers.

If you see an abused child whom you cannot stop thinking about, you could be heading for trouble. Talk about your feelings to a trusted colleague when you first sense that they may not be appropriate. Often we must become conditioned to the troubles we see. Few people feel relaxed when they first view surgery or a cadaver, but a few repeated exposures generally take the mystery and horror away. Anatomy students often eat lunch while studying in the morgue.

You must live through your first few experiences with difficult patient problems in order to build up your stamina and understanding. Be quick to recognize your own inner warnings of trouble. Then talk to a more experienced person for help in dealing with your feelings. Someone who has recently been a student may be of great help to you. Chances are that he or she also went through a similar time.

Occasionally we come upon a patient problem that overwhelms us because it strikes too close to home. For instance, if you were a battered child, you might react too strongly to an abused child's situation. Yet, if people in your field are to work repeatedly with battered children, you must do something about your reaction. Health care providers sometimes need help themselves. If your personal problems affect your work, you must resolve those issues in a manner that will permit you to function with all your patients. Otherwise, the patient you are overinvolved with might get a disproportionate amount of your time and your other patients might pay a price for your unresolved problems. Or you may be so upset in the presence of a certain patient that you cannot practice what you are hired for. All the sympathy in the world will not compensate for deprivation of treatment.

To avoid problems of overinvolvement, ask yourself these questions: What is my role here? What are the possible consequences (to me / to my patient) if I overinvolve myself? Will this affect my ability to function with other patients? Is there a better way to serve this patient?

Could you become overinvolved with a patient? With what type of patient might it be difficult for you to work? With what type of problem or patient might you identify? It is important to think about these situations before you must cope with them.

Self-preparation, early recognition of problems, talking with a colleague or a professional, and balance at home are keys to beating overinvolvement. In a few rare instances it might be best simply to remove yourself from a case. Doing so could be appropriate in an isolated incident, but if several cases are too much for you, you have work of your own to do.

Taking Things Personally or Becoming Defensive

Becoming personally involved may overlap slightly with another area of concern: taking things personally or becoming defensive on the job. We are focusing here primarily on practitioner/patient interactions. Personalizing issues with colleagues is another issue.

The health care provider who is trying too hard to make the world a better place or to win love from patients is very vulnerable. Patients often take their own frustrations and pain out on whoever is available. Although the nurse entering Mrs. Brown's room may be the kindest nurse in the world, Mrs. Brown may be hating **anyone** who is up and about while she is bedridden with pain. Our kind nurse will likely be attacked for no reason. If she is an experienced practitioner, the attack will simply key her in on how unhappy Mrs. Brown is. But, if she is overly sensitive, unsure of herself, or emotionally needy, Mrs. Brown's attack may be very damaging.

When patients attack, don't take it personally, paraphrase their anger.

As a health care provider, you cannot allow yourself to require praise and appreciation from your patients. If you do, you will often be hurt and disappointed. When you learn more about the needs of patients and the losses they are suffering, you can distance yourself from attacks. Attacks are usually a call for help and require attention and understanding. Defensiveness and arguments are not appropriate responses.

What do you do if you walk into a patient's room and are yelled at for no understandable reason? Well, you could cry or run or shout back but we hope you won't. So, what do you do? How about paraphrasing? Reflect back to the patient, in nonjudgmental tones, the complaint you are hearing. Don't panic. Chances are this approach will serve to soothe the patient and allow you to perform your job. Remember that patients are not really upset with you as an individual; they are angry with their own situations. Consider this example:

Patient: "Why can't you damn nurses do anything for this pain?!"
Nurse: "It must be overwhelming always to be in pain. I will check with your doctor about more medication. While I'm doing that is there anything else I can do for you?"

Receiving and Giving Feedback

As a student, you are often in the position of receiving feedback. Your instructors, especially in experiential / laboratory and clinical settings, must appraise you of your strengths and weaknesses. But, whether feedback is coming from teachers, friends, or colleagues, there is a set of responses that will best serve you as the receiver.

You may recall our discussion about defensiveness in the previous section. A defensive response means you are blocking out the value of any feedback that is directed toward you. Besides preventing you from developing your skills, a defensive response is like waving a red flag that reads "I am insecure."

Receiving Feedback

There are four steps to follow in receiving feedback. Note how they guard against defensiveness.
1. Thank the giver.
2. Paraphrase what the giver has said.
3. Seek any necessary clarification.
4. Discuss what you can do to correct weaknesses.

Thanking the Giver.   By thanking the person who gives you feedback, you immediately set a receptive tone. You are saying, in essence, "I am glad to have your input so I can profit from what you see." An automatic thank you gives you time and prevents you from making a short or defensive opening remark.

Paraphrasing.   In the context of receiving feedback, paraphrasing will do two things for you. First, it will allow you to be sure you have heard the feedback correctly. Even the best communicators can be ambiguous at times. And, when you're dealing with any form of criticism, oversensitivity can easily distort your hearing. You want to be certain that your understanding of the message is what the speaker intended.

Second, paraphrasing gives the speaker a second chance. Hearing his or her own words of evaluation repeated may allow him or her to see that it sounds too strong or too all-encompassing. Feedback will seem more appropriate following paraphrasing.

Seeking Further Clarification.   Once paraphrasing has occurred and you fully understand the issues, you may still need to clarify certain points. Consider this example:

Evaluator: "You are spending too much time with your patients."
Student: "Do you mean I am working too late?"
Evaluator: "No, I mean you should limit the time you spend with each patient so you can see all patients by noon. If there is a special needs case you can return to it once you've reviewed the needs of all the patients."

By seeking clarification, you are demonstrating a desire to fully understand what you might need to change. You are asking specifically what it is that the evaluator is suggesting you do. If feedback is not **specific and behavioral**, it may be impossible to follow as described below. Seeking to clarify feedback shows that you are willing to work on change if the evaluator can be clear about what you need to work on.

Discussing How to Correct Weaknesses.   Once you understand precisely what needs work, you can discuss how to make the necessary change.

Case 1

Evaluator: "I wonder whether I might speak to you in private? I have been getting complaints about your notes in the charts."
Student: "Thank you for bringing this to my attention. *(Para-*
(Thank you): phrase) It sounds like my notes aren't up to hospital standards. (Seeking clarification) What do I need to change?"
Evaluator: "You need to give more details when reporting your conclusions. Otherwise no one knows why you are picking up various patient problems the rest of us have not seen."
Student: *(Discussion of what can be corrected)* "If I take just a few extra minutes with each patient I should be able to describe the patient comments or behavior with which I am concerned. Would that take care of it?"
Evaluator: "Yes, that sounds very helpful."

Contrast Case 1 with the two that follow.

Case 2

Evaluator: "I wonder whether I might speak to you in private? I have been getting complaints about your notes in the charts."

Student: "Oh no! I've been writing down everything you taught us to. Who has been criticizing me?"

Evaluator: "Now please calm down. We are all trying to help you learn. But several persons have questioned your conclusions on patient problems. They especially want to know why you think Mr. London is upset by his daughter's visits."

Case 3

Evaluator: "I wonder whether I might speak to you in private? I have been getting complaints about your notes in the charts."

Student: "Oh dear! I'm so sorry. I knew I couldn't handle all this. Does this mean I am out of the program?"

Evaluator: "Heavens no. This is probably not at all serious, but we do need more information when you make a statement about a patient problem."

Which of these three responses would you most likely have made? Why? (We hope you picked Case 1.)

Giving Feedback

We have made several assumptions in the above discussion regarding the receiving of feedback. One is that the evaluator is **acting for the good of the receiver**. Another is that the problem can be corrected. These two assumptions are essential to giving feedback.

Whether you are giving feedback to a patient, a colleague, or a friend, you need to be aware of certain basic guidelines. The first is that you must examine your reasons for giving the feedback. Feedback that is not intended to help the receiver is bound to be received negatively. If you are angry with or want to hurt or punish the receiver, you can count on not being well heard.

One way to guard against giving punitive (aimed at punishment) feedback is to keep feedback specific and behavioral. Never suggest that someone change an intangible. Consider this example: "Why don't you just grow up? Your immature attitude is hurting the whole department!" What is the receiver to do? Wait five years and try the job again? Note, however, that if the criticism relates to specific behavior, there is hope for change: "It is difficult for the staff to work

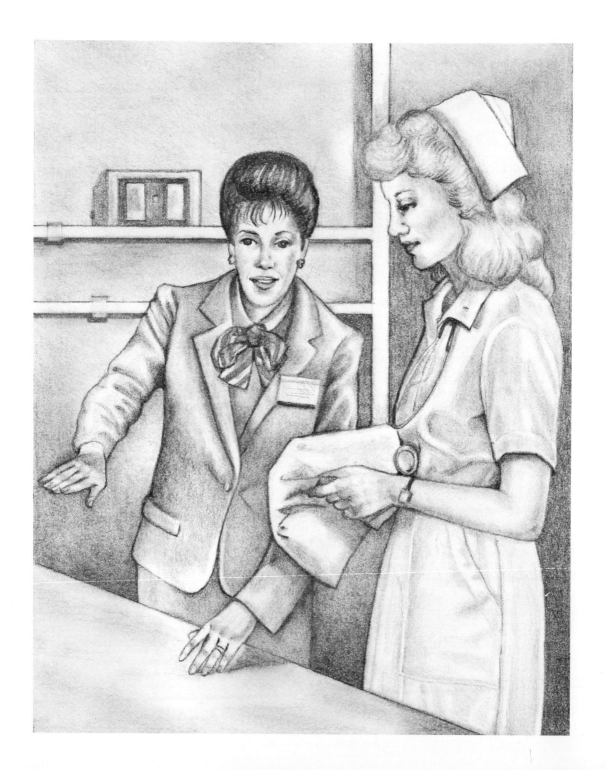

around your irregular hours. If you will give us an updated copy of your schedule from week to week I am sure things will go smoothly."

The first giver, who sounds hurt and angry, made negative character judgments based on hidden behavioral issues. When the behavioral issues themselves (irregular hours) becomes the focus, the giver makes more sense and the receiver knows what is bothering the staff. It is much easier to change a schedule than to try to "grow up."

Well-intentioned behavioral feedback is productive feedback; it is advice given expressly to help the receiver become aware of and change her or his behavior.

Knowing when and where to offer feedback so it will be best received is essential. Generally speaking, feedback should be given immediately so it is clearly connected to the event under discussion. Further, the receiver is less likely to be embarrassed that the situation has been allowed to go on with him or her being seen in a critical light.

There are a few exceptions, however. Most individuals prefer to receive feedback in a private setting. Although some classroom and clinical situations may offer the opportunity for everyone to learn from the errors of one, most feedback is best given in private. The impact of delayed feedback may not be weakened if the delay is for the sake of discretion. Giving immediate feedback in front of others at the risk of embarrassing the receiver is not productive.

Finally, remember to look for the positive. Begin a feedback session by reviewing the receiver's strengths. No one wants to feel they can do nothing right. Tell the receiver what you like before mentioning what you do not like. Doing so will increase the receiver's receptivity. To summarize, the rules for giving feedback are:

1. Begin with something positive.
2. Be specific.
3. Focus on behavior.
4. Be certain your motive is to be helpful.
5. Be immediate.
6. Be private.

What do you do if you follow these rules and the receiver becomes defensive anyway? First, remember that anyone can have a bad day. You may be giving feedback to a person who is undergoing a personal crisis. Or you may be offering well-intended feedback to someone who is too insecure to deal with it.

How should you respond when the receiver is clearly in distress? Your first reaction might be to clarify what you are trying to say to be sure there is no misunderstanding. Beyond this, you could choose either to back off and perhaps try again another time or to stick with the issues and pursue the receiver's difficulties in hearing it.

Either of these responses may be appropriate. Who the receiver is with respect to you and your role may dictate how you proceed. If you are responsible for the training or well-being of the receiver, the second approach may be more beneficial. Ideally, feedback is being given upon request; that is, it had been solicited or is expected by role definition.

Chapter Summary

This chapter described the value of good listening skills for health care providers. Even the greatest scientists cannot help others unless they are able to communicate their knowledge. Careful listening, using paraphrasing as its quality control gauge, is the most essential part of verbal communication.

To be most effective, you must go beyond the actual words a client uses and connect these words with the underlying feelings. Suspension of value judgments is an essential component of developing these empathic responses.

This chapter describes appropriate and effective timing of questions. Special emphasis is given to the use of open-ended questions.

Various communication hazards common in a social context are described. You must also learn to take responsibility for your own emotional health and to avoid patient overinvolvement as a way of "healing" yourself.

Finally, we discussed the important skills of giving and receiving feedback.

Acute: severe, sudden, usually short term

Cadaver: a dead body

Cognitive: of thought, factual knowledge, thinking skills

Intangible: something *without* form or substance, something that *cannot* be touched as a thought or idea

Mastectomy: surgical removal of a breast

Ostomy: surgically formed hole on abdominal wall coming from the intestine, usually involving a baglike receptacle

Paraphrase: repeat message in different words

Punitive: aimed at punishing or hurting

Tedious: boring, long, and tiresome

1. List five good reasons for paraphrasing.
2. What effect might it have on the world if every speaker had to be paraphrased before the listener could make an original response?
3. Why is it easier to empathize with a real live person, face-to-face, than it is to empathize with most problems as described in a text?
4. Discuss the pros and cons of overinvolvement for the patient and for the health care provider.
5. What types of patients or human problems are most likely to lend themselves to "overinvolvement"?
6. Describe your personal problems with giving feedback and receiving feedback. How might you overcome this?

Chapter

3

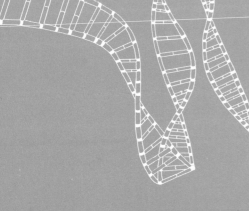

After reading this chapter, you should be able:
- To understand Maslow's hierarchy of human need.
- To understand Freud's concept of the unconscious mind.
- To understand Freud's theories of life and death instincts.
- To understand the terms Gestalt therapy, transactional analysis, and Rogerian counseling.
- To use the concept of defense mechanisms in analyzing social and professional situations.
- To define the terms repression, suppression, sublimation, identification, transference, countertransference, inversion, denial, displacement, compensation, symbolism, and rationalization.
- To give some examples of Axis I and Axis II DSM III classifications of mental disorders.
- To explain illness behavior, family traditions of illness, and sickness disorders.
- To recognize how a client's psychologic makeup determines the presentation, course, and management of physical illness.
- To understand what it is like to be a patient.

Basic Psychology

Human behavior can be analyzed in several ways. Much of what we talk about in this book uses the Rogerian approach. The Rogerian approach is client centered, which we advocate. By contrast, the older psychoanalytic approaches are more of a theoretic explanation of client behavior. We believe that combining both approaches will be helpful to the aspiring health care worker. This chapter covers many of the psychoanalytic explanations which form a framework for thinking about client behavior.

A Historical Perspective

A basic understanding of psychology will add a conceptual framework to the skills you have been developing. This chapter condenses an enormous field into the basic essentials for understanding human behavior. Also contained within this chapter are the definitions of many terms related to the field of psychology.

Ancient psychological beliefs seem bizarre by today's standards. Yet many people today regard physical suffering in a medieval way, as a punishment for sins. An example is the patient with an infected leg ulcer who commented: "It is the bad coming out of me." As we look at psychological theories, we can gain insight into human beings and illness behavior.

Maslow and the Hierarchy of Human Needs

Abraham Maslow (1908–1970) linked together existential philosophies (ideas relating to existence) and human psychology. He began by acknowledging a hierarchy of basic human needs common to all individuals. These needs, in order of priority, are:

1. **Physiological needs or survival needs to sustain life** — food and water.
2. **Deficiency needs** — Shelter (safety and security), sex, affection and a feeling of belonging, self-respect.
3. **Growth oriented or "being" needs** — Freedom, beauty, goodness, unity, justice.
4. **Inner-self needs** — Self-actualization or self-transcendence, or a realization of the inner self.

In simple terms, Maslow said that to understand a patient's motivation we first have to see at what level of human need she or he is being threatened. For example, a patient who is facing a grim diagnosis or extraordinary surgery may withdraw to varying degrees from friends or family. Further, such a patient may regress to a childlike state, exhibiting a decline of self-respect. These emotional and behavioral changes can be understood if we see at what level the patient is being threatened. If this patient believes that her life is at risk or her security is totally jeopardized, then we can understand her inability to relate to higher level needs.

Only those rare individuals who have become self-actualized can transcend disruption at lower levels. Such remarkable individuals live life always in search of more, taking every turn of events for its peak value. The self-actualized cannot, therefore, be threatened.

Self-actualization was a goal for which even Maslow himself continued to thirst. He did, however, describe a state of homeostasis that many persons experience during their lifetime. Homeostasis is not a zero point, which might indicate low motivation, boredom, or lack of challenge, but rather a sense of optimum functioning.

Finally, we must acknowledge something in human beings that goes beyond basic human needs. This is the autonomous self or pure psyche — the unique essence of the individual. Awareness of this essence can free up our definition of the authentic or healthy person, making us able to better value human beings and better understand motivation as defined by the individual's own right or uniqueness.

Pavlov and the Conditioned Reflex

Ivan Pavlov (1849–1936) is famous for his work on conditioned reflexes. He measured salivation in dogs in response to food. He then found that salivation occurred as soon as the dogs saw food coming. He then paired ringing a bell with presenting food. When he finally stopped bringing food, the dogs still salivated in response to the ringing bell, an unrelated stimulus. This was called a conditioned (that is, learned) reflex (that is, response to the stimulus). Consider this example:

> Every Sunday, Mrs. Benson's daughter would drive her mother to a local restaurant for dinner. But Mrs. Benson always felt sick in the car and eventually had to stop going out. Subsequently, Mrs. Benson developed severe nausea every time her daughter visited. She did not become nauseated at any other time.

> The car made Mrs. Benson sick. But when the stimulus was withdrawn, the unrelated stimulus (her daughter's company) still evoked the same response. This illustrates a conditioned reflex.

Behaviorism is a school of psychology founded by John B. Watson and William James. It held that we should be concerned primarily with an individual's behavior. Behavior therapy involves using conditioning to change a person's behavior.

Psychoanalytic theory might suggest that Mrs. Benson secretly disliked her daughter. Behavioral theory would say that we should accept Mrs. Benson's symptoms more at face value. Therapy might consist, for example, of a simple explanation of conditioned reflexes or counterconditioning (associating her daughter with another stronger cue to oppose the nausea; for example, the daughter always brings a present or ice cream).

Freud and the Subconscious Mind

Sigmund Freud was the founder of modern psychoanalytic theory. In *The Psychology of Everyday Life,* he explained unconscious motivation. Some events may be pure chance; others may be subconsciously motivated. Obviously, he said, it is not your fault if a brick falls on your head. But spending a day in bed with a splitting headache is an excellent way of missing work and gaining the family's attention.

Freud also explained the concepts of repression and resistance. **Repression** means pushing painful thoughts into the unconscious mind. **Resistance** means the conscious mind will not allow unconscious thoughts to enter. Emotions that are undesirable conflict with the conscious mind. They are repressed or pushed back into the unconscious. Once there they cannot re-enter the conscious mind because of resistance.

Mr. Green was told that his wife would be dead in a matter of weeks. She had advanced cancer. Knowing that she had always wanted to travel around the world, he bought tickets for the two of them to go on such a trip six months later. The painful thought was that his wife would die. He repressed this thought to the unconscious. We know he repressed the thought because he bought a ticket for her that she could clearly not use. We know that his conscious mind resisted the painful thought because he paid a lot of money for the tickets.

This kind of situation comes up frequently in psychology because it is conflict that is painful.

Another of Freud's theories involved the **life instincts** — sexuality and self-preservation. His theory of infantile sexuality became of profound importance to later psychologists. He believed that two drives were innate in a young infant: the drive for self-preservation and the drive to procreate (which he claimed was thwarted till later).

He noticed frequent reference by patients to three erogenous areas. On the basis of these references, Freud formulated his theory of libido or sexual drive. The child's interest in each of these zones follows a set chronological sequence. Until the end of the first year, interest is centered on the mouth. Eating and smoking therefore represent, according to this theory, a persistence of infantile libidinous (or lustful) instincts at the oral level. This is one reason why people who give up smoking tend to eat more.

From the end of the first year, until the end of the third year, the child's interest is centered on the anus. The bowel habits of the young infant are said to bear a direct relationship to later traits such as possessiveness or stubbornness. Feces become associated with belongings and especially with money ("He's got pots of money," "He's stinking rich," "She's rolling in the stuff"). Constipation represents the child's desire to hold onto possessions and indicates that the child is trying to assert control over the parent doing the toilet training.

From the end of the third year to the fifth year, interest is on the genital area. At this time Freud's renowned Oedipus complex arises. The boy is sexually attracted to his mother and sexually jealous of his father. The situation usually resolves itself through the castration complex, in which the boy fears that his illicit desire will be punished by his father through castration. Freud seems to have been rather uncertain about the girl. He explained the situation in terms of penis envy, which causes the girl to be sexually attracted to her father. Freud called this the Electra complex. This complex resolves itself more easily than the Oedipal complex because the girl feels that she **has been** punished, whereas the boy feels that he **may be** punished.

Freud later termed his sexual phases and instincts as **Eros** or **self-preservation instincts**. This can be explained as feeling that you do not wish to die, to be the underdog, or be controlled or defeated by others: you choose instead self-determination.

In contrast to the life instincts, the **death instinct**, or **Thanatos**, represents the individual's innate destructiveness and aggression either toward himself/herself or toward others. Here Thanatos plus libido produces sadomasochism. In Freud's theory, examples of self-aggressive behavior include addiction, accident proneness, and recurrent failures.

Another of Freud's theories involves the **id**, the **ego**, and the **super ego**. The id is the mass of undifferentiated instincts inherent in a new-born child, which later becomes modified and develops in the infant to form the ego. The ego represents the realization that the child is a unique person. The ego acts as a sort of arbitrator between the subconscious id and the reality of the outside world. When moral prohibitions of society are imposed, the superego emerges from the ego. Much of the superego is made up of the conscious mind and is responsible for most of an adult's character.

Adler and the Inferiority Complex

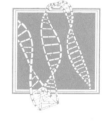

Alfred Adler (1870–1937) introduced the concept of inferiority feeling due to a real or imagined defect. This inferiority feeling determines what stance in life a person takes. A strong feeling of inferiority with undue pessimism is termed an inferiority complex. If a person consciously or subconsciously overcompensates for feeling inferior, it leads to a superiority feeling or complex.

Another corollary of feeling inferior is the natural tendency for people to move from a passive or feminine role, to a masculine or aggressive role. This is called masculine protest. The yin and yang of masculine protest (that is, the passive conflicting with the aggressive) was to Adler a major cause of anxiety.

Carlos, aged nine, injured his knee playing football with some friends in the street. When he saw the physical therapist, he was pessimistic. Rather than do the exercises the physical therapist prescribed, Carlos chose to sit around. He spent much of his time indoors. Despite a seemingly mild injury, he seemed convinced that he would never again be able to play football. This in turn would stop him from being able to get into his new gang of friends. He said he didn't mind that so much because he liked to spend time with his rabbit.

Clearly, Carlos has an inferiority complex. It is affecting his motivation to cooperate with physical therapy. The comment about his rabbit could be viewed several ways. It could be his rationalization of why his most important striving (to join the gang) did not matter. It could be simple displacement activity for something else that he would have rather done (playing with the gang). It could be a cry for help. "If I say something so pathetic, perhaps she will help me to do what I really want to do."

The physical therapist's mandate here is to attend to more than Carlos's knee. It is to use his knee to help him with his inferiority feelings. The physical therapist can accomplish this by first accepting the patient's problem. Although the patient may be exaggerating the knee injury, he may be using it as a symptom on the plate.

By accepting the symptom, we can use the patient's agenda and help him to achieve his goals. Additional questioning may allow the patient to maintain his control without undue threat: "How's the knee doing this week?" "Is it getting better?" "Do you think you'll be able to manage to get back on the football field in a week or two?" "Have you seen any of your friends recently?"

More than Carlos's knee may need attention. What should your role be?

Jung and the Collective Unconscious

Carl Jung (1875–1961) believed that all humans are born with a genetically preprogrammed unconscious. He called this the collective unconscious. He also introduced the idea of a complex, a group of ideas with a common feeling or tone. Jung described the inner self as the anima and the front a person puts on for the world as the persona. He also described the now well-known personality types called the introvert and the extrovert. An introvert is shy and introspective. An extrovert is sociable and outgoing.

It is obvious from this historical perspective that there is no "correct" explanation. Some old philosophies are simply viewed as inappropriate and sexist in today's world. There are many systems of psychological explanation to choose from. Each health practitioner will choose different items from the menu and will use them in individual ways. That is normal. What works for one health care provider may not work for another. What works with one patient may not work with another.

Other Theories of Human Behavior

We have dealt thus far with schools of psychoanalytic thought that seek to explain what makes the personality of one person unique. Some other theories are Gestalt therapy, transactional analysis, and Rogerian counseling.

Gestalt Therapy

Fritz Perls (1893–1970) developed Gestalt therapy. Or, as he might have said, he worked on **developing** Gestalt therapy, for Perls never considered Gestalt a finished product, just as he viewed all of development as a confirming process. The word *gestalt* is German for a pattern or whole that is more than the sum of its parts. Gestalt therapy treats the patient as a whole. It concentrates on finishing the patient's unfinished business by focusing on current feelings. Role playing techniques may be used to bring old unfinished situations into the present.

Transactional Analysis

In *Games People Play*, Eric Berne (1910–1970) developed transactional analysis. In their transactions, he said, people assume different roles at different times. He labeled each of these roles as a different ego state: parent (dominant), adult (equal), or child (submissive or immature). Any series of interchanges can be written as a diagram showing which ego states are involved (sometimes two are involved if the exchange has an ulterior meaning).

Therapeutic relationships usually call for a patient to assume a dependent role. Take the example of a female nurse giving a male patient a backrub. An appropriate response for him afterwards might be, "Thank you, nurse." Such a response establishes him in the child role and her in the adult role. If during the backrub he said, "That feels good, don't stop," he would be reversing the roles. Or he might say afterwards, "Thank you, that felt good, will you be in tomorrow?" This could be taken both ways: child to parent and parent to child.

People, Berne said, need "stroking," physically or socially. They structure their time to receive strokes through four activities: pastimes, games, intimacy, and nonsocial activity.

Pastimes are semi-ritualistic simple transactions used commonly at parties or during waiting periods. Games differ from pastimes in that ulterior transactions are involved or because there is a psychological payoff. The following exchange is a simple pastime: "Have you seen the latest Chrysler model?" "Yes, the Cadillac has that too. It looks very nice." But, if the response to the question is "Of course we ordinary mortals can't afford that — maybe I should raise my prices like you pharmacists," it is a game. Games can be very complex and can be played without the participants being aware. Games can involve a simple transaction, a life situation, a marriage, or a professional situation.

Rogerian Counseling

Carl Rogers (1902–1987) has been a major influence in the areas of behavioral prediction and control. Rogerian counseling initially was called nondirective or client-centered therapy. The basic idea is that patients have their own way of understanding themselves and getting better, and that a supportive, nonjudgmental, deeply caring therapist can activate this understanding and bring about change.

Rogerians focus on what the client is saying and then paraphrase and empathize. A key concept is positive regard. The therapist is careful to make the patient feel special. The patient is then free to trust that someone cares and understands. This judgment-free positive regard is thought to be especially helpful to those who have suffered from lack of parental support. Rogers also believes that psychotic patients should receive reassurances and warmth.

Roger's theory, like any of the others, can be criticized, but it has been used extensively. Much of today's therapy and inpatient mental hospital treatment has a Rogerian base. It has also led to the encounter group movement. Do you see any similarities between Rogerian counseling and the paraphrasing, listening, and empathizing that we discussed in Chapter 2?

Psychoanalysis has long theorized the existence of the subconscious mind and that two conflicting stimuli produce either psychic pain or resolution of the conflict. The psychic pain can manifest as anxiety or some other pathology. The conflict can be resolved through various mental mechanisms — also called defense mechanisms, ego defenses, or dynamisms. This theory is summarized in Figure 3-1.

Defense Mechanisms

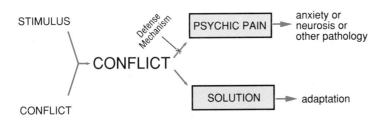

Theory of conflict resolution.

The simplest defense mechanisms are repression and suppression. **Repression** is an involuntary relegation of consciously intolerable ideas into the unconscious mind. **Suppression** is the conscious equivalent of this.

Mr. Cage, aged 85, is normally a model patient. But one night he developed a fever, became confused, and struck his nurse. The next day, after his fever was gone, he was told that he had struck his nurse. When the incident is mentioned to him a week later, however, he has no recollection of being told that he had struck his nurse. To Mr. Cage, the idea of striking his nurse was in conflict with his normal character. Rather than leave such conflicts in his conscious mind, he repressed the painful thought into his unconscious. He was not forgetting or lying. He was not being malicious. He found the memory too painful to bear; repression was the way he dealt with it.

Sublimation is finding a socially acceptable outlet for a socially loaded problem. For example, a normal devoted husband finds that his wife has lost all interest in intimacy. So he devotes his evenings to committee meetings of various charitable organizations. Another example is an avid athlete who develops multiple sclerosis and becomes a jazz fan instead.

Identification is the unconscious transfer of outside character traits into one's own mind. Identification is what makes you cry at the movies. Group identification is of major importance in the armed forces (for example, "I am a Marine. Marines are the best"). Parents often live vicariously through their children's lives. Fathers may, for instance, identify with the sporting achievements of their children. Mothers may push daughters to be popular in ways that they were not.

> The medical office assistant thought Mrs. Gefarb lived a boring existence. Meals on Wheels came once a day. Once a week her daughter brought some groceries and talked briefly about her children. Mrs. Gefarb had no television or radio and took no papers. Yet she didn't seem to be depressed. In fact, she always seemed very happy. Much of her conversation revolved around the achievements of her two grandsons, who were both at Princeton. The assistant thought of trying to increase Mrs. Gefarb's socializing, and she suggested getting a television set. She could not understand why her patient wasn't interested. Mrs. Gefarb was living a vicarious existence. By identifying with her two grandsons, she perceived fulfillment through their achievements. She didn't need any other fulfillment. Her daughter's weekly 15-minute conversation about her children was Mrs. Gefarb's weekly "soap opera." Remarkably, this kept her going all week long.

Transference is when a patient identifies the health professional with someone else. Commonly the health professional is viewed as a parent. Feelings the patient has toward his or her parent are transferred to the health professional. **Countertransference** is when the health professional has personal (nonprofessional) feelings toward the patient.

If you analyze your own feelings towards a patient, you find there are two parts. The first part is that your reaction toward that patient is similar to other people's reactions. A patient, for instance, may have a habit that you find annoying. This feeling will also show you how others may react to her or him. The second part of your feelings may be a response that goes beyond objectivity. You might recognize feelings of love or hate. These feelings are countertransference and can be a problem for **you**.

As a health care provider, you must strive for a subtle balance between overidentification and insufficient identification. You will find it through experience and learning. **To learn, you must be objective.** To be objective, you must examine your own feelings: Am I reacting to the patient objectively or for some need of my own? Am I feeling hate or prejudice?

Excessive identification makes the health professional too involved and he or she loses objectivity. Insufficient identification makes it difficult to understand the patient's point of view.

Establishing professional distance does not mean you are being impersonal. It means you are treating the patient as you yourself would like to be treated. Objectivity is most commonly lost when we step out of our professional role into the role of friend. This can happen, for instance, if we overidentify or become a friend with a patient outside of the professional setting.

> Irene, a middle-aged nurse, worked on the pediatric oncology ward. She chose this area because her six-year-old son died from leukemia 10 years previously. Unfortunately, all her patients became her substitute children. She was unable to switch from one patient to the next, became too involved, and soon had to transfer to a general pediatric floor. Once moved she worked much more effectively. Overidentification had caused her to lose her objectivity and her effectiveness.

Inversion is when a person does the opposite of what they want. For example, if you are rejected by someone you love, you may be able to deal with this more easily by hating that person instead. (The word inversion was used by Freud differently to refer to homosexuality.)

Denial is another defense mechanism in which painful truths are denied. Denial is the verbal equivalent of suppression.

> A girl who loved her father very much often came home from school to find him drunk. He often assaulted her physically. She found this so unpleasant that she simply did not think about it and so appeared to be quite contented. This is suppression. When a nurse asked her if her father ever beat her she said, "No, he loves me." This is denial.

Other common defense mechanisms include:

- **Displacement:** Putting feelings, especially negative ones, on someone or something other than the direct cause of those feeling; for example, yelling at your mother because you were embarrassed by your teacher.
- **Compensation:** For example, the polio victim who goes into professional athletics.
- **Regression:** For example, assuming childlike behavior. Repression, which is part of normal illness behavior, is described in detail later in this chapter.
- **Symbolism:** When one idea comes to stand for another; for example, money for love.
- **Rationalization:** When unacceptable events are made acceptable through a pseudo-logical argument; for example "I beat her because she talks back" or "I don't have enough time to do those exercises."

Classification of Psychological Diseases

Early classifications of psychological disease centered on mental retardation, dementia, and neurosyphilis (a venereal disease that sometimes affects the brain in its later stages). Later classifications broke mental diseases into retardation, neuroses, psychosis, and psychopathy. The neurotic lived in the real world but worried about it. By contrast, the psychotic lived in an unreal world, detached from reality. One old aphorism was that neurotics knew 2 + 2 = 4 but were worried about it, whereas psychotics knew 2 + 2 = 5 and were not worried about it. Another aphorism was that neurotics built castles in the air, psychotics lived in them, and in both cases the therapist collected the rent! The psychopath was simply unable to get along with others, the psychopath was later called sociopathic, and most recently is said to have an antisocial personality.

In 1980 the American Psychiatric Association rewrote a diagnostic and statistical manual of mental disorders (DSM III). In it, mental disorders are classified in five different "axes," a practice that many find pedantic. These axes are as follows:

Axis I   Clinical syndrome (for example, neurosis)
Axis II   Personality disorder (compulsive)
Axis III Physical disorder (dry skin from excessive washing)
Axis IV   Severity of stress (severe)
Axis V   Highest level of functioning in past year (cannot work because of bleeding hands)

Clinical Syndromes

Childhood disorders
- Mental retardation
- Behavioral problems

Organic disorders (Caused by known physical disease rather than mental disease)
- Dementia (also referred to as senility by the general public and chronic organic brain syndrome, COBS, in medical circles), in which the primary part of the problem is the inability to recall recent events.
- Substance-induced disorders (alcohol intoxication, cocaine-induced psychosis)
- Substance abuse (alcohol or other drug abuse)

Schizophrenia
Basically a psychosis, often with delusions or hallucinations. In paranoid schizophrenia, a primary delusion shapes a person's whole existence; for example, "I am Napoleon." Other types of schizophrenia are disorganized, catatonic, undifferentiated, and residual. A delusion is a belief that has no basis in reality; for example, "I am Napoleon." A hallucination is a sensory perception that has no basis in reality; for example, hearing voices.

Neuroses
- Affective neurosis (a disorder in which a disturbance of mood — depression or mania — is the major feature; for example, depression, manic depression, mania)
- Anxiety (phobia such as dread of spiders)
- Obsessive compulsive neurosis (behavior such as continuously washing the hands)
- Simple anxiety (nervous about everything)

Somatoform
Concentrating on the body; for example, hysteria, in which an impairment of some bodily function occurs in response to stress, such as sudden paralysis from the waist down from no obvious physical cause.

Hypochrondiasis
The persistent belief that one has various diseases. Also, the problem does not resolve itself after appropriate and reasonable investigation and reassurance that these diseases are not present.

Psychogenic pain
Real pain without organic cause, usually related to an underlying psychological feature such as guilt and self-punishment (for example, crippling back pain in someone who clearly moves and walks with ease).

Disassociative hysteria
A type of hysteria in which the whole conscious mind behaves independently at times (for example, split or multiple personality or a sudden loss of memory for a period, also called fugue).

Psychosexual disorder
- Homosexuality
- Paraphilia (fetishist, transvestite, exhibitionist, sadomasochist, voyeur)
- Dysfunctions (premature ejaculation)

Impulsive syndromes
Kleptomania, pathological gambling, pyromania.

> **Personality Disorders**
> - **Paranoid personality disorder** — patient seems to be unjustifiably suspicious, tending to suggest that others have ulterior motives.
> - **Schizoid personality disorder** — patient is socially withdrawn, has peculiar ideas, is unable to integrate into society, may be described as eccentric or bizarre.
> - **Histrionic personality disorder** — patient is overactive and dramatic and engages in attention seeking behavior.
> - **Dependent personality disorder** — patient has poor self-esteem, seeks approval, gets others to be responsible for important things in life.
> - **Passive-Aggressive personality disorder** — patient displays aggressive behavior in passive ways; for example, forgets intentionally, is obsequious and stubborn.
> - **Borderline personality disorders** — patient acts impulsively in ways that are detrimental to himself or herself, has unstable but intense interpersonal relationships, is temperamental, makes suicidal gestures, has many surgeries and frequent accidents, has an unstable mood.

Obviously, Axis I and II are what would commonly be called mental illnesses. The first is the clinical syndrome presenting itself, and the second is the underlying personality disorders (see accompanying boxes for descriptions and definitions).

Although you will not be making DSM diagnoses on patients, as a health professional you need to understand diagnosis, which is the short-hand of mental health. It is often helpful to create for yourself a picture, or vignette of a particular patient's problems. An example might be: nervous, self-destructive, alcoholic, or a paranoid dementia patient liable to be violent. This technique is intended only to provide a loose framework upon which to build patient understanding.

Illness Behavior

The key to understanding illness behavior is to remember that each patient is an individual. A common misconception is that people simply have or do not have diseases. Studies have shown that groups of people who see their physician frequently (more than five times a year) suffer in fact the same frequency of commonly reported symptoms like colds, backache, hemorrhoids, and headaches as do those who see their physician infrequently (less than once every five years). Illness behavior describes ways that different people respond when suffering the same symptoms.

You must think of a patient as a complex gestalt: in their relationships, within the family, to authority, within work and society, and developmentally within their culture, traditions, myths, and sickness beliefs. You must also take into account emotional and intellectual makeup as it affects illness behavior.

Each time you see a person before you, and particularly when things do not seem to be going as they should, think about this gestalt. Realizing this gestalt can make brief encounters with patients much more productive, as you will not always have the time for an in-depth analysis. Lack of time will occasionally put you in the position of taking short cuts. And, of course, you bring to each patient your knowledge from other patients you have seen. In a sense this is using a preconceived notion about the characteristics and needs of the individual. It is still important to spend time on paraphrasing, empathizing, and asking open-ended questions. But awareness about the patient as a whole can enable you to zero in on things more effectively.

Illness behavior is shaped by many relationships and factors. Can you think of any influences from your culture, traditions, myths, and sickness beliefs that have helped form your illness behavior?

Psychosocial Stress Level

Epidemiological work suggests that illnesses within a patient tend to occur in clusters. There is also evidence to show that these clusters occur at times of psychosocial stress. Illness at such a time can be seen as maladaption to stress. All people experience stress but the level alters during life. We must be attuned to likely stressors.

Recent bereavement is the most obvious major stressor; others include a recent geographical move when social support systems have to be remade, a change of job, pregnancy, and taking on a mortgage.

It is a fairly good bet, for instance, that most illnesses presented in the context of recent bereavement could be regarded as symbols of stress. Generally speaking, the best way to deal with such illness seems to be on a symbolic basis. A patient, for instance, who wants physical therapy on a knee in such a situation should be given the therapy (as long as it will not harm the patient) even if nothing abnormal is found. It takes a lot of courage for such a patient to present themselves to you in the way they feel is most appropriate, which is to come to you in your area of expertise. To deny that communication would be rejecting the patient. To accept it makes the pain a little easier to bear and can open up more significant underlying problems.

Family Myths and Traditions

A mother says, "My daughter has always been very delicate." One day mother and father argue about this issue. Mother then takes the daughter to the school nurse to complain of a cough. This is an example of a defense mechanism, in this case displacement activity. The threat of conflict with her husband is switched to a concern about her daughter's health. The school nurse examines the child and agrees that she has a cold. All it takes is a little pressure from the mother to obtain permission to keep the child out of school the next day. Mother comes home to dad and recounts the day's goings on, adding, "I told you she was very delicate." Father loses this game and so learns that it is best not to argue. If he has any frustrations, he will have to figure out some other way of dealing with them. He agrees that his daughter is delicate. To deny it would start a game that he knows he would lose again. Thus, a family myth has been perpetrated. The daughter will be raised in the **family myth** of a medically delicate person.

This behavior spills over into **family traditions of illness**. Mother may not take daughter to the school nurse each time she gets a cold because of any game. It may be simply a tradition. "When I sin I must confess to the priest, so when my daughter has a cold I must

Major Stressors According to Holmes and Rahe*

1. Death of spouse
2. Divorce
3. Marital separation
4. Jail term
5. Death of close family member
6. Personal injury or illness
7. Marriage
8. Fired at work
9. Marital reconciliation
10. Retirement
11. Change in health of family member
12. Pregnancy
13. Sex difficulties
14. Gain of new family member
15. Business readjustment
16. Change in financial state
17. Death of close friend
18. Change to different line of work
19. Change in number of arguments with spouse
20. Mortgage or loan for a major purpose
21. Foreclosure of mortgage or loan
22. Change in responsibilities at work
23. Son or daughter leaving home
24. Trouble with in-laws
25. Outstanding personal achievement
26. Spouse begins or stops work
27. Begin or end school
28. Change in living conditions
29. Revision of personal habits
30. Trouble with boss
31. Change in work hours or conditions
32. Change in residence
33. Change in schools
34. Change in recreation
35. Change in church activities
36. Change in social activities
37. Mortgage or loan for a lesser purpose
38. Change in sleeping habits
39. Change in number of family get-togethers
40. Change in eating habits
41. Vacation
42. Christmas
43. Minor violations of the law

*Institute for Stress Research

seek medical attention." She feels she might be seen as negligent if she did not check with the nurse. Health education — telling her it isn't necessary to seek medical attention for every cold — may not work. Her tradition is part of her ego system, which, if undermined, may increase rather than decrease her stress level. Both myths and traditions are reinforced when the health professional agrees to participate in them.

Sickness Roles

Normal illness confers roles on the patient and the health provider. The most usual role in terms of Berne's transactional analysis is for the patient to be child and the health provider to be adult. The patient's role has been labeled dependent as opposed to independent.

> A hard driving businessman suffers a heart attack, is admitted to the coronary care unit of a hospital, and gives the nurse a difficult time. He pulls out his intravenous lines, refuses to take medication, and insists on having a phone by his bedside so he can continue to run his business.

This patient, who is used to playing an adult role, now finds he must regress into a dependent, childlike role. Although this would be good for him under the circumstances, his lack of "adaptive regression" puts his life at risk.

A normal healthy person can drop the dependent role as she or he recovers. Some people, however, demonstrate excessive regression, which is a defense mechanism caused by anxiety. It can be difficult to loosen the patient's clinging grip. Although health professionals may feel flattered by such dependency, it usually becomes emotionally draining very quickly.

Another way of looking at the sick role is to consider the advantages (or secondary gains) that might be accrued outside the health professional / patient relationship. For example, a patient is unable to work at home or at his job, although he is needed there. If he cooperates with what the health professional says, he gains the privileges of the sick role. This allows him to be off work or to avoid duties at home.

These roles are difficult to apply to all illnesses; however, they apply best to acute illness. Consider, for example, the difference between chronic disability and a health risk. A patient with a chronic disability may play any role from chronic dependency (child / parent) to mutual cooperation (adult / adult) to excessive assertiveness (parent / child). A patient with high blood pressure has a health risk rather than a sickness.

Irene went to a screening clinic and was told that she had high blood pressure. Her doctor prescribed medication and a low salt diet. A nurse practitioner was asked to see her because she would not take her pills or follow the diet. The nurse explained to Irene that she was not sick. Further, she would not become a sick or disabled person if she took care of herself. After a while, Irene came to understand that taking pills was acceptable and that it did not signify that she was an ill person.

Primary and Secondary Gain

Mrs. Sanger, a middle-aged housewife, tells the nurse that she is ill. She says the doctor diagnosed a prolonged viral infection. She does not seem particularly upset by the idea. Indeed, she seems somewhat pleased. What has she got to gain from being ill?

First, she has the illness itself. It has become a new center of attention. The doctor listens to her. The nurse listens to her. She does not usually have such an audience. She can be egocentric and talk about her illness and nothing else. This is called primary gain. It is the advantage the illness itself creates.

But there are more advantages. Mrs. Sanger can tell her husband that she has been advised by her doctor to avoid housework and rest in bed for the weekend. This is called secondary gain. It is a consequence of the illness that has a bonus aspect for the patient.

The worst case of secondary gain is maintaining or producing illness only because of its advantages. One patient suddenly developed paralysis of his legs and was unable to go to work. No physical cause could be found. He had a little electric repair shop in his back room where he sat in his wheelchair and enjoyed his lifelong hobby of electronics. This released him from his boring factory work and gave him a disability pension. These were the secondary gains of his hysterical paralysis. Behaviors are maintained when they are rewarded. We discuss this further in Chapter 7.

Another patient was a passenger in a car crash. He suffered a whiplash injury that gave him neck pain and headaches. He talked with an attorney and found that he might get a lot more than his medical bills paid. Soon he was unable to work. He won an out-of-court settlement of $80,000 and decided to apply for disability. This is another example of secondary gain.

The rewards of sickness to children can be just as real. They get to stay home from school, watch television in bed, have favorite foods brought to them, and get more attention from mother. They do not have to worry about schoolwork, teachers, or peer criticism. Sometimes the thought of returning to the real world can be downright threatening.

Perceptions of Who is Actually the Patient

Mrs. Smith is an aging, senile woman who has lived for many years with her daughter, who cares for her devotedly. Mrs. Smith's urinary incontinence means that her daughter must wash bedclothes constantly, and the house looks like a laundry. The caregiver daughter, the doctor, and the visiting nurse were all aware of a gradual overall deterioration. From time to time, Mrs. Smith's second daughter from California comes to see her mother. She had not seen her mother for several years when she arrived on her latest visit. Although she had certainly heard stories from her sister, she expected to find her mother not much different from when she last saw her. What she found shocked her. She immediately called the home health aide agency, which in turn called the visiting nurse. The visiting daughter reported that Mrs. Smith had fallen, was covered with bruises, and needed to be admitted to the hospital.

Who is the patient? Certainly we can all see that the first daughter, who regularly cared for her mother, was likely to be severely stressed. But she is not the patient. She and all the other caregivers have acknowledged the deterioration. They also acknowledge that, given the circumstances, the mother would like to continue to be cared for at home. But was the mother really the patient? No. This is the **distant relative syndrome**, not uncommon in geriatric care. The situation, previously stable, is a surprise for the guilty relative, who is shocked. The visiting sister from California has not seen her mother for several years. By precipitating a crisis, she has assuaged her guilt that she has not cared for her mother. If she did not feel guilty she would have grasped the fact that multiple caregivers had already acknowledged the situation, decided what was best, and given their best. The true patient is the visiting sister. It is she to whom the health professional must talk.

A **stressed mother** brings her children to the nurse practitioner approximately monthly for colds. The children are not necessarily the patients; the mother needs more help than they do.

The wife of an Iranian engineering student constantly visits the student health clinic. The nurse practitioner can never figure out what is the matter with her. This may be an example of the **lonely**

immigrant syndrome. Is the Iranian woman or the society she lives in really the patient? The problem is that she needs to socialize, but she has no one who shares her culture and language.

What is Perceived as Disease

Health is defined as a state of complete mental, social, and physical well-being, not simply as the absence of disease. Some may see a cold as an illness requiring treatment. Others may ignore a cold unless there is extreme suffering.

A couple who have sexual difficulties to the point of contemplating divorce may see the pharmacist to ask for sexual stimulants. The pharmacist may be infinitely more helpful if she or he refers them to a counselor. Although low sexual drive could be seen as an illness (and treated with medication), such a perception might limit or restrict actual help.

A problem viewed as an illness by the patient may not be seen as one by the health professional. An example would be the onset of normal menstruation in an unprepared pubescent girl.

Cultural Determinants of Sickness Behavior

Sickness beliefs may depend on a patient's upbringing. A patient may choose a medical model, see a physician, accept treatment, and present physical symptoms. Or a patient may have a psychoanalytical model and expect their illness to be treated through psychological insights. Or they may have a primitive model of illness — that suffering is a retribution for sin, for example. Is mental illness an illness? Is drug addiction an illness? Is gambling an illness? It depends not only on the health professional, but also on the patient and on the society.

Certain cultures may have styles for expressing sickness. Pain, for example, is often expressed differently in different cultures. Minority groups may have their own health beliefs that persist in a different country. Any minority group may cling to early beliefs of their country of origin — a sort of medical expatriate syndrome.

Manipulative Patients

Manipulative patients cancel their appointments or fail to show up for them. They may switch from one health professional to another as though they were shopping for tuna fish. They may seek multiple consultations for no apparent reason without proper communication. If, for instance, they are seeing you as a physical therapist, you may be unaware that they are seeing two other physical therapists also.

Manipulative patients do not get better in ways that health professionals devise, desire, or control. They may do some or all of what they do because they cannot tolerate the dependent role, because they deny illness, or because they wish to manipulate their own treatment. They need to be in control.

The reason for being manipulative can be analyzed on several levels:

1. It may be an expression of a passive-aggressive or of a borderline personality disorder.
2. It may be in the terms of transactional analysis that they cannot accept the sick role; that is, they cannot assume a dependent role because of an ego disorder (like the businessman in the coronary care unit example).
3. It may be a defense mechanism. They are being dictated to and they do not want to be. This conflict either produces anxiety or can be resolved through defense mechanisms such as:
   - **Denial** — "I forgot my appointment."
   - **Rationalization** — "My sister told me the physical therapist down the street specialized in back pain."
   - **Substitution** — "The pills you suggested I try, didn't work, so I decided to try acupuncture."
4. It may be a social phenomenon. Some patients may use manipulation as a style. It is the only way to assert themselves, especially when they know they may spend the rest of their lives on the bottom of the pile. Because manipulative behavior is such a common difficulty for the health professional, we include the following somewhat detailed example as an illustration.

George, aged 61, frequently worked at the hospital as a volunteer. He was an epileptic and had been hospitalized many times, though usually not for epilepsy. Chest pain frequently brought him to the hospital, although cardiologists said there was nothing wrong with his heart.

When he first saw the nurse practitioner at the health center, George was charming. His medical story was extremely complex. Soon letters started arriving from a cardiologist, two neurologists, and a gastroenterologist. None of these referrals had been made by the health center.

The nurse practitioner called his previous family practitioner and discovered that he switched primary care specialists about every two or three years. The family prac-

titioner also revealed that he had learned not to criticize George. He had heard through the grapevine that George would tell the nurses and the patients at the hospital negative things about all his caregivers. George had already had a run-in with an x-ray technician at the local hospital and so refused to have anymore x-rays there.

The nurse saw George's pattern of behavior as a problem. One day George cancelled his appointment at the last minute. He said his car had broken down. She called his house hoping to speak to him, but instead got his wife, Mabel. She said he was out, but she did not know where. Mabel knew what was going on. Once, she said, she had tried telling George that he must tow the line. Within a month of their conversation, George visited six different specialists and ran up medical bills of $2,000. Mabel said she simply could not afford to risk that again.

That same night, George called the nurse at home. She had no idea how he got her unlisted number. George told a long convoluted story about several different symptoms and how everyone was turning against him. He said that she was the only person to whom he could turn. After a long conversation, George thanked her profusely and apologized for calling her at home.

She never heard from George again until a request arrived three weeks later to transfer his records to a new HMO clinic in town.

This story portrays a man who uses manipulation as a lifestyle. He manipulates his health caregivers, his wife, and probably his friends as well. He uses illness as a substitute for interaction and as a focus in his life. Subconsciously he can change his symptoms at will. Who knows which symptoms are real and which are subconsciously motivated? He is dramatically the center of attention. Commiserating volunteers at the hospital are his audience. This is a lifetime game, and as the star player he cannot be beaten. No relationship is likely to give him as much attention as his game. Counseling (to try to get him to realize what he is doing) would likely be yet another game for him. If he found it more challenging he would switch. But chances are that with his experience and contacts, a medical model gives him more primary and secondary gain.

What could you, as a health professional in such a situation, do? First, you would have to give the patient the benefit of the doubt. You would have to allow some time to pass for a pattern to establish. Only then could you reliably define the situation. You might accept the situation if the manipulative behavior is mild, or if the behavior is not too detrimental to the patient or to society.

If the behavior exceeds these guidelines you would have to set some boundaries. You might set some, for example, if the patient calls frequently after hours or frequently fails to appear for an appointment. Discussing such behaviors with a patient may actually be therapeutic for him or her and is likely to be helpful to you as a health professional.

Illness Behavior Related to Work

As already described, the sick role involves permission to stop work and get better. The housewife with flu who goes to bed can reasonably expect some help looking after the children.

A person who is the dominant figure at her or his place of work may find it difficult to accept a dependent role in sickness. Recall the businessman in the intensive care unit.

Many people have learned that physically demanding work is hard, and that looking busy makes life a little easier. Likewise, time off makes life a little easier. If you are allowed to take two weeks of sick time per year, you soon learn that a cold, previously not much of a problem, will give you a welcome break from work.

Others have a very strong work ethic. One hospital dietitian only took two days off in her entire life — on each occasion to have a baby!

Some types of work have traditions. Physicians, for instance, are likely to take little time off. Psychiatrists have a higher smoking rate. Military personnel have high rates of alcoholism.

Cartesian Dualism

Rene Descartes (1596–1650) first postulated a philosophical difference between the body and the mind. Ever since, it has been difficult to bridge the gap between the psychological and the physical.

In particular, patients have a difficult time relating anxiety to sickness. A patient can suffer a purely physical problem such as pneumonia, or can present pure anxiety to the health practitioner. Some symptoms of anxiety are tremors, sweating, palpitations, jitteriness, insomnia, or feeling physically exhausted. Some anxious people find specific symptoms more bothersome during periods of anxiety; for example, diarrhea, loss of appetite, headaches, or frequent urination. Because pure mental illness is still taboo or is looked down upon in our society, a patient may come to the health professional with these physical symptoms, thinking they are more acceptable. Often, how-

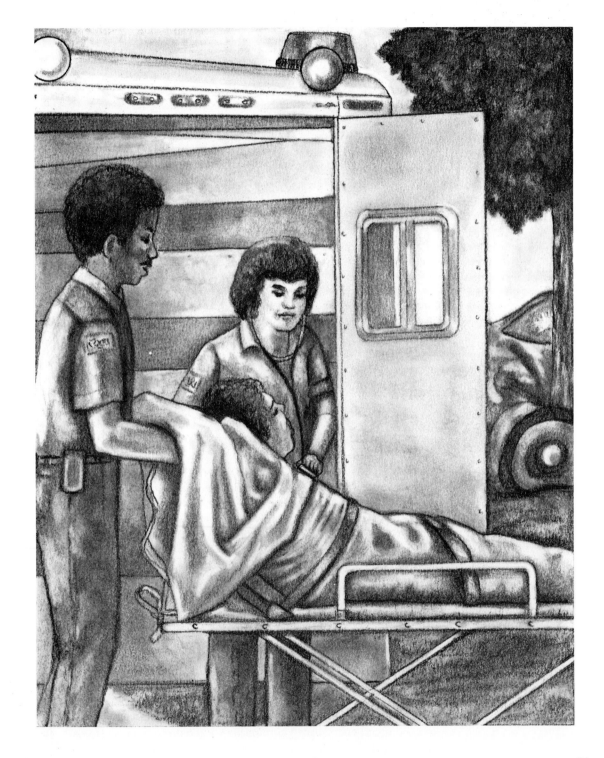

ever, a patient understands how close such symptoms are to simple anxiety, is afraid of rejection, and therefore believes that he or she must present the correct ticket to the health care provider. This has been called the "symptom on the plate."

Rather than say "I grind my teeth," a patient may prefer to present a toothache to the dentist. Perhaps he is already aware that tooth grinding is a symptom of anxiety. Presenting a toothache will at least prevent the dentist from telling him that the problem is anxiety. The patient may simply want reassurance or fixing so that his teeth will not fall out.

The dentist can still treat the patient, but a new sensitivity can make him or her more receptive to the patient's world and symptoms. If the dentist can probe (psychologically!) in the right way, even the slightest hint from the patient may enable the dentist to respond more appropriately and learn what is really bothering the patient.

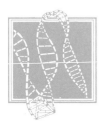

Personality Types in Illness Behavior

The histrionic personality (a person who displays emotions for effect) is apt to play out in the health profesional's office as much as in the outside world. Symptoms are exaggerated, dramatic, sudden, and presented in an alarming fashion. Understanding what the style of such a person is likely to be can help the health professional see such symptoms in their true perspective.

Dependent personalities may quickly reveal themselves to caregivers through their desire to please ("Yes, nurse", "Whatever you say nurse"). Of course, the way a patient comes across to you also tells you how they may deal with other people. Perhaps they are also dependent on their spouse or their peers. If a patient's problems are psychological, excessive dependency on a health professional may block the patient's ability to stand on his or her own two feet again. The aim of psychological treatment is to promote independent functioning.

Obsessive compulsive personalities may dwell excessively on particular symptoms, especially their bowel habits.

A lot of interest has been paid to **Type A and Type B personalities**. Type A behavior entails a sense of urgency, striving for perfection, and difficulty in accepting things if they are not the way the person wants them. Most successful businesspeople are Type A. Type B's are not bothered by lateness, accept people and events as they are without frustration and feel no compulsion to compete. Type A's are thought to be more prone to heart attacks than Type B's possibly because Type A's produce more adrenaline due to the hostile part of their personality. A chronic high adrenaline level may stress the heart.

Intellectual Capacity

As a health care provider, it is important for you to be particularly sensitive about a patient's literacy level. Illiterate patients do not announce the fact. An illiterate person will accept written information graciously. When asked to fill out forms, the person will have a friend or family member do it for them, offering an excuse such as forgetting their glasses that day. It is difficult to detect that a patient is illiterate, but you must learn how to do it so you can provide effective treatment. Literature or schedules for pills are, of course, inappropriate for an illiterate person. Pill tables can be constructed by taping each pill to the left of a table that has check marks indicating when pills should be taken. Graphs also would be inappropriate; pictures are best.

Whether patients can read or not, communication is of vital importance. A study of discussions with patients about informed consent for operations showed patients remembered or understood virtually nothing at a later date. Patients remember best what is said first. Older and more intelligent patients remember about the same as younger or less intelligent patients. Most patients can consistently and easily recall only two statements.

More educated patients tend to visit multiple health care specialists for various problems. By contrast, the less educated may take their financial, moral, psychological, and legal problems all to their primary caregiver be that the parent figure in a dependent relationship, their landlord, a grandmother, a nurse, or a physician.

How Illness Affects Behavior

Each illness has its own story, and illnesses do not have the same psychological effect. A patient with chronic renal failure on dialysis has needs that are different from those of a patient with paraplegia, diabetes, chronic pain, or terminal cancer. Multiple sclerosis patients often seem to be inappropriately euphoric, despite a seemingly disastrous future, although underlying depression is common. Alcoholics frequently use denial — a part of the illness itself — as a defense.

It is important that you, as a health care provider, not be sidetracked by behaviors that may be part of the illness itself. For example, you cannot assume that every MS patient who seems to be happy is happy.

Secondary depression in illness is also common. Such depression can be regarded as a grief reaction to learning the diagnosis of some chronic problem. If the patient can adapt, life will become enjoyable again. If not, the patient will suffer from chronic grief, a surprisingly common and hidden reaction in chronic sickness.

Appointment Negotiating

No discussion of illness behavior would be complete without an examination of how patients handle the making and keeping of appointments in the outpatient world. Many patients, regardless of the diagnosis, take a distant appointment to mean that they are doing well. They may resist having appointments close together because they see this as a symbol of how ill they are. Never mind that they need the appointment!

Other patients may wish to have frequent appointments regardless of actual need. They may be frightened and want extra support from the health professional, or they may be using their health problems to get attention. Frequent appointments mean that they get attention from the health professional, or they may get sympathy from their family and friends for having to see a health practitioner so often.

Other patients use the breaking of appointments to manipulate the health care provider. Providers may be wise to refuse service to patients who break appointments frequently. The symbolic implications around the scheduling of appointments make their negotiating a phase of treatment to which you and all health care practitioners must be alert.

Appointment scheduling can have many implications for the patient. Be sure you understand the psychological aspects of "sooner" dates versus "later" appointments.

The Patient's World

It is important to think of what life is like for your patient. But you cannot simply put yourself into a patient's world because you probably would take your own value judgments with you. (Look back at the section on empathizing in Chapter 2.)

An important factor in the patient's world is their **primary relationship**. Leo Buscaglia, a popular contemporary author who writes about the dynamics of love, defines the primary relationship as "the closest person with whom you presently choose to relate, or are forced to on a regular basis in your daily life." For most people this is a family member or a friend. But some people have their primary relationship with a dog or cat, with themselves (they may be isolated, depressed, alone, withdrawn, or narcissistic), or maybe with their landlord. As a simple example, an elderly woman whose primary relationship is with her dog is, unfortunately, unlikely to find many health care workers who realize that.

One barrier to understanding can be the health practitioner's class assumption that primary relationships are the most important thing to patients. For some people, the struggle for survival, money, food, sex, or drugs may be most important. Remember our discussion of Maslow's hierarchy of human needs at the beginning of this chapter.

Sensitivity is the key to digesting the information in this chapter. You need to have your ears open to the unique qualities of your patients. You need to build an understanding of the things that all human beings need and value. You need to understand what it is like to be healthy and what it is like to be ill.

Chapter Summary

Many different theories have been suggested to explain human behavior. Notable contributors are Pavlov, Freud, Adler, Jung, Perls, Berne, and Roger. There are no "correct" theories. Just as many different word processing programs are available for computers, so different theories may all be used for a satisfactory insight into the patient's problems.

An important insight into everyday life is the use of psychological defense mechanisms. Beyond a simple understanding of classifying psychological disorders, you are urged to consider illness behavior, illness traditions, and sickness roles.

The health care provider should also analyze the interaction of the patient in the patient/health professional contact, looking for the true essence of the patient's problem, not just "the symptom on the plate."

Review

Behaviorism: school of psychology focusing on patient behavior
Complex: group of ideas with common feeling or tone, e.g., inferiority complex which is a strong feeling of inferiority with undue pessimism
Conditioned reflex: a learned response to a stimulus
Defense mechanism: psychological method of reducing psychic pain from mental conflict
Delusion: abnormal idea which has no basis in reality
Denial: defense mechanism in which painful truths are denied
Ego: the realization of a person's conscious mind as a unique individual
Gestalt: form of therapy treating the patient as a whole, and focusing on current feelings
Hallucination: abnormal perception which has no basis in reality
Identification: defense mechanism in which there is unconscious transfer of outside character traits to one's own mind
Libido: sexual instinct
Neurosis: group of psychological syndromes manifest by an exaggerated worry, though oriented to reality
Psychoses: group of psychological syndromes manifest by detachment from reality
Rationalization: defense mechanism in which unacceptable events are made acceptable through pseudological argument
Repression: pushing painful thoughts into the unconscious mind

1. Give examples of layers of the human mind.
2. A client has just been told of the presence of terminal cancer. Discuss how Freud's theories of life and death instincts may play a role.
3. What is the difference between an inferiority complex and introversion?
4. List three situations where you can identify games played by people or clients. Discuss in each game the ego state and motive for the games.
5. "There are no illnesses, only ill people." Discuss.
6. "Always remember to ask yourself who is really the patient and what is really the disease." Discuss.
7. Why must you be objective to learn about people?

Berne, E. *Games People Play.* Ballantine Books, New York, NY. 1973.

British Medical Journal. The Future General Practitioner. Working Party of Royal College of General Practitioners. London, England. 1972.

Purtilo, R. *Health Professional/Patient Interaction.* W.B. Saunders Co., Philadelphia, PA. 1978.

Buscaglia, L. *Loving Each Other.* Fawcett Columbine, New York, NY. 1984.

Chapter

4

After reading this chapter, you should be able:
- To define and identify the five Kübler-Ross stages of loss.
- To understand the interrelationships of these stages and how they apply to losses such as death and dissolution of a relationship.
- To respond appropriately to patients by using this understanding empathically.
- To discuss death with the dying.
- To recognize the psychological issues connected with loss of positive body image.
- To define thanatology, positive and negative euthanasia, and the philosophies connected with "right to die" issues.
- To assist the family in dealing with the dying patient.

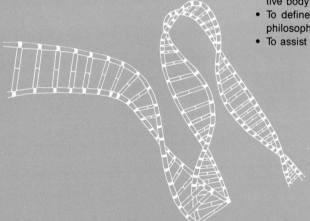

Understanding Grief

Until recently, health care workers generally were not taught to deal with the psychological aspects of loss or death. Curing disease and maintaining life were the primary goals of health care providers. Although it was acknowledged that people did die, this harsh reality was seen as a defeat and was thus regarded as unworthy of attention. It seemed more appropriate to focus training on the positive goals than to put valuable time into a negative outcome.

It was not until the 1960s that a physician named Elisabeth Kübler-Ross challenged health care workers to view loss and death as natural. She focused her work on understanding and helping the dying. She pointed out that denying reality doesn't change it. What was being gained by living in a death-denying society? Perhaps the living could avoid looking at reality for an infinite period of time, but who then comforted the dying?

Kübler-Ross worked with hundreds of people as they learned of their own terminal illness. She and her staff supported these individuals until the end. What the dying taught them has become a cornerstone for the education of all health professionals. Kübler-Ross stages of loss have far-reaching implications. They enable us to understand and to help not only the dying but all grieving people. They help us to deal with those who are about to die, those who have lost a loved one to death, and those who have lost a body part or the use of their body. Further, they help us gain insight into those

The Kübler-Ross Stages of Loss and a View to Body Image

who are losing a preferred lifestyle, such as those who face divorce or economic loss. Gaining understanding of these stages will enhance your ability to empathize.

Stages of loss.

Briefly, the stages of loss are as follows:

1. **Denial:** A defense mechanism that generally serves as a buffer against too harsh a reality. Patients may describe themselves as simply feeling numb when faced with bad news. Or they may actively deny the existence of a problem until or unless they become able to handle it. When first told that a breast lump is cancer, a patient may say, "This lump is nothing. I've simply bumped into something."

2. **Anger:** Rage at the world for the victim's misfortune; the "why me" stage. Patients are preoccupied with the unfairness of their situation and see everyone else as lucky by comparison. They appear to hate anyone who is well. The bereaved may direct their anger at others with such statements as "She would still be alive if you had given her the injection when you should have" or "If only Harry had brought him to the hospital sooner." Or they may direct their anger at themselves: "It was all my fault, I should have seen how ill he was."

3. **Bargaining:** Usually a spiritual stage during which victims hope to postpone the inevitable harsh reality by promising a sacrifice to their God should they be allowed to live a bit longer. Sometimes this bargaining is played out with health care workers as well. If, as a medical office assistant, you permit them to schedule their

next appointment in the distant future, they see it as a way of gaining time. An appointment next week may mean they are in serious trouble. An appointment next month may mean they are not so bad off.

4. **Depression:** A stage of quiet grieving during which victims face their loss squarely. Often they withdraw from all but their closest contacts.

5. **Acceptance:** The stage during which victims become resigned to their fate and plan for it. A patient at the acceptance stage may update her/his will, write an obituary, put old grievances to rest, and say goodbye to family and friends.

As we review these stages indepth, bear in mind that the stages **are not mutually exclusive**. People pass through stages and go back again. Most often stages overlap. Some individuals miss stages entirely or never reach them.

Denial

Denial is a reaction that commonly follows the first news of impending death or significant loss. It is a defense mechanism. When information is too harsh for an individual to face, denial acts as a psychological buffer. It is an emotional escape hatch, for it tells us that the thing we do not wish to hear is not true. Denial comes in a variety of degrees, lasts for an unpredictable length of time, and is demonstrated in various forms.

A healthy amount of denial might be described as follows: An individual is told that he has inoperable cancer. His first thought is that this just cannot be true. He seeks a second opinion. While waiting for the retest results he begins to think about putting his life in order and what he would do if this horrible news were, in fact, true. When the second opinion confirms the first, he begins to let go of his screen of denial and progresses through the other stages.

Sometimes a longer lasting form of denial is also helpful. An individual who is dying may still need to accomplish many things. For some, only the hope that they will actually live allows them to continue. They may handle situations bravely and be helpful to and encourage family members.

Denial becomes a problem when it goes on too long, makes the patient emotionally fragile ("Please don't say anything that will chip away at my defense"), or gets in the way of positive actions. Some individuals remain in almost a zombie-like state of denial. They cannot make appropriate plans, either for themselves or their family members, and they may engage in a variety of activities designed to convince themselves that they could not possibly be dying. These activities may include making grand vacation plans, buying new cars, having elaborate elective dental work, or procuring new pets. Such individuals focus more on beginning activities than on tying up unfinished business.

Others may be so afraid of facing their illness that they may delay treatment or other help. As mentioned above, the story is well-known: Aunt Matilda discovers a lump in her breast but says she must have bumped herself and does nothing about it. In some instances, then, denial can cost individuals their lives.

We do not wish to sound judgmental as we discuss denial. Can you sense the panic or fear you would feel if you were to discover a lump that could mean cancer? Can you understand both the power and comfort denial could offer to someone facing something so frightening?

See if you can tell which of the following responses are empathic (the answer is at the bottom of the page). Then practice by creating your own empathic responses to the patient comments. Remember to suspend your judgments.

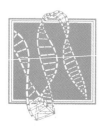

Patient: "I know the cancer is in both lungs now, but I won't give up. I'm sure others have been this ill and survived and I'm going to be one of them."

Response A: "You will not stop fighting the cancer."

Response B: "You are desperately determined to live despite the odds."

Patient: "I don't care how many doctors tell me I will never walk again — I know I will. If I have to leave the country to get treatment then that's what I'll do."

Response A: "You'll go anywhere in the world to find help in walking again."

Response B: "You're angry with anyone who interferes with your determination to walk again, and you will fight to get the support you need."

Anyone associated with a dying person — family members, friends, other patients, and health professionals — may go through stages of denial, anger, bargaining, depression, and acceptance. Sometimes the emotional stages of friends, relatives, and others coincide with the same stage in the patient. Often, however, individuals progress through the stages based on their own personal needs.

For three years a daughter dutifully visited her mother in the nursing home. She came for at least an hour every day. She read to her mother, fed her, and helped to bathe

---

Answers: **A** responses are paraphrasing; **B** responses are empathic.

her. Throughout these three years the mother was expected to die any time. Her condition, the result of hardening of the arteries and stroke, went from grave to critical. The health care providers involved made assumptions about the daughter's preparation for her mother's death. They believed the daughter was devoted to her mother, but they thought she would be tired of caring for her and worrying about her. Further, they reasoned that the daughter had come to accept death as the inevitable release for both. The nursing home staff was not prepared for the daughter's reaction the day her mother did die.

The daughter was called at her home at 7 a.m. She was told that her mother had died quietly during the night. When she heard these words, she began screaming hysterically, "She can't be dead, she can't be dead!" Fifteen minutes later, still wearing a nightgown, she arrived at the nursing home and dashed to her mother's door. There she flung on her mother's bed and sobbed and moaned. It was not until her own daughter was summoned from a nearby town that she was comforted.

Apparently the daughter had been existing in a state of denial and bargaining. If she took good enough care of her mother, she reasoned, she would never lose her. It was weeks before she attained a level of acceptance. During these weeks she went through the stages of grieving as though her mother's death had been a complete surprise. Perhaps attention to the daughter's needs would have enabled the staff to predict her behavior. Better still would have been intervention **prior** to the mother's death. No one realized that this woman was stuck at an early stage of adjustment. What could a health practitioner have said to the daughter in this case? How do you tell a woman that her mother will die soon?

Problems like this one can be avoided if family members ask about the future of their loved ones. A gentle but truthful response is then the best one. When family members do not allow themselves to hear the truth, a family conference may be necessary. The conference, which would bring together all close members of the patient's family, not only would clarify health information, but also would allow family members to form a support group for themselves as well as for the patient.

In our example, the patient's daughter had a grown daughter of her own. The daughter might have become more involved with the patient's care in a way that would have permitted her to comfort her own mother. Or the granddaughter might have helped the staff to identify the depth of her own mother's denial if she had reported the disparity between her mother's comments about her grandmother and her grandmother's actual condition. Even if the patient's daughter had no other family, there might have been ways of detecting her denial. The biggest clue might have been the daughter's intense devotion to her mother's care. Perhaps it was too intense. When anyone seems to do **too well** in a difficult situation, we must be on the alert to discover if this might be a form of denial and the extent of the denial.

Health care workers who deny feelings for dying patients may, in a sense, atrophy. They can become cold and clinical with the dying. Their scientific skills may be excellent, but they hide warmth and humanness from the patients who need it most. The job environment also can affect a health worker's development. Think of a warm, caring, involved provider who works in an environment that is not open to mourning. For how long can a person choke back grief before it causes additional harm? Not long, we think. It is not an unusual occurence that staff in nonsupportive environments burn out early and leave.

Obviously those who provide continuous care to a patient are most likely to be affected. But even those health practitioners who have less frequent contact with the dying patient may require the right to grieve when a special patient dies.

There is a fine line between professional detachment and coldness. The experienced health practitioner will have developed a skill that permits closeness and understanding without setting up an incapacitating identification with the patient. Accepting grief as a necessary part of our work with the dying helps us to deal with it promptly and properly. Unfortunately, we are not untouchable with respect to life's pains. Predicting this helps us to take better care of ourselves and of our patients.

Another area of loss with which we must be familiar is that connected with the end of a relationship. When a spouse or family member dies, the remaining family generally receives caring support. There is a formal, prescribed set of social responses connected with death. Friends send flowers, food, and memorial contributions. People come together even from great distances to be there for the survivors. All the people who knew the deceased praise his or her accomplishments.

Proper response to a divorce or the end of a relationship is not so universal, however. Friends often do not know what to say. Yet the dynamics of a breakup are strong and potentially dangerous. A patient who is divorcing may feel both rejected and like a failure. It is very difficult to resume living when self-esteem is so shattered.

Typical responses to a breakup may be well-intended but are not always supportive of the person they're said to. For example:

"Oh, he was no good for you. You're better off without him."
"You two were never compatible."
"I knew for years that she was cheating on you."
"I know you'll be fine, it's just the kids we feel sorry for."
"I told you you were working too many hours. If you'd been home more I bet he wouldn't have gotten bored."

This list may sound humorous, but haven't we all heard such misguided advice being given? As health care providers, we need to be a lot more sensitive. Remember that during the first part of a breakup one or both parties may be in a denial state. Typically this means that the persons involved are ignoring any evidence of an impending breakup. A wife may refuse to believe that anything is wrong with the marriage even though her husband fails to come home several nights a week. A husband may not let himself think there is anything wrong at home even though his wife will no longer share a bed with him and is hinting at separate vacations.

When people in denial-like states are hit with reality, they become panicky. Learning that their partner has left brings out feelings of desperation: "This can't be true. I'll never survive without her." The response "I think she'll come back" gives no support.

You will be better able to understand the breakup of a relationship if you examine it in the context of the stages of loss. Patient problems and illnesses make more sense when you place the patient with respect to these stages. Remember that there is often overlap between stages. Treatment will improve when you focus on how patients are progressing with their grief.

Anger

Anger generally follows denial. You may have detected an element of anger already in the denial stage. Recall the patient who said "I don't care how many doctors tell me I won't walk again . . ." This statement shows anger. The way the denials are worded almost screams out that the patient knows the truth.

As the patient breaks out of the denial stage, screaming may, in fact, take place. Facing the harsh reality of a tremendous loss makes most people very angry. This is the "Why me?" stage. There is often bitterness and turmoil as the patient experiences loss and isolation coupled with a sense of unfairness regarding his or her plight.

Patients are angry with their disease and with their poor fortune. Because the objects of their anger are intangible, the anger usually spills over onto other objects. Patients in the anger stage are often difficult to be around. The young, healthy health care worker makes a good target. The worse the patient is feeling and the younger the worker appears to be, the more angry the patient may become. These angry outbursts require caring and gentleness. Responding in anger is most inappropriate; even **not** responding in anger becomes difficult when the patient lashes out as if to blame the health professional for her or his imminent death.

When both denial and anger are operating, patients or their families may sue for malpractice because of the terminal diagnosis. "If this or that had been done *or* had not been done *or* had been done sooner, then perhaps Dad would not be dying now." Most such responses are scapegoating. It is so hard to accept loss that anger and blame temporarily ease and divert the involved parties. Unfortunately, this may unduly tax the health care system. After all, Dad may still need help from those who are being blamed.

When health care providers and family members rationally discuss prognosis and possible causes, the patient seems to suffer least. In fact, if health care providers attempt to avoid all dealings with the family's anger, they are more likely to be sued. Stating that you understand the family's grief and pain may help them to fix blame on the disease and not on the bearer of the bad news.

Patient's Spouse: "Oh, it's easy for you to stand there and say 'we'll do everything possible to make him comfortable.' What's it to you. I bet your husband is healthy!"

Health Professional: "It looks to you as though I might have no problems in my personal life and no understanding of how difficult this is for you."

By staying with the speaker, you will generally calm them. A defensive remark such as "Where do you get off thinking you're the only one with problems" will only generate more anger. By letting people vent and helping them to feel understood, you decrease their **need** to lash out.

Anger shows up as human beings struggle to understand and accept all types of loss. It may take years to accept a disability. Generally, the more severe the limitations are, the longer it takes to accept them. A 24-year-old who awakes to find that a car accident 10 days earlier has left her a paraplegic probably spends years adjusting to her loss. Think of the number of losses this news involves. Not only

can she never walk again, but her body image, sexuality, family planning, work ability, general mobility, and long-term health will all be affected. Can she still drive? With what adjustments? How will she control her bowel and bladder? Can her chair fit through the doors of her home? Will she need an attendant? How will her boyfriend and friends react?

Anger and depression can be very strong for those adjusting to loss. Suicide attempts may occur for several years after the loss. The more the individual tries to cope with the disability, the more frustration he or she encounters. When people try and try to make things better the proportion of effort they must expend is sometimes outweighed by a too-small degree of change. When they feel helpless and frustrated, they sometimes give up. Still others simply become angry at the world. They feel bitter that everyone else appears to "have it all" when they have "lost it all." Until they can deal with their anger, they have little chance of developing independence. Anger will keep tripping them up.

Remember that anger is a natural reaction to loss. When loss is tremendous, anger is likely to be more pronounced. Health professionals need to empathize and respond by acknowledging the patient's anger and the patient's right to feel angry. Who wouldn't be angry facing loss? When a patient holds on to anger for years, more treatment is necessary. Patients will not readjust if they are angry with everyone they meet for not suffering as they do.

When divorcing people hit the anger stage, they often gain comfort from friends. If you can share anger with a friend you may not feel so out of tune. Problems occur when the anger stage is denied or displaced. People who deny anger toward their spouse often develop emotional and psychosomatic illnesses. They may feel very unwell and develop something like indigestion, for instance, because they cannot admit how angry they are about their spouse's rejection.

Those closest to a breakup often are injured by displaced anger. A mother may not be able to admit how devastated she is at being divorced, but she becomes an overcontrolling nagging dictator with the kids. She throws her anger and her need to feel in charge on those who are less threatening to her.

Health care providers themselves frequently need a place to be angry. Some facilities, especially those connected with hospices, have screaming rooms. These are private, soundproof rooms where individuals can close themselves in and scream. This helps to ease sorrow by releasing the burden of keeping it all in. Remember that anger at a patient's imminent death is common among the staff who work closely with the dying. It is difficult to care for your patient while losing her.

Understanding Grief

The anger stage is painful and difficult for everyone — families, health care workers, and patients. But, like the denial stage, it is normal and necessary to most people. Remember that the dying person is losing everything. While others are grieving over the loss of an individual, the dying person must say farewell to all he has known: people, sunsets, puppies, ice cream, Christmas, music, everything. It is natural and emotionally appropriate to be angry.

Some elements of the anger stage may remain throughout the dying process. Generally, however, there is an acute angry period followed by considerable calming if the anger is brought out and dealt with properly.

Bargaining

The bargaining stage is similar to denial. It is another safety zone or buffer from the full force of unbearable reality. The bargaining stage generally has a religious overtone to it. When faced with death, even the least religious person seems to invoke her or his God. The patient will often offer a sacrifice of sorts if God will only save his or her life. If, for example, a patient thinks he has worked too hard and hasn't shown his children enough consideration, he will promise to undo this wrong in exchange for a return to health. "I will spend all my time with my children." Another patient may say, "Please God, let me live long enough to attend my grandson's wedding." If she should live to the wedding date, she may renegotiate the contract: "Please God, let me live to see my first great-grandchild born."

Patients may also bargain with the health professional. A dentist gently told a man with terminal cancer that there was no real need to continue his root canal work. She was surprised by the patient's zealous insistence that the tooth must be treated! By convincing the dentist to finish the root canal work, the patient had a sense of gaining proof that he would continue to need his teeth.

Bargaining may provide comfort and hope when all seems lost. Generally, however, the patient sees that the "deal" is not going to be met. This generates feelings of frustration and anger, which usually dissolves into depression.

Depression

Depression occurs when a patient believes that hope is lost. He has cracked through initial denial, raged at the world, and even pleaded with a God in whom he may have had no faith. But everything he has thought and done has been to no avail. He is not getting better and he knows it.

Although we never wish to see a patient suffering through depression, it is a normal and necessary state. During this time the individual examines her life, what she has done, and what she will never do. She becomes introverted and withdrawn, and may sit alone in a darkened room. She may refuse most visitors, seeing only a few family and friends who mean enough to her.

Although subdued in tone, the depression stage still contains turmoil. Elements of denial, anger and bargaining may still creep in. Remember that no previous stage is ever discrete (separate and distinct) or complete. But during depression the patient actually comes to believe in his own mortality and thinks over what he has done and what he has missed.

This stage, like all others, is somewhat mediated by who the patient was before the disease. For example, certain resilient individuals will show similar spunk even when faced with death. Other less emotionally strong people will have more trouble passing through the stages and facing reality.

If depression lingers for a long time, medication and psychotherapy may be indicated. Certainly the patient should receive all the emotional support possible. The threat of suicide is a very real possibility during this stage and mandates referral to a psychologist or psychiatrist.

Reminiscing, reviewing life, and sleeplessness are behaviors that commonly accompany depression. (These behaviors are reviewed in more detail in Chapter 5 in the section on senescence.) Basically they can be viewed as normal. Life review helps a dying person gain perspective on what she or he has accomplished and will leave behind. Not sleeping well as part of depression may be the mind's way of working to reconcile the sorrow of grieving and is therefore necessary. For how long is depression normal? Generally speaking, after losing a loved one, a person should be back at work within a month and able to mix socially within six months. Although some sorrow may continue indefinitely, a person who is still having a lot of difficulty handling the loss after six months may need special help.

Acceptance

Acceptance, the final stage in the emotional process, follows depression. Acceptance is not a happy phase, but the patient is generally calm and demonstrates a subdued interest in the world and in attending to unfinished business.

Usually the patient wishes to talk out loud to a trusted friend or two. There seems to be a need to verify many of the thoughts conjured up during depression. And there is a need to touch base with someone who knows about the patient's life and can thus validate his or her worth.

Generally, the more loving the patient's support group is, the easier acceptance comes to the patient. There seems to be a stronger sense of self-worth and of having mattered in the world if many people love you. Such support provides the environment necessary for a patient to face death and to put her or his life together with dignity.

To reiterate: remember that none of these stages is discrete. Although denial will generally come before depression, there are elements of both in each. Some individuals skip stages. Others work through stages very quickly. Passing through stages must be at the patient's own pace. A patient or family member who is suffering because of being stuck at a particular stage may require assistance to progress. If a disease progresses rapidly, the patient may never reach some stages.

Denial, anger, bargaining, depression, and acceptance are the feelings of loss most dying and grieving people must pass through. The more you can learn about these stages, the better able you will be to help your patients, their families, and yourself.

Because denial and anger generally occur at the beginning of the grieving process, they tend to be prominent among the stages. Another reason they are noteworthy is that they can confound and complicate medical treatment. It is essential that you understand both the stages of and responses to denial and anger because they generally entail more of a health challenge than do bargaining, depression, and acceptance. Of course, being familiar with all the stages will enable you to better understand and provide service to your patients.

> See if you can identify the Stages in the following examples:
>
> Patient 1: "I've always gone to church and worked hard. This is so unfair. My sister never does a thing for anybody and she is healthy as a horse!"
>
> Patient 2: "I know that if I just eat more carefully this whole thing will reverse itself. No way can I be so sick at my age.
>
> Patient 3: "At this point I want to rewrite my will and fix up the obituary. That will make things easier on my wife.
>
> Patient 4: "If it is God's will that I die, so be it. But I know that he wants me to see my last child through to graduation and I'm going to do it.
>
> *Answers:* Patient 1 = anger; Patient 2 = denial with some bargaining aspects; Patient 3 = acceptance; Patient 4 = bargaining.

A View to Body Image

The area of body image warrants examination. Too often we do not realize the emotional pangs of looking different. As health care workers, we often reason that if a patient's life is not threatened and there is no pain, that patient is lucky. But burn patients who are fully recovered in terms of physical abilities often remain depressed and suicidal. *And some patients refuse a medication because it distorts their facial features,* even though taking it may improve the quality of their physical health. These examples demonstrate a form of denial that overlaps with other psychological features. Undoubtedly a breast lump is more difficult for some women to face than other lumps might be. The fear of cancer may remain the same, but the fear of disfigurement is crippling. Few women react as directly and purposefully as Nancy Reagan — to have the breast removed quickly and go on about the important matters in her life.

Positive body image is a valuable commodity. To better help your patients, you must ask yourself what they are risking in this area as well. To assume that adequate functioning is sufficient for happiness is a gross oversight.

Thanatology is the study of death. It encompasses religious and philosophical issues as well as practical issues. Whether or not we personally believe in an afterlife, modern medicine provides us with numerous ethical dilemmas related to dying. Only a few years ago the notion of an artificial heart beating inside a human being was purely science fiction. Today we all remember the heroic struggle of Dr. Barney Clark with the Jarvic heart.

Such fast-paced scientific achievements leave many questions regarding the **quality of human life**. It is not enough simply to prolong life if there is no enjoyment for the patient. Questions such as this have led to organizations that actively promote the right to die.

Right to die groups are typically political. They focus their time and money on influencing state legislative bodies. For example, in California in 1987, as in previous years, another attempt was made to pass right to die legislation. This legislation would allow patients who are terminally ill to declare that no heroic life-sustaining efforts should be made to prolong their lives. This is **negative euthanasia**. Negative euthanasia is tacit noninterference with the process of death; for instance, leaving pneumonia untreated. **Positive euthanasia** involves *directly* taking a life. The terminally ill would not simply be allowed to die but could be put to sleep. Philosophically, supporters of this bill argue that it is inhumane to allow dying human beings to suffer. If there is no hope, why force a patient to die slowly and painfully when we would do more for a beloved pet.

These issues have been fought repeatedly in nearly every state. Negative euthanasia is common practice in most hospitals. The hopelessly ill simply are not revived when problems develop. "Do not resuscitate" orders are written by physicians in a hospital setting when a patient is in the final stage of an incurable medical condition, or sometimes if an older patient requests it. For a 65-year-old who is otherwise healthy to resist aggressive treatment might be seen as parasuicide. But for a 96-year-old blind person to resist aggressive treatment could not reasonably be seen as parasuicide. Somewhere between these two extremes lies a dividing line. In practice, that line is usually drawn by the competent patient and his or her relative after informed discussion with health professionals. Competency is the ability to understand relevant risks and alternatives and to make a decision that reflects the patient's own choice.

A "do not resuscitate" order in no way means that health care providers abandon or cease treating the patient. It simply means that cardiopulmonary resuscitation would not be performed should the patient's heart stop beating or should breathing stop.

However, even this form of euthanasia is not totally without legal ramifications. Proponents of the right to die movement want to ensure that physicians can administer lethal doses of drugs to a dying person (upon the person's request) and be protected from legal ramifications.

Obviously, there are more issues surrounding dying than simply providing comfort. Health care workers need to be aware of the legal and ethical ramifications of their treatment of the dying. Some health professionals may even wish to lead the way in finding solutions to death with dignity issues. But for most of us, the number one concern is how to help dying patients directly. There are five specific ways in which you, as a health care provider, can help the dying. You can: listen, focus through paraphrasing, respond from your own "gut," leave hope intact, and assist the family to be with the patient.

Listen

When a dying person wants to talk, listen. As part of progressing through the Kübler-Ross stages, the patient needs to gain a perspective on what is happening. Talking can help patients work their way toward acceptance. A big problem for the dying is to find someone who is willing to listen.

Most people freeze up when confronted with a grieving person. They feel ill at ease. They are afraid to say anything lest it be the wrong thing. Health care workers must work very hard to overcome this kind of fear. Students who are just beginning their clinical training often fear dealing with dying people more than they fear any other aspect of patient care. A dying person will often pick a young health care worker to confide in. What should you do if you are the one chosen? First, listen. Take a deep breath. Do not panic. Remember that it is okay if a patient needs to talk about dying. You do not have to have years of experience to be of help. You may need to schedule more time to work with such a patient, however. Their emotional needs and your ability to respond will be enhanced by extended and frequent visits. Remember, a dying person does not have time to wait.

Focus through Paraphrasing

Listen and then focus through paraphrasing. Stick with what is being said. A typical response to a patient's statement of grief blocks rather than encourages talking.

Patient: "I wonder what it will be like to be dead."

Health "Oh, now don't think about that. Think about getting
Practitioner: well."

Such a response is obviously inappropriate. How much easier dying would be if the patient were allowed to talk instead of being closed off.

You do not have to be brilliant, supersensitive, or even vastly experienced to say the right thing. All you have to do is paraphrase.

Patient: "I wonder what it will be like to be dead?"

Health "It seems that you're getting curious about death at this
Practitioner: point."

Patient: "Yes."

Offering such a response encourages the patient to keep talking. It says that you understand what the patient is saying and that it's okay to talk with you about it. Once the patient gives more, an empathic response is generally appropriate. But, simply paraphrasing throughout the dialogue would be far better than closing off discussion.

An empathic response to this patient's statement would be: "It sounds like you're frightened of what lies ahead. Maybe you could tell me what you think death may be like."

Respond From Your Own "Gut"

Kübler-Ross teaches her students to make a "gut" response. This approach ties in with the use of empathy. Your gut response would be an empathic one, for you would be responding to your patient with an honestly felt emotion. If a patient asks you a question, even a personal or difficult one, you need to answer it. The dying need to know what you think.

"Do you believe in God, doctor?"
"Will it hurt to die, nurse?"
"Will I see my baby brother in heaven?"
"Are you afraid of death?"
"Do you think there is an afterlife?"

Problems occur when, as health care workers, we have not dealt with these issues for ourselves. After all, we live in a death-denying society, and health professionals may regard death as failure. How do we as individuals break through denial to share our honest feelings? Your instructor will assign several class exercises that will help you feel in touch with your own mortality. Only when you have faced the reality of your own death will you be comfortable in responding from your gut to your patients. Responses that are not honestly felt may seem safe to the giver, but rarely will they fool the receiver.

Leave Hope Intact

There is a subtle difference between denial and hope. Hope can be looked at as a bright spot or an escape hatch. For a dying man to have hope may simply mean that tomorrow won't be taken away from him, even though he has no long future ahead. Most human beings, even during stages of depression and acceptance, want hope.

The dying have been asked how they want to be told about their illness and its consequences. They have responded that they want to be told the truth, but that they need to believe there is some hope, some reason to fight. If an illness is very serious, then say so. But never convey that it, or a patient's situation, is totally hopeless. Do not lie, but do not give up. In such an atmosphere, the terminally ill can manage to live better until they die.

Most of us will probably not be giving such news directly to a patient. But it is important to understand this frame of reference. Even when you are assisting in the breakdown of denial, you don't want to convey a sense of hopelessness.

We need to be sensitive to the words we select to convey the nature of a patient's illness. Must we always refer to cancer as cancer? Avoiding the word *cancer* may prevent some patients from shutting down their senses and giving in to deep denial. Substituting the word *tumor* may be less emotionally devastating for some patients. Observing a patient's body language and concentrating on matching their level of questions may key health professionals in on how best to phrase difficult news. If the patient says, "Is it malignant?" or "Is it cancer?", then the health professional can respond using such words. But if the patient obviously avoids the word *cancer*, then using a less direct term may be in order.

> Patient: "Do you think the doctor got it all? They said it was a long operation."
>
> Health Professional: "The whole breast was removed and nothing was found outside the area."

Assisting the Family to be with the Patient

The people who work in hospitals can make a sterile environment less cold and more inviting. With a caring staff of health care workers and enough time in the institution, a patient may find that the hospital begins to feel like home. Hospitals that are run like hospices are set up to closely simulate the home environment, a difficult task when medical equipment makes up part of the furnishings. The hospice concept promotes home death whenever possible. Dying at home is thought to be more natural. Imagine how much more gentle it might be to die in your own bed surrounded by familiar things and people who love you than to die in a hospital.

Unfortunately, dying at home is a luxury that not every family can manage. Some families cannot cope with taking care of a physically infirmed loved one. Lifting, feeding, bathing, and bathroom use present insurmountable hurdles. The physical abilities of the family must be considered along with the condition of the patient.

But the emotional strength of the family is probably the most important consideration. Can the family deal with their loved one and her terminal disease 24 hours a day? How will they react to her pain or nausea? If she becomes severely confused, will they become frightened? How prepared are they for death? Have they enough support systems for their own emotional well-being? If the family wants the patient at home, there is usually a way that home care can be managed. If sufficient community services are available, or if money is plentiful, then home care may be possible with even frail family support.

Ideally, medications will be sufficient to keep pain at a minimum. Often medication and other aides to comfort can be adjusted when the health care team makes house calls. The team also can assist family members in making time for themselves away from the patient. If a patient's condition becomes too much for the family, intermittent inpatient care can be arranged. When all goes well, death — as the final stage of life — occurs naturally, at home.

When hospitalization is constant and prolonged, a patient can suffer a tremendous sense of isolation. He or she may believe that friends and family do not care. When visitors come only infrequently, a long stay in the hospital gives patients a message of rejection or abandonment. Sadly, visitors do tend to avoid the dying. Many people find it painful to acknowledge the possibility of death, especially in a friend. They may fear that the dying person will put them on the spot. Thus your job as a caring health care practitioner must be to encourage supportive visits. You can do this in several different ways.

1. Encourage the patient's family to let friends know what is going on. The patient's illness and prognosis need not be a secret. Friends may need to hear that their visits are desired and that the patient is not too ill to want to see them. This may be the time to key in on a family's denial. Not spending time with the sick relative may indicate that the family is blocking the message of how serious the patient's condition really is. The family conference mentioned earlier in this chapter then becomes essential. It is not unusual that the harsh reality has to be spelled out for relatives at such a meeting.

Relative: "When she gets home will she need a lot of help for a while?"

Health Professional: "If she gets home she will require all the help she can get. But she most likely will not be coming home. Have you thought about taking time off and who will handle arrangements after she dies?"

2. Be as flexible as possible with visiting hours. Don't lock the door on a friend who arrives outside visiting hours unless it is absolutely necessary. It may be difficult for friends to visit during hospital hours. The importance of the visit generally far outweighs the importance of rules.

3. Be certain that friends receive positive feedback. Tell them how much their visit has meant to the patient. Suggest that they come again. A cheerful reception and a friendly goodbye may keep friends coming for as long as they are needed.

After a loved one is gone, the family continues to need support. They will feel better about themselves if they have been with the patient while he or she was dying. If the family was fortunate enough to have a hospice worker assigned to them, they will be followed for one full year from the time of death.

A year's follow-up permits the bereaved to have comfort and assistance through all the anniversaries that they connect with their lost loved one. Holidays that were special to the deceased will especially touch those who are left behind. The deceased's birthday and the wedding anniversary when a spouse has died become hurdles to climb. Living through the occasions once permits a natural strengthening.

Having advanced notice of death allows family members to do anticipatory grieving. Writing "This is Dad's last Christmas with us" on all the cards may mean that the next Christmas will be less traumatic. In most cases, having time to prepare for death is easier on the family than is sudden death.

Many terminal patients prefer the familiar surroundings of their family and home. For families that can manage it financially, emotionally, and physically, having a loved one at home until death is a more natural process. The home setting is much less intimidating than the hospital, so that other family members and friends are more likely to visit. As a health care provider, you must be aware and supportive of the patient's needs and the family's needs, whether in the hospital or home setting, and be as flexible as possible consistent with good medical care.

Chapter Summary

The Kübler-Ross stages of dying are: denial, anger, bargaining, depression, and acceptance. Being familiar with these stages will enable you to recognize different stages and to intervene as appropriate. You need to develop an understanding of these stages as they apply to other forms of loss; for example, death of a loved one, death of a patient, disability, or dissolution of a relationship. It will be easier for you to respond empathically once you know how loss affects most human beings. You also need to understand how losses that alter body image affect human behavior.

Negative euthanasia is not providing heroic measures to sustain life in the terminally ill. *Positive euthanasia* is an active measure — taking someone's life for the good of that individual.

Finally, this chapter describes five ways in which you, as a health care provider, can help the dying. You can: listen, focus through paraphrasing, respond from your own gut, leave hope intact, and assist the family to be with the patient.

Review

Discrete: separate and distinct

Displaced: transferring of emotion from an area of conflict to a safer or more neutral area

Euthanasia: "a good death" or mercy killing; positive euthanasia is directly taking life, and negative euthanasia is not taking efforts to prolong life

Hospice: supportive medical and home care focusing on dying with dignity; an organization that helps the dying and their families

Psychosomatic: physical illness with cause related to emotional factors

Thanatology: the study of death

1. How is it possible for a patient to experience both anger and denial at the same time?
2. What counseling strategies will help us the most when dealing with dying patients?
3. What must we do to prepare *ourselves* to work with dying patients?
4. Why might a mastectomy patient suffer more emotional side effects than a patient who has just lost a kidney to cancer surgery (assume the same prognosis for each)?

5. We are living through a period of history in which many children regularly die of starvation and neglect. How do we justify putting financial resources and energy into prolonging the lives of the elderly and terminally ill?

Additional Reading

Kübler-Ross, E. *On Death and Dying.* Prentice Hall, Englewood Cliffs, NJ. 1968.

Kübler-Ross, E. *Death, The Final Stage of Growth.* Prentice Hall, Englewood Cliffs, NJ. 1980.

Meisel, A., Grenvik, A., Pinkus, R., and Snyder, J. *Critical Care Medicine.* Hospital guidelines for deciding about life-sustaining treatment: Dealing with health "limbo." Williams and Wilkins, Vol. 14, No. 3, 239-246. 1986.

Scott, H. D. *Rhode Island Medical Journal.* Some Thoughts on Long Term Care. May, 1987, Vol. 70, 213-215.

Chapter

5

After reading this chapter, you should be able:
- To recognize the primary issues of early childhood development.
- To develop skill in appropriately treating young children.
- To recognize issues typical of the adolescent.
- To develop skills in the treatment and understanding of the adolescent.
- To develop skills in the appropriate involvement of the parents and other family members when treating small children or adolescents.
- To recognize the abilities of seniors.
- To recognize the complexities and issues of adaptation in physical and social health at senescence.
- To evaluate the physical and social issues of the elderly in order to maximize treatment and appropriate family involvement.

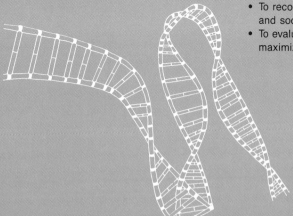

Developmental Issues

Humans have for generations viewed the birth of a child not only as the astonishing unfolding of new life but also as a challenge to society's caregivers. An array of responsibilities and demands comes with this new life. Dynamic creativity on the part of parents, siblings, educators, and health care workers is necessary. The health care worker's success in meeting the needs of children depends on an understanding and respect for the child's physical, emotional, and cognitive uniqueness.

Early Childhood

In early childhood, little can be accomplished unless parents or primary caregivers accept the plan for care and play a role in the child's compliance with the designated intervention. For example, the clinical dietitian has little hope of eliminating a particular food from a child's diet unless mom, dad, and sometimes grandma and grandpa or other significant adults avoid offering the child the food.

Expectancy and Perfection

All parents have visions of what their unborn child will be like: a healthy child, a happy child, a physically attractive, well-behaved child who sleeps and eats, sits and crawls, and talks and walks according to Benjamin Spock's timetables. At some point in the baby's early months, every parent sees their expectations of perfection blurred.

Expectations can be blurred temporarily by a string of sleepless nights, or they can be all but destroyed by severe illness or deformity.

Time and interaction between parent and child modify parental expectations, decreasing the discrepancies between expectation and reality. Most of the parents that health care workers encounter are experiencing an ongoing evolution of acceptance. The success of the parent/child relationship depends on the evolution of acceptance, a process that differs little from the stages of loss described in Chapter 4.

Obviously, parents want to be in control of the expectations they have for their child. The greater the gap between reality and their expectations of perfection, the more parents blame themselves and question the observations of others. Discrepant expectations of perfection contribute to parental behaviors ranging from forced feeding to stress-related colic and from verbal abuse to physical abuse. Sometimes little reconciliation occurs between what the parent wants from and for the infant and how the infant acts and reacts to the parent. Conflicts are then set up that affect the health professional's relationship with both the child and the parents.

In high-risk nurseries and in early intervention programs, the health practitioner must help the parents reconcile their discrepant expectations in an empathic, sensitive, and supportive way.

Joey, born three months premature, has been discharged from the neonatal unit of a major research hospital. Despite what the hospital staff has done to prepare the parents, Mary and Dan perceive the discharge from the hospital as a sign that everything is okay. Threats to their expectations of perfection soon arise, however, when family and friends are surprised by Joey's frailty and his lack of head control for a three-month-old. Friends offer comparisons with their children or grandchildren. These discrepancies conjure up new fears of imperfection for Dan and Mary.

Joey's weight and development are not unusual given his premature birth. The reassurance of the hospital staff that Joey was indeed doing "better" than the other infants who continued to stay in the hospital originally decreased Mary and Don's discrepant expectation of perfection. But friends and relatives are noticing differences. Joey's problems are emphasized by the fact that a home visitor is providing special help for the family. Because parental denial is a reasonable reaction, the home visitor or pediatric nurse practitioner may find that Dan and Mary don't welcome suggestions. Parents need to feel comfortable to share their fears, hopes, and concerns with the health care provider. Until they can relate openly with the health professional, efforts to begin a positioning program or feeding schedule will not succeed.

Most health professionals focus on the problem and ways to treat the problem, making each encounter with the parents difficult. Why?

Because with this approach, health practitioners ask the parents to focus on just those things that are discrepant with their expectations for the child. That is why textbooks suggest that you treat the parent as well as the child. Working hard to build parental trust, and listening and incorporating the parents' concerns and priorities into the intervention is essential.

Pamela L. Roberts, R.P. T., M.S., is the author of the early childhood section of this chapter. She has been associated with the School of Allied Health Professions, University of Connecticut, Storrs, since 1974 and served as Academic Coordinator of Clinical Education from 1977 to 1986. She has practiced extensively as a physical therapist, has been active in the American Physical Therapy Association serving on the Board of Directors, and is currently completing an Ed.D at Clark University. Her area of specialization is pediatrics.

Bonding and Dependency

Even a casual observer sees the special relationship between parent and baby when eye contact and touching bonds a baby to its caregiver. For the baby, the bonding stage focuses on basic needs and safety. While being held securely and receiving warmth from the mother's body, both the bottle-fed and breast-fed baby experience a satiation of hunger. The baby is so dependent on this satiation that early in infancy the baby may only be able to fall off to sleep in the mother's arms.

Although experts agree that this bond develops rapidly under ideal circumstances, bonding is not automatic. Opportunities for fondling and immediate gratification are essential to bonding. Situations that separate the parent from the baby during the first few hours and days of life interfere with bonding for both the infant and the parent. Close proximity, relaxed cuddling, eye contact, and secure handling facilitate bonding.

The necessity for medical intervention such as incubation or use of a respirator makes bonding more difficult. Problems such as cerebral palsy, cleft palate, and respiratory difficulties make feeding a frustrating experience for both parent and infant. Frustration with feeding leads to satiation delay, which has the potential for threatening bonding.

Experts predict that bonding sets the stage for the parent/child relationship. Lack of or delay of bonding can affect the child's eating habits, academic success, and self-esteem. For example, high self-esteem is associated with strong bonding.

Because bonding is so important, early intervention programs focus heavily on this issue. Health care workers and educators become consultants and facilitators, teaching the parent ways to foster physical, emotional, and cognitive growth. While minimizing separation and fostering bonding, this model allows the parent to assume control in the situation without placing unrealistic demands on the parent's skills and resources. Because successful feeding is so important to bonding, clinical dietitians as well as speech, occupational, and physical therapists all encourage programs that help both the infant and the caregiver enjoy feeding.

Separation and Body Schema

Separation Anxiety. As a result of bonding, infants perceive themselves as one and the same with their sustainer and nurturer. The infant/parent pair is often referred to as the infant/parent dyad. Eventually, either intentionally or because of circumstances, both parent and child find themselves playing a risky game of separation. Light patterns dancing nearby, music in the background, other people in the room, colors flashing past, or hands encountering a textured sweater serve as stimuli luring the infant to give up that tightly swaddled position of comfort. Little by little the intensity of feeding and sleeping is broken by brief periods of concentration on the outside world. Within the trusting relationship of the dyad bond the child explores new sights and sounds.

The infant soon begins to explore emotional and physical separation from the nurturing adult. He or she begins to develop reaching and grasping ability, allowing contact with more and more environmentally distant objects. Mother's role in presenting the objects diminishes, and the child and the object develop a new and distinct relationship.

While mother is nearby the infant tolerates this risky business of exploration well. There comes a time, however, when physical separation is a crisis. When the child sees the nurturing adult leave, inability to understand that the adult will return puts the child ill at ease. Until experience with separation proves that the mother consistently returns, separation anxiety occurs. Consider this example:

> Jane, a nine-month-old infant, plays happily exploring toys in the room while keeping watch on her mother. When

Mom steps out of the room to answer the phone, Jane searches desperately about the room for her. She is soon screaming shrilly. Another adults tries to comfort her to no avail. Toys that delighted her five minutes ago are now rejected without even a glance. The only thing that calms Jane is Mom's return.

This crisis of separation can interfere with all attempts by health care workers to provide a service. Although separation is difficult for children between the ages of nine months and two years, it can be a problem for children of all ages. With the increased stress often characteristic of encounters with health care workers, even adults find separation from loved ones difficult.

Separation anxiety.

Even very young children respond better when prepared. Preparation can take the form of a simple explanation like "In a few minutes I'll be going out of the room, but I'll be right back." A simple explanation like this can be used for short separations until the child builds confidence that Mom will return. Playing separation games like peek-a-boo and hide and seek when there is no crisis can also help. The child builds trust in the return of the adult through these low anxiety situations.

What can health care workers do to prevent separation from interfering with care? For the very young child, health professionals can provide systems of care that minimize separation. Parental overnight stays with hospitalized children are options in many pediatric facilities. When possible, young children can be examined while they are sitting on the parent's lap. Opportunities for preparation, transition, and structured routines allow the child and parent to be more comfortable. Physical spaces can be designed to be more like home environments. Sensitivity to separation issues allows the health care worker to integrate an understanding of separation anxiety into a child's plan of care.

Separation anxiety poses a special problem for working mothers. Often care is given outside the home by day care workers, baby sitters, or other family members. If the child has a health problem or disability, separation is often more difficult than normal. It is essential, then, that child's caregivers be competent in positioning, feeding, and caring for the special needs of the child. Often this means that the health care worker — the physical or occupational therapist, for example — must teach these techniques to day care workers. When substitute caregivers can make the child feel secure and safe, separation will be easier.

Working with the parent and child to make the transition to a day care situation smooth is important not only to the child's emotional security but also to the parent's emotional well-being. Parents often feel guilty when their child cries as they leave. Separation routines help to ease the transition. Preparation followed by some physically structured and consistent routine often helps the child cope with separation.

For example, Bobby a 20-month-old child, is left at the day care center at 8 A.M. every workday morning. Bobby's mother and his therapist have met with the day care center staff on several occasions to describe the physical care Bobby requires: The therapist has taught the staff how to hold Bobby so his lack of head control and muscle weakness do not make him feel insecure. Even with these precautions, Bobby's Mom finds that each day she has to force herself to walk out the door while Bobby screams. The day care staff plan a parent conference to discuss ways to work with Bobby and his mother to alleviate this daily crisis. The routine that the staff and Bobby's mother work out goes like this: Bobby and Mom sit together with the center teacher for a few moments while Mom talks quietly with Bobby. She tells him that in a little while she will be going to her office, reminding Bobby that he's been there before! Mom talks about the photograph of Bobby on her desk, creating for Bobby a concrete picture of exactly where Mom will be. This way Bobby can visualize Mom somewhere during the day even though she is not with him. Mom goes on to say that she will be back after his afternoon nap, giving Bobby an easily identified reference for her return. Mom gives Bobby a kiss and hug, gets some in return, and then reinforces her return by saying, "See you after your nap!" as she walks out of the room. Mom walks away, Bobby's teacher picks up on the reinforcements of permanence and return that Mom had already introduced. She tells Bobby about Mom going to the office and gets him involved by asking him whose picture is on her desk. She reinforces the fact that Mom loves Bobby and will come back after his nap.

Although this routine may not eliminate the crying on the first day, eventually it will take the place of the crying routine.

Structured routines continue to be important as children get older. If, for example, a nine-year-old child arrives home an hour before her working Mom, she will handle this separation better if a routine can be maintained. A routine might suggest a snack. A phone call from mom or a neighbor could help alleviate concern.

As with most situations that lead to growth, separation is not all bad. Without separation from the nurturing adult, the child could not develop his or her own identity.

Body Schema. Cognitive, language, and motor development all depend on the child's development of body schema — the child's ability to use herself or himself as a reference for understanding the world. Hands go to the mouth and bring everything from the world to the mouth for exploration. Distance concepts develop from the child's reach for objects close and far. Communication focuses on "me" and "mine," emphasizing the link with the environment. Self-feeding begins, separating nourishment from adult dependency.

The development of a competent and confident separate self ushers in the beginning of self-control. The potential for toilet training and independent choices for food and clothing arises. Parents and health care workers begin to feel this self-directed emphasis in their interactions with the child. They begin to hear that word most feared by all parents of two-year-olds, no!

Negativism and Control

Somewhere between the ages of 18 months and four years, the "terrible twos" descend. A child's relationships with adults and other children are strained. If you call a child who is in this stage, he runs the other way. If you suggest reading a book, he insists on going outside. If you offer his favorite food, he refuses to eat. Parents who have revelled in their child's cautious encounters with independence wonder where their control has gone.

Eating problems are a common manifestation of negativism. Fearing that their child isn't being adequately nourished, the parents force the child to eat. The child retaliates. A vicious circle is created. Parents and health care workers need to recognize that young children do not starve through simple negativism. If a child refuses a meal, the quickest way to combat the problem is to accept the child's choice.

This new self-confidence is born out of the battle of separation as the child's understanding of self solidifies. Parents and health professionals must understand and recognize the child's need for control and self-direction. Recognizing the need for choices and presenting acceptable choices or alternatives can save the adult from the wrath of the sometimes defiant two-year-old.

Offering unlimited choices won't work, however. The two- or three-year-old's choice may threaten the child's safety or the parent or caregiver's sanity. Given limited, feasible choices, the child will delight in self-determination, and a new ability to manipulate the world will emerge. "Would you rather have fish and carrots or chicken and corn for supper tonight?" offers acceptable alternatives. "What would you like for supper tonight?" opens the door for disaster. The child could easily choose candy and cookies, leaving the parent no alternative but to try to convince the child to accept a more appropriate alternative. Creating and maintaining the parameters of acceptable behavior is the most important task the parent assumes at this time.

Health care professionals may find working with the negative child particularly challenging. Parent presence may or may not lead to compliant behavior. How should you approach the child? How should you react to negative responses?

Encouraging acceptable behavior for the child at this stage of development includes structuring the setting to decrease opportunities for unacceptable behavior. Remove delicate objects to limit the need to say no. Provide alternative tasks that lead to the behavior you seek. Use "if . . . then" statements to mold behaviors. Avoid "Don't," which is a command. Remember that the child needs to be in control. "If you . . ." sentences give the child the information she needs to make an informed decision. Be sure that the consequence you use is related to the specific behavior you want to avoid. For example, in the statement "If you throw the toy, I will take the toy away," the consequences (removing the toy) is directly related to the behavior.

Avoid vague consequence. Consider this example: "If you throw the toy, you will not be allowed to play with these toys the next time you return." The consequence in this example is far too removed in time for the child to see it as an immediate consequence of her behavior. The consequence should be related directly to the interaction between the child and the toy. "If you throw the toy, I will spank you" focuses on a consequence not directly related to the child's interactions with the object. Most authorities think that threats of spanking do not deter future behavior. More importantly, threats of punishment affect the child's self-esteem and interfere with the development of a good relationship with the child. For the health care worker, physical contact must be monitored carefully to avoid any questions of physical abuse.

Positive reinforcement is the most effective form of behavior modification for the child at this stage. Remember that a child at this stage is in a mode of rejecting suggestions. Many adults, including health care workers, find that they pay attention to a child's behavior only when it interferes with adult tasks or interactions. Such an approach sets the situation up for failure. Instead, health care workers should focus constantly on identifying appropriate behavior for positive reinforcement. The child who delights in praise and reward will increase the frequency and intensity of those behaviors that led to adult approval. As the frequency of these appropriate behaviors increase, the frequency of inappropriate behavior will decrease.

Positive reinforcement is especially effective when you deal with more than one child at a time. Consider this situation:

Sally and David are siblings brought to the outpatient laboratory by their mother for blood tests. As the medical technologist begins to tell them what she will be doing to perform the finger prick blood test, Sally listens intently while David begins to talk loudly and interrupt. If the medical technologist stops the instruction and tells David to stop talking and listen, David is likely to reject this adult control and continue to talk and interrupt. But, if the medical technologist instead says quietly to Sally, "What good listening, Sally. I really like the way you are paying attention," David may stop his ranting for a moment. At that moment, the medical technologist could say to David, "What good listening, David. Now let's see if you remember what we were talking about."

In this example, the health care professional used positive reinforcement of Sally's behavior to indirectly point out the importance of good listening. As soon as she saw an approximation of appropriate behavior in David, she rewarded him. For some children, a verbal reward is enough to mold behavior; for others a more concrete reward may be necessary.

Any rewards you use must be considered appropriate by the parents and the agency in which you work. For example, the small objects like the tiny figures often found in the treasure chest at the dentist office are hazardous for the children under three.

It is sometimes impossible to control behaviors through positive reinforcement. When the child's safety or property in the room is threatened, it may be necessary to gently restrain the child. In all situations, however, both the child and the parent must still feel your acceptance and respect. Even when you must express disapproval for some action, your disapproval should be specific to the behavior so that it cannot be perceived as general dislike for them as persons. Communication skills are especially important here. Paraphrasing the child's or parent's response so they can further define their wants and needs can clarify the situation and may prevent conflict.

The rebellious stage can create ambiguous feelings for the parent of an ill or handicapped child. There is a tendency for the parent to rejoice in the child's attempts at interacting with the world even if the child's behavior is manipulative and inappropriate. Spoiling the child by giving in during conflict deprives the child of the consistency and structure that can assist him or her in organizing the cues from the world. Adults guide the alternatives offered to the child in a way that allows for choice but that structures or limits the child's alternatives. Given some practice with structured decision making, the child will grow in ability to make appropriate decisions that support safe and productive actions. Without such experience, a child's interactions with the world are likely to be compromised.

The health care professional needs to be able to recognize when the parent may need help in determining appropriate behavior and applying limits consistently. Inability on the part of the parents or the health care professional to deal with a child's negativism may affect the overall success of any necessary evaluation or treatment. Making referrals for help in handling behavior problems that interfere with health care may not only be appropriate but essential. All children of any age normally have times during their development when behavior is a problem. The health care professional who recognizes and understands the parents' struggle can provide helpful modifications in the health care program to make the interaction more successful for the child, the parents, and the health professional.

Modeling and Competence

When the young child learns that within acceptable behavior many options for control exist, adults and other children become strong models. The young child watches the activities of others and then imitates the activity and practices the skills necessary for success in movement, speech, play, and feeding. Success is exciting for the child.

As the child imitates the action of others, the relationship between the action and the outcome (cause and effect) intrigues the child. Persistent repetition of tasks is often a focus of the young child's activities. Even the nine-month-old shows signs of persistent repetition during throwing activities. We have all seen the child in a high-chair or playpen who throws all the toys or objects onto the floor for the sheer delight of hearing them hit. The action (throwing) is reinforced by the outcome (the toy hitting the floor), and the child repeats the action over and over again. Adult and peer feedback reinforces attempts at dressing, eating, and construction type tasks. Through this reinforcement and repetition the child gains competence.

Being competent means meeting a goal. Nine-month-old John works diligently to remove his shoe and shrieks with delight when he succeeds. His mother puts the shoe back on, and John takes it off again. Sometimes parents misinterpret this repeated goal-directed activity. A fine line exists between negativism and the stubborn persistency to be independent and competent.

An adult must make allowances for competence development. A successfully completed task for the child need not be at adult standards. Sharon, age three, diligently works at spreading peanut butter on bread for her sandwich that she can eat without any help from the supervising adult. Acceptable behavior for the adult may include a clean counter, no peanut butter on Sharon's shirt, and evenly spread peanut butter without any holes in the bread.

Developmental Milestones

As health professionals we are likely to be asked to give our opinions on the appropriateness of a child's abilities at a particular point. Usual age ranges for the child to sit, walk, talk, copy shapes, etc., are called developmental milestones. Lists and charts showing age ranges and skill criteria for developmental milestones are used as a reference by health professionals, parents, and educators in evaluating the development of a child. These lists and charts can guide us in setting realistic expectations. Developmental testing also meets the parents' need to know that their child is making good progress toward competencies expected at each age level. Additionally, the sequence of one task followed by another gives us cues for structuring the child's environment to maximize the potential for growth.

Developmental Issues

Denver Developmental Screening (DDS) is one such guideline used by a variety of health professionals to assess a child's progress in successfully completing age-appropriate tasks. (If one wishes to use the norms depicted by the bars, it is essential that each item be administered and interpreted in the prescribed manner. Failure to do so negates use of the norms.) Refer to Figure 5–1 as we discuss the way such a chart might be used by a health care worker.

The purpose of the chart is to give the health care provider specific tasks to observe and criteria for indicating whether a child is competent in the task. DDS allows the professional to draw a vertical line through the adjusted age of the child. The adjusted age of the child is chronological age minus any weeks of prematurity. The adjusted age line will intersect on the chart with those skills typical of a child at the age. After short periods of observing the child, the health care practitioner can determine whether the child is performing below or above average for her or his age.

Using a chart like the DDS chart is especially appropriate when an inexperienced health care worker is asked by a parent whether their child is slow in some areas. When used to measure strictly against a standard or to compare one child's performance with another's, however, the chart can strip a child of the unique competence he or she has been developing. Developmental testing is, after all, only an approximate estimate of a child's level of skills in various areas. It can be helpful, however, in discussing and planning opportunities for a child to grow in areas where competence is still evolving.

Developmental assessment may be necessary to validate a need for special services that offer the child additional opportunities for developing skills. Unfortunately, labeling a child as developmentally delayed may be necessary to receive special services. And labeling can have a permanent effect on the child's access to services and the child's social acceptance. A health care provider makes this determination only after careful, repeated assessments and full consideration of medical problems that might be affecting skill development.

Determining language delay in a young child is a good example of the need for careful and comprehensive assessment. "Failing" items on the DDS chart related to speech sounds may indicate mental retardation, or it may indicate that the child has a hearing impairment resulting from repeated ear infections. The courses of action would, of course, differ dramatically. In one case, repeated and expanded testing might indeed show a tendency for the child to have difficulty in many related skills, resulting in a diagnosis of mental retardation. In the other case, treatment of the ear problem might resolve the speech problems, making formal speech therapy services unnecessary.

R DRESSES WITHOUT
3 SUPERVISION

R SEPARATES FROM MOTHER EASILY

R BUTTONS UP

R DRESSES
3 WITH SUPERVISION

R PLAYS INTERACTIVE
GAMES e.g., TAG

R WASHES & DRIES HANDS

DRAWS
13 MAN
6 PARTS

R PUTS ON CLOTHING

12 COPIES □

R HELPS IN HOUSE-
SIMPLE TASKS

IMITATES □ DEMONSTR.

R USES SPOON, SPILLING LITTLE

13 DRAWS MAN 3 PARTS

R REMOVES GARMENT

11 COPIES +

R IMITATES HOUSEWORK

PICKS LONGER LINE
10 3 OF 3

R DRINKS FROM CUP

IMITATES
BRIDGE

PLAYS BALL WITH EXAMINER

TOWER OF 8 CUBES

R INDICATES WANTS
(NOT CRY)

9 COPIES O

R PLAYS PAT-A-CAKE

IMITATES VERTICAL LINE
WITHIN 30°

R INITIALLY SHY WITH
STRANGERS

DUMPS RAISIN FROM BOTTLE-SPONT.

2 RESISTS TOY PULL

TOWER OF 4 CUBES

50%   PLAYS PEEK-A-BOO

SCRIBBLES SPONTANEOUSLY

87%

WORKS FOR TOY OUT
OF REACH

DUMPS RAISIN FROM BOTTLE-DEMONSTR.

TOWER OF 2 CUBES

20 COMPOSITION OF/3 OF 3

R FEEDS SELF CRACKERS

8 NEAT PINCER GRASP
OF RAISIN

19 DEFINES WORD/6 OF 9

SMILES
SPONTANEOUSLY

OPPOSITE ANALOGIES
18 2 OF 3

R BANGS 2 CUBES HELD IN HANDS

R SMILES
1 RESPONSIVELY

87%

7 THUMB-FINGER GRASP

R RECOGNIZES COLORS/3 OF 4

REGARDS
FACE

COMPREHENDS
PREPOSITIONS/3 OF 4

RAKES
RAISIN ATTAINS

17

SIT, TAKES
2 CUBES

COMPREHENDS
16 COLD, TIRED
HUNGRY/2 OF 3

SIT, LOOKS
6 FOR YARN

R GIVES 1ST &
LAST NAME

PASSES CUBE
HAND TO HAND

R USES PLURALS

28 BACKWARD HEEL-TOE/2 OF 3

REACHES
FOR OBJECT

15 FOLLOWS DIRECTIONS/2 OF 3

BALANCE ON 1 FOOT
10 SECONDS/2 OF 3

REGARDS
RAISIN

14 NAMES 1 PICTURE

CATCHES BOUNCED
27 BALL/2 OF 3

GRASPS
5 RATTLE

R COMBINES 2 DIFFERENT WORDS

26 HEEL TO TOE WALK/2 OF 3

R FOLLOWS
4 180°

R POINTS TO 1 NAMED
BODY PART

HOPS ON 1 FOOT

HANDS
TOGETHER

R 3 WORDS OTHER THAN MAMA, DADA

BALANCE ON 1 FOOT
5 SECONDS/2 OF 3

R FOLLOWS PAST
4 MIDLINE

DADA OR MAMA
SPECIFIC

25 BROAD JUMP

EQUAL
MOVEMENTS

*100% pass at birth

BALANCE ON 1 FOOT
1 SECOND/2 OF 3

R IMITATES SPEECH SOUNDS

FOLLOWS
TO
MIDLINE

DADA OR MAMA
NONSPECIFIC

R PEDALS TRICYCLE

TURNS TO VOICE

JUMPS IN PLACE

R SQUEALS

24 THROWS BALL OVERHAND

R LAUGHS

R KICKS BALL FORWARD

R VOCALIZES-
NOT
CRYING

R WALKS UP STEPS
23

R RESPONDS
TO BELL

WALKS BACKWARDS

R WALKS WELL

R STOOPS & RECOVERS

R STANDS ALONE WELL

R STANDS MOMENTARILY

R WALKS HOLDING ON FURNITURE

R GETS TO SITTING

R PULLS SELF TO STAND

R STANDS HOLDING ON

SITS WITHOUT
SUPPORT

BEAR SOME WEIGHT ON LEGS

22 PULL TO SIT
NO HEAD LAG

R ROLLS OVER

STO-CHEST UP
21 ARM SUPPORT

SIT-HEAD
STEADY

STO-HEAD
UP 90°

STO-HEAD UP 45°

R STO-LIFTS
HEAD

1. Try to get child to smile by smiling, talking or waving to him. Do not touch him.
2. When child is playing with toy, pull it away from him. Pass if he resists.
3. Child does not have to be able to tie shoes or button in the back.
4. Move yarn slowly in an arc from one side to the other, about 6″ above child's face. Pass if eyes follow 90° to midline. (Past midline; 180°)
5. Pass if child grasps rattle when it is touched to the backs or tips of fingers.
6. Pass if child continues to look where yarn disappeared or tries to see where it went. Yarn should be dropped quickly from sight from tester's hand without arm movement.
7. Pass if child picks up raisin with any part of thumb and a finger.
8. Pass if child picks up raisin with the ends of thumb and index finger using an over hand approach.

| 9. Pass any enclosed form. Fail continuous round motions. | 10. Which line is longer? (Not bigger.) Turn paper upside down and repeat. (3/3 or 5/6) | 11. Pass any crossing lines. | 12. Have child copy first. If failed, demonstrate. |

When giving items 9, 11 and 12, do not name the forms. Do not demonstrate 9 and 11.

13. When scoring, each pair (2 arms, 2 legs, etc.) counts as one part.
14. Point to picture and have child name it. (No credit is given for sounds only.)

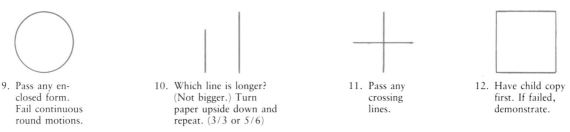 

15. Tell child to: Give block to Mommie; put block on table; put block on floor. Pass 2 of 3. (Do not help child by pointing, moving head or eyes.)
16. Ask child: What do you do when you are cold? . . . hungry? . . . tired? . . . Pass 2 of 3.
17. Tell child to: Put block *on* table; *under* table; *in front of* chair; *behind* chair. Pass 3 of 4. (Do not help child by pointing, moving head or eyes.)
18. Ask child: If fire is hot, ice is ?; Mother is a woman, Dad is a ?; a horse is big, a mouse is ?. Pass 2 of 3.
19. Ask child: What is a ball? . . . lake? . . . desk? . . . house? . . . banana? . . . curtain? . . . ceiling? . . . hedge? . . . pavement? Pass if defined in terms of use, shape, what it is made of or general category (such as banana is fruit, not just yellow). Pass 6 of 9.
20. Ask child: What is a spoon made of? . . . a shoe made of? . . . a door made of? (No other objects may be substituted). Pass 3 of 3.
21. When placed on stomach, child lifts chest off table with support of forearms and/or hands.
22. When child is on back, grasp his hands and pull him to sitting. Pass if head does not hang back.
23. Child may use wall or rail only, not person. May not crawl.
24. Child must throw ball overhand 3 feet to within arm's reach of tester.
25. Child must perform standing broad jump over width of test sheet. (8-1/2 inches)
26. Tell child to walk forward, ⚬⚬⚬⚬⚬→ heel within 1 inch of toe. Tester may demonstrate. Child must walk 4 consecutive steps, 2 out of 3 trials.
27. Bounce ball to child who should stand 3 feet away from tester. Child must catch ball with hands, not arms, 2 out of 3 trials.
28. Tell child to walk backward, ⚬⚬⚬⚬⚬→ toe within 1 inch of heel. Tester may demonstrate. Child must walk 4 consecutive steps, 2 out of 3 trials.

DATE AND BEHAVIORAL OBSERVATIONS (how child feels at time of test, relation to tester, attention span, verbal behavior, self-confidence, etc.,):

Figure 5.1 Denver Developmental Screening Test (Reproduced with permission from Denver Developmental Materials, Inc.)

The health practitioner must be careful to discuss his/her assessment of any developmental milestones supportively and positively. Emphasis on isolated deviations from the norm can stifle both the child's and the parent's confidence in other skill areas and can decrease the child's feelings of self-worth. Questioning competence is especially crucial when the child already perceives himself or herself as different. The blind child, the deaf child, the physically handicapped child, the learning disabled child all tend to receive special services to assist them in gaining the competence to be productive adults. In providing those services, educators, parents, and health care workers find themselves in the role of evaluator, teacher, and enabler. As helpers they must support the child's intact competence.

Helping a child to become more competent often involves the painfully difficult task of pointing out inadequacies in the child's approach to a task. In other words, what they are doing "wrong" must be pointed out. Making concrete suggestions for substitute strategies is more successful than directing the child to avoid doing something. For example:

> Sharon holds the spreading knife in a cutting fashion. An immediate response might be, "Sharon, you are making holes in the bread. Don't hold the knife that way." A better response would be, "Sharon, when you hold the knife flat like this, the peanut butter spreads better."

Reinforcement for what is successful builds a child's self-esteem. Criticism for unsuccessful attempts destroys a child's energy and enthusiasm for seeking competence.

Communication with parents about developmental milestones requires tact, sensitivity, and an understanding of parental expectations of perfection. The parent bond with the child makes it inevitable that criticism of the child's performance will be interpreted as criticism of the parent. It may help to remember that the child who focuses on cognitive tasks in school and motor skills in sports uses the same competence-seeking behaviors as does the infant who is learning to walk or talk. In fact, adults who choose to continue growing in skills and developing in areas of competence use these same behaviors as well. Linking act with outcome, persisting with repetitions and practice, and being sensitive to criticism of success at the task are competence-seeking behaviors characteristic of all age groups.

If you are a health care student who anticipates primary involvement with children or who fears interactions with young children, you should work on gaining a basic understanding of the forces responsible for the typical behaviors seen in children. The first 12 years of life entail a fascinating array of complex interactions with people and objects. The health care provider who understands the stages of child development will be better able to understand the actions and reactions of young children and their parents and will develop skills that motivate children to participate in health care activities. Such a professional can transcend the accomplishment of tasks associated with the role of professional and focus on unique and rewarding relationships with the children and their parents.

The transition from childhood to adult life is often difficult. Adolescents are still dependent on their parents but must struggle to prove otherwise. Remember when you were 15? Much of what you needed still had to come from your parents. You had to have their permission and approval every step of the way. Their money subsidized outings with friends, your wardrobe, your ability to train for the future, and eventually even your auto insurance.

Adolescence

Ideally, parents recognize and reward teenagers with increased privileges as they demonstrate increased ability to take responsibility. This approach allows for some stability in emotional support. Adolescents are in conflict, wanting to be independent yet needing emotional support. No single aspect of adolescence illustrates these difficulties better than puberty.

Puberty/Sexuality

Following the advent of walking the transition to sexual maturity is undoubtedly the most important physiological and social event in a child's life. The hormones work in ways that produce both longed-for developments like pubic hair and breasts and embarrassing developments like increased sweating and acne.

Changes in **primary sex characteristics** refer to changes in the reproductive organs. These changes soon lead to the possibility of reproduction if a sexual union were to take place. In males, wet dreams (the nocturnal emission of semen) generally characterize reproductive readiness. In females, the onset of menses (the menstrual period) generally indicates reproductive readiness.

If reproductive readiness coincided with social and emotional readiness, life would be a lot simpler. Sadly, the adolescent usually experiences a strong attraction to the opposite sex at the same time she or he feels awkward and insecure.

Peer groups of the same sex serve a valuable function as adolescents learn from each other. Experienced peers may be admired for their knowledge of what sex is really like. Less experienced peers serve as a baseline of support. Peers encourage each other through the heroic tasks of meeting possible mates. They brag and joke about the aspects of sexuality that make them nervous. They comfort each other in the face of romantic rejection.

Discussion and valuation of **secondary sex characteristics** are among the most important roles of the peer group. Secondary sex characteristics are other physical features associated with reproductive readiness. Both males and females develop pubic hair by puberty. Males now also develop facial hair and a deepened voice. Females take on the characteristic hour glass shape with an increase in hip size and breast development.

Although secondary sex development is normal, it is a time fraught with insecurities for the adolescent. The recently developed female may feel self-conscious in settings that call attention to her body. Going to the beach, for example, may create a pronounced discomfort. Further, the female who develops later than her peers is generally perplexed and unhappy over her fate.

Males are anxious for the outward signs of manhood to appear. But when an adolescent boy's voice first cracks in public or his kid sister teases him about peach fuzz, these signs may feel humiliating. The boy who is slow in developing is doubly humiliated, he fears that nature has played a cruel trick on him.

We can see here the basis for peer pressure toward conformity at this age. Everyone wants to be recognized as normal. Early adolescents often dress alike, talk alike, buy the same music, worship the same heroes, and generally imitate all possible characteristics of their group. As adolescents become more mature, they begin to make decisions on their own. Conformity during the early stage has given them enough stability to become more individual in the later stages. Still, we cannot fail to recognize the value and influence of the peer group.

Adolescents Who Are Different

And what about those who are different? Children who are too fat, too short, or too tall or children who are truly disabled in some way suffer acute anguish, especially during early adolescence. Imagine already being insecure and not thinking of yourself as normal. Then add the difficulties of puberty. These children are often rejected by peer groups. Rejection is so strong that they may fail to date. They tend to withdraw from events like school dances, events that are designed for their developmental benefit. They may spend years feeling ostracized and depressed. Kids who feel the "outsider" role most strongly are likely to end up in serious trouble.

What does this mean to you as a health care worker? Well, if your patient is an adolescent you may have to consider whether any emotional or developmental damage is being inflicted. Diseases in general threaten a potentially frail self-concept. Any health problem that can be seen by others (the loss of a limb, facial disfigurement, hair falling out, skin problems) threatens the victim's self-concept further. When the body image of an adolescent is threatened, the psychological stress is devastating. When your patient is a child who has grown up with a disability, puberty may signal the temporary loss of stability. The onset of sexual issues, which demand normalcy and acceptance, may make kids who are already different feel terrible.

Sexual Activities Among Adolescents

Teenagers who are aggressive or hostile usually feel rejected, inadequate, or too dependent. They may get into trouble in numerous ways as they struggle to prove themselves. Drinking and sex are favorite activities of adolescents who feel inadequate. What better way to prove your maturity than to drink a lot and make a baby!

Moral values around sexual activities differ from culture to culture. Even within our own society, various groups view sexual behavior in differing ways. If the peer group believes that only a fool is still a virgin at 15, then there is extraordinary pressure on young adolescents to become sexually active. If sex is considered appropriate only between those who intend to marry, then permissive behavior is looked down on. "Well-adjusted" behavior, then, has to be seen in the context of its subculture.

Homosexuality is thought to be practiced by approximately five to ten percent of our population. Although having sexual relations with someone of the same sex is considered a sexual preference rather than a mental illness, homosexuality is still not well-accepted. It is believed that many individuals who have homosexual feelings do not act them out due to this social stigma.

As a health care worker, you will need to cope with your own beliefs because what you believe may have an impact on others. You may be asked to counsel or guide an individual whose sexual practices differ from your own. If you are straight and must help a person who is exploring their own gay feelings, you may **need to know your own limitations**. At times, referring a patient to someone more like themselves may be a tremendous help.

In any event, being homosexual in our society is not easy. We must be careful that our patients do not perceive referral as rejection. Adolescents are, of course, extremely fearful of homosexuality. Since all adolescents fear that they are not themselves normal, the fear of being rejected by society is enormous. Males whose voices fail to change on schedule or who have the misfortune of a feminine appearance, live in dread of being pointed out as a "faggot." Females who don't feel feminine because of their size or shape may shrink with terror at being called "butch."

These issues are especially pronounced as each adolescent goes through the phase of feeling homosexual. Feelings of sexual attraction for a close friend are both pleasant and frightening to the adolescent. Not infrequently, sexual experimentation occurs. In the straight adolescent, such experiments are usually prior to age 18 and are short-lived. When they occur frequently and well beyond age 18, the individual is usually homosexual or bisexual. Because bisexuality is also different from the norm, it raises additional obstacles. Acceptance by family and friends is badly needed by all who are different.

Identity and Breaking Away

A 16-year-old boy slams the bedroom door, shouting, "I wear the same crummy clothes everyday! The other kids must think we're on welfare!" A 15-year-old girl exclaims, "Don't you know anything about nutrition, mother! You serve so much cholesterol and salt we'll all be dead in 10 years!" Another adolescent shouts, "Sure, you'll let me get my license if I make the honor roll. By then cars will be out of style and you'll have kept me nice and trapped!"

These youths are all complaining about the same thing. They want to differentiate or separate themselves from their parents; they are struggling to break away. Rejecting the clothes and food the family

Breaking away.

provides is symbolic of demonstrating independence. Anger at, or rejection of, family values is another expansion of independence.

Most adults view this as destructive, rebellious behavior. It is difficult for a family to accept the rejection of family values, and the adolescent knows it. The more parental resentment and hostility the youth has built up, the more she or he will try to destroy the values she or he has been raised with. This is the time that a child raised in a religious home is most likely to reject God, whereas the child of agnostics might embrace a cult. Staunch Republican parents may find their child on a Democrat's campaign committee. Avid hunters and fishers may have children joining Green Peace. And whatever hair style looks best to the folks, John and Jane are certain to wear the opposite.

"The acorn never falls far from the tree," but don't tell a 16-year-old. Although most children eventually end up not too dissimilar from their parents, they will put on a good act of being opposite as they struggle to break away. This is normal and healthy. Without this struggle between parents and child, differentiation would not take place. The child's message is, "I am not you. I have to find my own way of doing things, even if you don't approve of my way." Obviously, this is a difficult time for parents as well as the adolescent. The more the parent understands the dynamics of the adolescent's behavior, the better the family unit survives.

Without parental understanding, rejections of parental values may be carried to extremes and cause real trouble. In homes where the young person's sense of self or identity is weak, pathology may emerge. Such teenagers seek to define themselves by doing what they think will get peer approval. The more impact these approval-seeking behaviors have on parental control, the better they look to such youngsters. The overuse of alcohol gets peer approval. Show the group what a daredevil you can be while intoxicated. If mom and dad are devastated, so much the better.

Adolescence is also the prime time for eating disorders to emerge. The young women who fall victim to eating disorders define beauty and perfection by the impossible quest for thinness. The only way they know who they are is if they push themselves to be perfect. Naturally no one can define, let alone achieve, perfection. Such young women may make themselves vomit to lose weight. The control issues at the core of most eating disorders also provide fuel for the adolescent. Perhaps mom and dad have always been in charge. The young woman with an eating disorder may not have found ways to strike out on her own or to be in charge of herself. With food and purging, she finds a way to gain control.

Parental Responsibilities and Dilemmas

The experiments of the adolescent who is struggling to find maturity can spell disaster and create parental nightmares. Does a parent allow a teenager to drive? At what age? How does the parent gauge when the child is mature enough to avoid speeding or drinking and driving? For that matter, what does a parent say to a child about drinking? Can the child be trusted to attend parties where alcohol will be used? Does the parent have to check up on the adolescents' stories: Can the parent believe it when a child says, "Of course Johnny's parents will be home"? How does a parent deal with sex and birth control issues or information about venereal disease (VD) and AIDS?

For decades, parents stuck their heads in the sand when it came to the sexual activities of their children. Parents simply could not deal honestly with this topic. If their son got a girl pregnant, or if their daughter became pregnant, they would then find some way to cope. Otherwise, it was the ostrich approach, that is, no news was good news.

More recently, enlightened parents have told their adolescents about birth control. Some parents have helped their children obtain birth control and thus avoid unwanted pregnancies. But the issue of adolescents practicing birth control has been fraught with controversy. Much of society believes it is wrong to condone teenage sexual activity. Many people believe teenagers should be told that sex is wrong before adulthood or marriage.

With the advent of AIDS, a sexually transmitted disease, the only safe advice that can be offered to any age group is to have only one sexual partner in a mutually monogamous relationship. The use of condoms is the best protection against sexually transmitted disease, but there is still some risk even with condoms. With one risk now being a horrible death, parents and adolescents have new nightmares to grapple with.

Some people think that the chance a condom will be used in initial sexual encounters in teenagers is so small that the contraceptive pill is the most logical choice for preventing pregnancy. The pill, however, offers no protection for VD.

There are no easy solutions to such parental dilemmas. We can only repeat that adolescents are healthiest when their responsibilities are increased as rewards for prior responsible behavior. Generally, until teenagers reach the age of 18, parents may have to serve as gatekeepers in order to protect the lives of their children.

Children of Divorce

How do the children of divorce cope with separating themselves? Consider first what it is that adolescents need to do. At 15, children want to have their friends accept them. They want to build their own social network. They want to attract and be attracted by the opposite sex. They want to plan their own future, look forward to a driver's license, and prove to their parents that they are capable and trustworthy.

When mom and dad have separate addresses, additional difficulties may arise. There are several reasons.

1. **Lack of security.** Security is the springboard for independence. If early security has been shaken by divorce, children may have had to become independent at an early age. Often the oldest child is left to fill in for the missing parent. Conversely, a lack of security may decrease a child's eagerness to break away. Such a child may express a fear of leaving a parent alone but in fact may be afraid of aloneness.

2. **Mistrust of the Family Ethic.** The idea of forming their own family may not hold much appeal. Their attitudes about love and marriage may show a cynicism inappropriate for their years and stage of development. They do not wish to be like the adults they've seen.

3. **Uncovering Repressed Anger.** Children of divorce may choose adolescence as a time to act out the rage from bygone days. Perhaps Mary, who was 10 when her parents divorced, was overwhelmed by anger at that time but never let her anger show. At 17 she may still be angry and now has a strong urge to demonstrate her rejection of her parents. This urge may illicit far more than the average aggression.

4. **Playing Parents Off Against Each Other.** Children of divorce may use animosity between their parents as a powerful weapon. Parents who communicate well together have a chance of surviving their children's teenage years. Parents in separate households who do not often speak with each other may become victims of their separateness. The adolescent may use misinformation from one parent to the next to get what she or he wants. When all else fails, such a child may threaten to leave one parent for the other as emotional blackmail for power and control.

5. **Loneliness.** Whether the family is intact or not, teenage isolation is a serious problem. Isolation may mean rejection by the peer group and the family. The family may be too busy to notice. Teenagers generally do not do well when consistently left alone and ignored. Even in homes that give every appearance of normalcy, a family member may feel very much alone. Isolation and depression contribute heavily to the high suicide rates of adolescents.

Treating the Adolescent

Parental Involvement. When health professionals treat adolescents, they need to think to what degree parents should be involved. Some parents will not trust a minor child to represent his or her symptoms accurately. The parent thinks that she or he must be present to explain the child's problems or the health care worker will never understand what is going on.

A health professional who has good communication skills can usually well understand a teenager. Having a parent present may actually lead to confusing or conflicting information. If hostility exists between parent and child, the child may deny the accuracy of what the parent says simply to get even with the parent. Or the child may be hiding information from the parent and will not give the health practitioner accurate information while the parent is present.

Topics that are especially likely to be distorted when the parent is present involve sexual behavior and the use of alcohol and other drugs. A teenage girl was brought to the doctor's office because she had been menstruating for six weeks. It wasn't until her mother left the room that the girl told the nurse she'd had an abortion six weeks before. This example is only one of many that could be used to demonstrate how important it is to question adolescents privately. Also, if parents are present, children may simply be afraid to ask the questions they need to ask.

As a health professional, you should be assertive in making some alone time for the adolescent unless the child appears to be afraid of you or unless the disease or situation make time alone unnecessary. Generally young patients are more comfortable and open if they are treated alone. Most treatment plans require parental consent and understanding. As noted, when, how, and even if parents must be involved can be controversial. Such decisions often depend on the situation.

Gauging Maturity. As a health care worker, you must be careful not to put too much responsibility on the adolescent patient. Don't be fooled into thinking that a physically mature person is an emotionally mature one. Take extra care to ascertain to what extent the adolescent is really aware of her responsibilities and the consequences of her behavior. You also need to consider how to appropriately involve parents as a safeguard or backup. Remember that it is easier to work with parents if the treatment does not involve possibly controversial social issues.

Figure 5.2 illustrates the progression from childhood to adulthood and indicates the individuals who are significant at each stage.

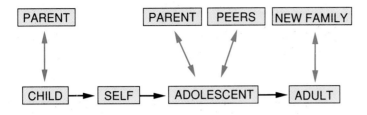

Figure 5.2 Significant individuals at different developmental stages.

In a society that worships youth, it is easy to forget that the older person has a lot to offer. Although the elderly are held in high esteem in many socieities, in ours only the fortunate among us get to know them and garner the knowledge they have. Our first lesson working with those who are in senescence (that is, growing old) is to be open to learning from and respecting the older person. We must remember that despite the changes and difficulties that can arise, this time of life is a time of enjoyment for the majority of the elderly. We must remember that most older people still have the adaptability to deal with problems because they can draw on their experiences in life. We must refrain from thinking of the elderly as collections of "worn out parts" and instead look at issues that are important to older people.

Senescence

Adaptability

There are two reasons that the body eventually wears out: because of wear and tear and because of built-in obsolescence. We now know that certain cells are genetically programmed to age in order to ensure reproduction and adaptability. If a species lives too long, it becomes too unadaptable in evolutionary terms.

In general, elderly people show a lack of biological adaptability across the board: physically, socially, and psychologically. A young person quickly adapts to an artificial limb, a 90-year-old may never adapt. Young people make friends easily, something the older person may find difficult. Young people may adapt well to life in a concentration camp, to a serious infection, to the loss of a loved one, or to surgery. But an older person cannot adapt so easily.

Mentally, this lack of adaptability often manifests as rigidity. Older people are said to be set in their ways. There may be reasons for this; the elderly person may be afraid of failure, or their rigidity may give them a feeling of security.

Older patients are often slow physically and **sometimes** mentally. By working within their system and showing some patience for their slowness, we can often better help them. A physically slow patient usually responds to "take your time" better than to "come on, hurry up."

On the other hand, many older persons have superior adaptive skills when compared with younger persons. How often have you heard the comment "he's mellowed since he's gotten older"? A lifetime of experience teaches many of us such things as better ways of handling people, how to get around shyness, and confidence in our own decision making.

Much has been made of a fall off of cognitive skills with age. However, the drop in intelligence quotient with age starts several decades before the age of 65. The decline is very small and it is more than compensated for by experience. Some areas of cognition apparently improve in older age, for instance, the ability to learn foreign languages.

Retirement

Although transition to old age generally begins at 65, there is no biological reason for setting 65 as retirement age. It started in Germany before the First World War, when the government decided the old could retire. An investigation into the financial cost of such a program led to picking the arbitrary age of 65, and it has been with us ever since.

Retirement changes lifestyle. A place of work — like a family — gives a person a role, a purpose, time-structuring activities, and a circle of friends and acquaintances. Retirement removes all this in one fell swoop. Is it any wonder, then, that retirement often causes stress? If the patient still has a good relationship with her or his spouse or has another work interest after retirement, then retirement may be less of a blow. If retirement has been planned in advance, the shock may be less.

Who you are before retirement is a good predictor of who you will be after. Sociable, adaptable people with multiple interests are likely to remain so. For many, however, the hobbies and activities they have put off until retirement never materialize. Instead, a sort of boredom or a feeling of having been put out to pasture sets in. Such feelings may turn into a chronic grief reaction. The elderly person may feel that his or her self-image has been stolen and cannot adapt to a new life. Instead of exploring and savoring a new environment, such a patient withdraws.

Further fuel is added to the fire when societal attitudes become manifest if retirees see themselves as a burden on society because they are economically unproductive.

If we think of the retiree's experience and the lifetime of work she or he did for our society, then the retiree becomes a person to be honored. Looking at the retiree in terms of his or her own life situation can help direct the patient. For the patient who is well motivated to keep himself/herself occupied and who has strong primary relationships and a strong social support system, retirement may be a joy. But the patient who has a poor primary relationship, has lost her social support system through retirement, and isn't motivated to occupy her time needs help. Volunteer work is often a good choice because it can strengthen self-image. For some, becoming a parking lot attendant, a clerk, or a janitor may fill the bill; others may find such a job damaging to self-image. Activities that may help are clubs for the elderly, bridge groups, senior centers, religious work, travel, and education.

For the children of the elderly, who often need help with their own children, grandparents can offer considerable stability. Children who have significant relationships with their grandparents often benefit considerably. And grandparents thrive with the young. Grandparents who have contact with their grandchildren remain happier and healthier than do those elderly people who are isolated from the young.

The disengagement theory postulated by E. Cumming and W.E. Henry states that the elderly sever friendships as part of a more general disengagement from society.

They may disengage because of stigma. They may feel, for instance, that drawing social security and no longer being productive is known to people around them. Thus they may feel that they no longer "belong" in their former circle of friends.

They may disengage because they feel they will soon die. Why bother learning new skills or games or making new friends if they may be dead in a few years anyway?

They may disengage because fewer roles are allowed in friendships. Roles formerly may have included work mates, boss, helper at work, mother, father, or confidante. When the children are grown and live in other cities and the elder is retired, many of these roles are lost.

Discrimination and withdrawal of the elderly may intensify this role reduction. The roles left may be grandmother, grandfather, money giver, or money needer. This smaller number of roles may reinforce the elder's disengagement.

Society has deprived older people of their right to be village elders. In part, this is because of our socially and geographically mobile society. For some elderly people, however, mobility becomes their salvation. They travel around the country in their mobile homes, or they join retirement communities. They may disengage from the rest of society but not from each other.

Primary relationships remain important as people age. Once the children are gone, the husband and wife may draw closer together. But sometimes they withdraw from each other, or they may have problems relating to their now adult children. Couple or family counseling may be essential for seniors in maintaining their primary relationships.

An unmarried person often maintains close ties with a brother or a sister or perhaps a cousin. If such a tie is a person's primary relationship, health care providers need to know about it. If a patient's spouse dies, we expect a grief reaction of some severity. But we may discount grief behavior after the death of a cousin unless we realize that the patient has lost his or her primary relationship. Separation from others is a part of life. For the child who leaves home, for the parent whose child grows up, or for the person who loses a dear friend, separation drives home a new reality. As the names of more and more old friends appear in the obituaries, the old person becomes increasingly aware of separation. The finality of death may hit home. Sometimes an elderly person feels regret about what feels unfinished in a relationship with a deceased friend. As time goes by, some older people withdraw from making new friends.

Illness

The incidence of illness in the elderly is much higher than for the young. Although people over 65 accounted for only 11.7 percent of the population in 1983, almost half of the hospital costs for that year were for people over 65. People may, however, have an unnecessarily pessimistic view of life expectancy for the elderly. Consider the survival figures in Table 5.1.

A 75-year-old woman who thinks she is too old to have an operation might be amazed to learn that, statistically speaking, she may live another 12 years and maybe even longer.

Another view many people have of the elderly is that they are all in nursing homes. Not so; even in their 90's the great majority of elderly persons are independent. Only about 5.1 percent of people over 65 live in institutions for the aged and dependent. A person who is institutionalized eats, sleeps, and works — or spends what would be working time — in the same place. The vast majority of elderly who live in institutions are there because of dementia, which is discussed below.

Table 5.1

STATISTICAL SURVIVAL RATES AFTER AGE 60*

Age, years	Statistical survival, years		Yearly chance of death, percentage
	Men	Women	
60	78	83	1.3
65	79	84	2.0
70	82	85	3.0
75	84	87	4.0
80	87	89	7.0
85	90	92	—

*U.S. Census Bureau, 1983 (latest available statistics).

What do the elderly die from? In order of frequency for both men and women over 65, leading causes of death are:

- Heart disease — sudden death, heart attack, and heart failure.
- Cancer — in men, lung, intestinal, and prostate cancer are most common; in women, intestinal, breast, and lung cancer are most common.
- Strokes.

The 10 most common causes of death in the population as a whole are heart disease, cancer, strokes, accidents, chronic lung disease, pneumonia and flu, diabetes, cirrhosis, suicide, and homicide (U.S. Census Bureau statistics, 1983). See Figure 5.3.

Although disease is common among the elderly, most elderly people are still independent and healthy even in their 80's and 90's. Disease is a fact of life to some, however, and it is often chronic disease. People who have chronic diseases often have multiple problems. One patient may, for instance, have diabetes, heart failure, high blood pressure, and osteoarthritis.

The medication regime for a person who has multiple problems is often highly complex and may change frequently. It is not uncommon for such patients to be on a half dozen medications on a regular basis. The fact that elderly people can adhere to such regimes is evidence that they have been able to adapt to their illnesses. Younger people would be less likely to comply with or consent to such regimes.

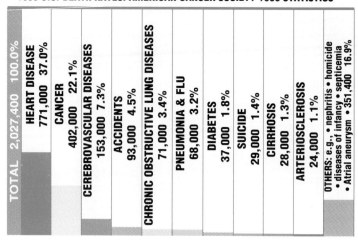

1985 U.S. DEATH RATES: AMERICAN CANCER SOCIETY 1988 STATISTICS

Figure 5.3 Most common causes of death.

Dementia, a common disease syndrome in the elderly, is also known as chronic organic brain syndrome (COBS). Many patients describe it as "going senile." The initial problem in dementia is a loss of recent memory which leads to a gradual loss of orientation. The patient cannot remember what year, month, date, and day it is, because he forgets what he was told this morning. If he is at home and has lived there many years, he will know it is home. But if he is brought to the hospital, he may say it is the pharmacy or home. He has no memory of being told where he was going.

If you, as a health care worker, ask a victim of dementia whether she recognizes you, she may say yes. If you ask her what your name is, she may ask you what your name is, or she may pause and say that your name escapes her at the moment. If you ask her what you do for a living, she may say something like "sell ice cream." If you ask her what she had for breakfast, she may say cornflakes, waffles, and coffee. When you check with the attendant, you may well find that she had scrambled eggs, doughnuts, and orange juice.

This example describes disorientation and confabulation, two characteristics of dementia. **Disorientation** is a loss of memory for time, person, and place. **Confabulation** is a coverup in which the patient fabricates, or makes up, events. It is similar to the lying a small boy does in telling his mother where he has been. But the dementia patient is not lying, nor is the patient using some subconscious defense mechanism. Confabulation is a natural process that is part of dementia and other organic conditions such as stroke or toxic states.

It is typical for the demented patient to cover their disorientation. If instead of covering up, however, a patient you work with constantly answers, "I don't care," you must suspect depression. Typically, demented patients — often with a tinge of paranoia — will answer questions with such replies as "You think I'm crazy, don't you?" or "You're just trying to trick me, aren't you?" or "I'm not going to answer these questions." Often correct answers will only come from the spouse, who may try to cover up their loved one's intellectual deterioration.

The **emotional reaction** to dementia, then, is most commonly reactive depression, paranoia, or both.

The following example describes one individual's reaction to dementia.

> A health care worker visited a demented woman at home. Earlier in her life, this woman had an obsessive, compulsive personality. As the worker walked through the hallway, he noticed that the entire living room was covered with tiny scraps of paper. In places they were several layers deep. They covered the top of the television set, the mantel, the sofa, the chairs, and the tables. On each scrap the woman had written a brief instruction to herself: "Put milk, butter out this morning." "Put the cat out tonight." "Bundle up the newspaper." On her coat she had pinned another message that said, "Glasses appointment this morning." This woman was mostly disoriented, but as her intellect started disorganizing, her compulsive personality had obviously started organizing.

Preservation of distant memory in a dementia victim may trick you into thinking that there is nothing amiss. A demented person may be able to recount with amazing detail and accuracy the history of his hometown before the Second World War, but he does not know where he is or who you are. Demented patients cannot remember current affairs or what you or their spouse told them five minutes ago.

As the process of dementia advances, more of the brain is involved and long-term memory begins to be affected. Victims lose the ability to speak, become spastic, and lose control of both bowels and bladder. In terms of the nervous system, the dementia patient gradually becomes similar to a newborn.

We do not know for sure what causes dementia. COBS, the syndrome just described, is most commonly due to a degenerative process that affects the cerebral cortex, the part of the brain that coordinates thinking, memory, and other higher activities of the nervous system. This degenerative process is called senile dementia of the Alzheimer's type or SDAT. Sometimes depression masks as dementia (called pseudodementia) or multiple strokes. Occasionally it is produced by unusual conditions like an underactive thyroid gland, a brain tumor, hydrocephalus (water on the brain), or a lack of vitamin B_{12}.

In the early stages, a victim may know that she is becoming demented and will compensate with defense mechanisms until she is no longer aware of what is happening to her. Some patients become depressed or withdrawn. They may become cranky so that people will not ask them questions and expose their dementia. Many victims become paranoid. One reason is that when a dementia victim puts an item down, he cannot remember where he put it and so presumes that someone stole it.

The caregiver, usually the spouse or a daughter, has to continue caring long after the patient has forgotten even who their caregiver is. It is extraordinary that so many caregivers are able to continue so long. But, as a senior nurse once said, "Our parents never abandoned us when we were helpless children, so why should be abandon them when they become helpless."

The example that follows illustrates how difficult dementia is for both the victim and the family (in this case, the spouse).

One day Ben noticed that his wife, Sally, 10 years his senior, was becoming less concerned about her appearance. The forgetfulness that he ascribed to inattention, disinterest, or simple absentmindedness, was gradually becoming a real problem. The previous evening, when he'd told her to get ready to go out for dinner with friends, she had gone upstairs, but, when he checked on her a few minutes later, he found her sitting on the edge of the bed looking at old photos. When he told her they were going out, she acted as though he had never said that before.

Ben soon discovered that unless he gave Sally a bath, she would never run the bath herself or get into the tub. Every time she wanted a cookie, Ben had to fetch the cookies, no matter how many times he told her where they were. He found this behavior particularly irritating despite the explanations the visiting nurse patiently offered him.

Eventually Sally began to get up in the middle of the night and start dressing herself. Often she would get upset because she could not pull her stockings on over her head like a pullover (dressing apraxia). Sometimes she got up to go to the toilet and, if she couldn't find the bathroom, would urinate on the floor.

Ben now had to start cutting back on his own activities. He could no longer count on sleeping through the night. He had to install a high lock on the bedroom door so Sally wouldn't fall down the stairs in the middle of the night. When she did fall or bump herself and a bruise would appear she would ask repeatedly how she got it.

Sally would turn on the gas stove and forget to light it, or turn on the iron and leave it. She began to wet herself more often and to wander outside after dark. Twice she was picked up by neighbors and once by the police when she wandered into the road and couldn't find her way back.

All this Ben could put up with. But when Sally started accusing him of stealing from her, he could take no more. It was painful enough that the person he once loved was slowly becoming like a toddler who needed constant watching. The suggestion of distrust was too much. When all the rewards for coping seemed to be gone, Ben gave up and put Sally in a nursing home.

Fortunately, dementia affects less than 5 percent of people over 65. More than 95 percent continue to live their lives with their mental faculties fully intact.

Disability and the Stigma of Aging

Disability Among the Elderly.   Because they are susceptible to disease, the aged are more likely to suffer serious disability. An important factor with the elderly is that they suffer more from multiple pathologies; their disabilities compound. Arthritis caused by aging in the knees and hip may prevent walking. Cataracts (clouding of the lens of the eye) may cause blindness. A weak heart may cause chronic tiredness and shortness of breath. And one person may have all these afflictions together. The patient may also live alone, be below the poverty level in terms of income, and be morbidly obese (more than 100 pounds overweight or more than 100 percent overweight).

For the person with such a complex list of disabilities, the important questions are not what sort of arthritis does she have or how bad is it or which joints are affected. Rather, they are: Can she walk through the supermarket? Can she read the labels on cans? Can she get on and off the toilet, cook her meals, and make out checks? These **activities needed for daily living** (ADL) become the new standard. Whether the patient can do them determines whether she can make it alone. Independence is as important to the elderly as working or parenting is to the young adult.

The elderly also suffer from what we might call the "bits" syndrome. Maybe Uncle Jack can make it with his cane, despite his arthritis, but if his cataracts get worse, he can't see his way so well. If he also gets dizzy because of his high blood pressure pills whenever he walks, he may not make it. Now the nerves to his legs are wearing out and he feels as if he's walking on cotton wool. He has arrived at the point where he cannot make it on his own. A single disease or symptom may not be too much, but all the bits together create a problem. Sometimes one little bit cured can make a remarkable difference, however. Examples include:

- Cutting painfully ingrown toenails and removing corns.
- Getting a new prescription for glasses or simply cleaning them.
- Fixing a hearing aid or getting new batteries for it.
- Arranging for a high toilet seat so the patient can use the toilet alone.
- Lining a patient's dentures so they fit better.
- Getting a pair of shoes that fit properly.

As health practitioners, we need to question the elderly or those who care for them about falls, abuse, continence, ADL, and memory, for such information is seldom offered spontaneously.

Falls may imply a loss of independence. The patient may fall and then be afraid to walk because of a fear of further falls. Falls can have medical causes (low blood pressure from too many medications) or be accidental (tripping over a scatter rug or a small dog, or slipping on a polished floor or in a wet bathtub).

If an elderly patient's injuries appear to be unnatural or cannot be accounted for, or if the patient seems generally fearful, you should suspect abuse. Approach the patient gently and in private with your questions. (Abuse is discussed in Chapter 11.) Continence and ADL are integral to a patient's independence. Review the accompanying ADL evaluation and short memory evaluation material.

One important point to keep in mind when you work with the elderly is that you need to be patient. You must not rush your patients, and you must allow them to prepare themselves with their wigs, dentures, hearing aids, jewelry, and canes. Remember that they may not feel right without these normal aids to their everyday existence. Hospitalized patients in particular should not be expected to respond without these accoutrements of existence. The equivalent to a young person would be to converse with them while they were still in the nude without having had a chance to get dressed.

Memory Evaluation

Question	Testing Recall
Where are we now?	Place
Where is this place located?	Place
What day is it?	Time
What is today's date?	Time
What month is it?	Time
What year is it?	Time
How old are you?	Recent or remote memory
What is your birthday?	Recent or remote memory
What year were you born?	Recent or remote memory
What is your spouse's name?	Recent or remote memory
How long have you been married?	Recent or remote memory
What are your children's names?	Recent or remote memory
Who is president of the U.S.?	General information — memory
Who was president before him?	General information — memory

It is sometimes difficult to strike a balance between treatment of every symptom and dismissal of every symptom with "you're just getting older."

Mrs. Olshaw, aged 81, lived alone in the country. She was a little confused and quite nervous about her nine different medicines for high blood pressure, breast cancer, heart failure, and arthritis. But despite this, she still smoked about 15 cigarettes per day because she said "I would be nervous if I stopped." She shopped once a week. For eight years she had used "Meals on Wheels" on whom she relied for a daily meal. One night she was awakened by severe shortness of breath, was admitted to the hospital, and was told that she had a heart attack. Sandra, a dietician, was called in to see her for a low cholesterol diet. Mrs. Olshaw's cholesterol was mildly high at 288 mg%. What should the dietician do?

She could treat this new finding or she could view the patient in a different perspective and realize the difficulties it would involve, and then discuss the situation with the physician. The dietician could tell the physician that since Meals on Wheels does not have a low cholesterol diet, the patient should be advised to avoid butter and egg containing products if they are served. (This patient leaned heavily on Meals on Wheels and ate virtually nothing else.) Sandra had found out from the patient that she would try to stop smoking if she could keep her Meals on Wheels. Although Sandra did not tell the physician, she had looked up an article on cholesterol after heart attacks. She found data on the poor predictive value of serum cholesterol levels after a heart attack and minimal evidence of treatment being worthwhile at the age of 81.

Stigma is another important problem in the elderly. Stigma is an integral part of disability and further compounds disability in the aged. Stigma against the elderly is called "agism," analogous to "sexism" or "racism." East Asian societies and some other groups often honor their elders but in American society the elderly are not so revered.

Stigma is associated with:

- **Retirement.** As discussed earlier, retirement brings with it a loss of image as a useful and productive member of society.
- **Economic loss.** Fifteen percent of the elderly live below the poverty level. The elderly are generally much poorer than the young.
- **Social isolation.** About 5% of people in their 20's live alone,
    10% of people in their 50's live alone, and
    30% of people over 65 live alone.

    Of those over 65 years old,
    31% live alone (15.4% for men and 40% for women),
    54% live with a spouse,
    15% live with relatives, and
    2% live with friends.
- **Touching.** The elderly, with their wrinkled, spotted skin, are often seen as unattractive, not to be touched. As a health care provider, you will quickly find that a handshake often turns into handholding. Sometimes the therapeutic effect of touching will be the major content of a patient's visit to you.

It is also made easier because touching the elderly does not have the social connotation of a sexual advance, which it may in young people. Touching is of particular importance in the elderly, and even more so in terminal illness, skin disease, and cancer patients.

- **Sex.** We don't see sex among the elderly on television or in the movies. Instead, the elderly are seen in comfortable nightclothes and a safe distance apart. Many jokes are made about the elderly having sex. The expression "dirty old man" attests to a feeling of disgust that the elderly should even be interested in sexual matters. But, although the frequency of intercourse often declines as people age, many elderly people still have sex regularly.

Discrimination and prejudice against the elderly are subtle and pervasive. If you can shake off your prejudice, your older patients will hold you in high regard and you can be more effective in helping them.

Loss

To the elderly, the loss of friends, acquaintances, and loved ones is a part of life. They also anticipate their own death as the time draws nearer. How an elderly person accepts the prospect of dying depends on many factors. If the person has a disease or disability that makes the quality of life borderline, death may not be unwelcome. To some, the approach of death is neutral, expected, even longed for. Many old people say they've lived long enough or ask why God doesn't take them. Others say, "I'm no good to anyone" (indicating a loss of positive self-image) or "I've been through enough." Because pneumonia is so often the cause of death, it has been called the old person's friend.

To many old people, loss of independence is actually a greater threat than death. Some individuals fiercely maintain independence even in seemingly dangerous circumstances. An elderly person who has had recurrent dangerous falls may stubbornly insist on continuing to live alone. Even accepting help may signify a loss of independence to such a person.

Loss of health and vigor is also part of aging. Aches and pains last longer and come more frequently. As one elderly physician put it, "It's not the heart that wears out first, it's the knees!"

As already discussed, the elderly also face loss of occupation, which can be attended by boredom or a state of suspended animation. Another kind of loss can arise from the realization that all those jobs and hobbies the person was going to get done one day are never going to get done.

Common coping mechanisms for the multiple losses of growing old include:

- **Excessively Defensive Behavior.** "I don't need a visiting nurse because I don't have high blood pressure."

- **Withdrawal.** The patient may shun contact with others because she or he is afraid of exposing loss or suffering further loss.

- **False Humor.** Such a defense keeps the interaction from getting too close to the real issues.

- **Dependence.** An elderly person usually depends on a spouse or a relative. Occasionally the dependence is on a friend. "I can't be left alone at night," the dependent person may say, "I may have a heart attack." Many older people are not as afraid of dying as they are afraid of dying alone.

- **Depression.** Depression is a state of chronic grief often with physical as well as mental symptoms. Symptoms can include sleep disturbances, weight loss, and mood changes, slowing of thoughts and actions (psychomotor retardation), loss of drive, loss of sexual drive, dementia (more accurately, pseudodementia), and somaticism (converting concerns to bodily health).

- **Reminiscing.** This reaction can be explained in many ways. The elderly person may be undergoing a review of his or her life in preparation for dying. Reminiscing may allow an older person to reorganize her or his attitudes, which may be beneficial, given the older person's rigid and more obsessive thought system. Reminiscing may simply be an equivalent of daydreaming — a device to counteract boredom. A rigid person may feel more comfortable thinking about what is familiar. In contrast, the young are more likely to explore with their daydreaming. Or rather than think about her current miserable status, an elderly patient may want to identify with proud moments in her past that she can live again.

  Reminiscence in the elderly has a different significance. Using reminiscence therapy is something positive health workers can do to help the elderly. Ask about their photos, their life when younger, their knickknacks. Ten minutes looking at their photo album with them may have immensely more therapeutic benefit than hours of our professional skills.

All humans must face loss. Again, we must stress that the vast majority of elderly people can accept these losses as part of life. And most lead fulfilling and satisfying lives.

Death and Suicide

The young are sure they are immortal, but the elderly often have a realistic view of death. The older person may say, "I've lived my life. It's time to go now." When an Eskimo has reached this point, she or he walks off into the snow and lies down to die.

Dying from a broken heart is another phenomenon in the elderly. Studies show a high mortality rate in the first year after the death of a lifetime mate.

Some patients seem to decide that they have had enough and simply go downhill. The psyche can cause death, albeit slowly. This is not really suicide, but more a subconscious speeding up of the end of life.

An aspect of living and dying that we health professionals must keep in perspective is that the quality of life is just as important, if not more important, than the quantity (length) of life. This question can arise when there is concern about an elderly person's safety. The issue may be loss of independence versus risk of death. You might help guide a patient by pointing out, for instance, that a fall and a fractured hip would most likely bring a loss of independence, whereas using a walker might enable the patient to hold on to his or her independence.

Religious questions inevitably enter into the older person's attitudes toward dying, often easing the passage from this world to the next. Some cannot wait to join their previously deceased spouse, believing that death will reunite them.

Suicide is common among the elderly. It is the eighth most common cause of death in all age groups. An elderly person may commit suicide for altruistic reasons: "I've lived my life, I'm just a burden now." Or the person may be tired of living. Often diseases take their toll more because they are chronic than because they are severe. The cancer patient may wait for the end to come naturally. The isolated blind man with severe arthritis may be unwilling to wait.

Depression, alcoholism, and accidents also are common among the elderly; all are associated with suicide. Who is to say whether the elderly alcoholic who falls down a flight of stairs does so intentionally? Any attempted suicide must be taken very seriously. The likelihood of repetition and success are very high in those over 40. People over 65 rarely fail to succeed the first time.

The annual incidence of suicide is 12/100,000 persons (in 1985 that translated to 29,000 successful suicides with approximately 10 times that many unsuccessful attempts). Men are three times more likely to be successful than women, but women attempt suicide three times as often as men do. This means that women may out number men by nine to one in unsuccessful suicide attempts. These figures refer mainly to adolescents and young adults, however. Older persons who attempt suicide are all **much more likely** to be successful.

The risk of suicide increases with the following independent risk factors:

- over 65 (40/100,000)
- separated, widowed, or divorced (42/100,000)
- living alone (71/100,000)
- unemployed or retired (25/100,000)
- males (34/100,000)

As you can see, the elderly widowed retired man living alone is at high risk for suicide.

Not all suicide is death-seeking. The patient may be crying out for help, trying to communicate psychic pain, seeking revenge ("see what you made me do"), or trying to relieve boredom or physical pain. For some, suicide is part of self-destructive behavior. Chronic suicide is a term used to describe chronic self-destructive behavior. Examples of such behavior include alcoholism, drug abuse, refusal to comply with an important medical regime, and morbid obesity due to overeating.

Suicidal patients often talk about it. Actually, 80 percent of those who commit suicide tell someone about it beforehand. Fifty percent see a health professional within a month of suicide; 7 percent see a health professional the same day of suicide.

As a health practitioner, you must ask about suicide. There is no evidence that asking about it puts any ideas in a patient's mind. You might ask the patient whether he feels that life is not worth living or whether he ever feels like ending it all. If he asks you what you mean, you might respond "Have you ever thought of doing away with yourself?" To establish whether suicide is a real risk for a patient, you must ask a question such as "Do you think you would ever actually kill yourself?" Once suicidal risk has been established, appropriate referral or hospitalization is mandatory.

The cause of suicide is not "being crazy," it is not "just in your genes," it is not just an effect of the weather or the phase of the moon. Rational people commit suicide; psychotic people usually do not. Endogenous depression (depression that has no obvious cause and

Developmental Issues

may be lifelong), which can be inherited, may dispose a person to suicide, but most suicides are not the result of endogenous depression. Male suicide often is associated with financial concerns for those that will survive.

Once the crisis that may have precipitated the suicide has passed, the patient is still at risk and needs continued support.

Parasuicide includes chronic suicide, dying from a broken heart, giving up, and living life dangerously; in some situations, it may include accident proneness. Some of these behaviors are common in the elderly and can be regarded as the equivalent of suicide.

The attitude of the older person who is obviously worn out from life may be different. As health professionals, we cannot condone suicide, but we can allow a patient to take risks if it allows continued independence. When a patient develops a terminal illness, she or he may want to be allowed to die should God decide it — a sort of Russian roulette.

Some older people sign a living will and give it to their physicians so they will not be put on a ventilator or be resuscitated if their heart should stop beating. Living wills are created by mentally competent people and should be respected.

As discussed in Chapter 4, do not resuscitate orders are written by physicians in a hospital setting when a patient is in the final stage of an incurable medical condition, or sometimes if an older patient requests it. To repeat, a do not resuscitate order in no way implies that a patient is to be abandoned or that treatment is to cease. It simply means that CPR would not be performed should the patient's heart stop beating or should breathing stop.

In dealing with the issues of senescence discussed in this section, we do not want to convey the idea that anyone over 65 is "over the hill." On the contrary, most senior citizens continue to live happy, healthy, and socially useful lives. Remember that 95 percent of people over 65 live at home, many continue to work, and many continue to live active lives. In fact, some people say life begins at 65.

Remember, too, many people over the age of 65 are high achievers. Consider these examples:

- One elderly grandmother who lives in Harlem continues to raise up to 50 foster children at a time. For many years she did this single-handedly, but she now has help. These babies have drug related problems.
- Grandma Moses started painting at the age of 78. She painted every day for 23 years, until she was 101.
- Harland Sanders retired at the age of 65. He then started a franchise we all know as Kentucky Fried Chicken.

Evaluation of Daily Living Activities

Name: _____ Diagnosis: _____

Date of Birth: _____ Occupation: _____

Key to Grading:

Independence Grades:

5   Normal performance

4   Adequate performance, but involvement noticeable and/or dependent on special apparatus, heights, weights, etc.

4– Adequate performance but needs improvements, slow, awkward, etc.

Dependence Grades:

3   Supervision needed to complete

2   Assistance needed to complete

1   Activity impossible

X   Not indicated for testing at present time

NA Not applicable

Small letter beside grade indicates:

w Possible in wheelchair only

b Possible in bed only

o Circle about grade indicates use of special apparatus

_____

_____

Apparatus

Wheelchair _____ Armsling _____

Brace _____

Cane _____ Mobile Arm Support _____

Handsplint _____ Crutches _____

_____

	Date:					
	Initial:					
Bed Mobility						
1. Operate signal light						
2. Hold book and turn pages						
3. Operate bed lamp						
4. Operate radio						
5. Procure object from night table						
6. Sit up						
7. Turn over						
Eating						
8. Eat with fingers						
9. Eat with fork						
10. Eat with spoon						
11. Cut with knife						
12. Drink from glass						
13. Drink from cup						

Evaluation of Daily Living Activities (cont.)

Date:						
Initial:						
Hygiene						
14. Use handkerchief						
15. Wash hands						
16. Wash face						
17. Brush teeth						
18. Comb hair						
19. Care for nails						
20. Shave or make-up						
21. Get on and off toilet – arrange clothes						
22. Use toilet paper						
23. Bathe self						
24. Get in or out of bath or shower						
25. Shampoo hair						
26. Lock and unlock braces						
27. Put on – remove braces						
28. Put on – remove slings or M.A.S.						
29. Put on – remove hand-splints						
Dressing						
30. Put on – remove overcoat						
31. Put on – remove underclothes						
32. Put on – remove button shirt						
33. Put on – remove slipover garment						
34. Put on – remove slacks						
35. Put on – remove shoes						
36. Lace and unlace shoes						
37. Put on – remove hose						
38. Tie bow or tie						
Utilities						
39. Operate light switches (all types)						
40. Operate faucets (all types)						
41. Flush toilet						
42. Operate locks requiring 1 hand						
43. Operate locks requiring 2 hands						

Evaluation of Daily Living Activities (cont.)

Date:						
Initial:						
44. Plug in cord						
45. Wind watch or clock						
46. Open and close drawers						
47. Open and close windows						
48. Use scissors						
Communication						
49. Write name						
50. Handle own mail						
51. Handle money						
52. Use dial phone						
Locomotion						
53. Wheel chair forward 30′						
54. Wheel chair forward 100′						
55. Wheel chair turning						
56. Wheel chair up ramp						
57. Wheel chair down ramp						
58. Get in and out of wheel chair from standing						
59. Get in and out of chairs						
60. Get in and out of car						
61. Get in and out of bed						
62. Get in and out of bathroom						
63. Walk forward 30′						
64. Walk forward 100′						
65. Walk backward 10′						
66. Walk sidewards						
67. Walk carrying object						
68. Cross street with traffic light						
69. Do 7″ steps with rails						
70. Do 7″ steps without rails						
71. Do bus steps						
72. Open and go through door with sills						
73. Operate automatic elevator						
74. Pick up object from floor						
75. Get down and up from floor						
76. Move on floor not in upright position						
77. Get wheelchair in and out of car						

In the early childhood section, we reviewed the strong relationship of parental expectations of perfection to the problems of preparing a parent to cope with a "less than perfect" child. We examined the importance of bonding and dependency and how these lead to appropriate body schema and separation development.

The developmental issues of negativism and control were also reviewed. Here the health practitioner is encouraged to use positive reinforcement and to encourage parents to do the same. Modeling and competence are further ways that young children will develop. Adults are cautioned to remember that the child's expectations may not match the adult's expectations.

This section closes with a discussion of developmental milestones. While these milestones provide valuable cues, they are best interpreted individually and with caution.

Puberty causes rapid physiological and emotional changes, as discussed in the section on adolescence. Coping with these changes involves family and social support. The more different the teenager feels, the more support is required.

Differentiating from parents nearly always means a struggle on the home front. No matter how good things are at home, adolescents fight for independence by rejecting what their parents offer. Rejection is especially difficult for parents when they see their values being trampled. The more problems a child has had in the past, the more she or he is likely to act out aggressively during this breakaway phase. Families survive best when they have provided long-term stability and offer the adolescent emotional support. Adolescents should be rewarded on the basis of responsible behavior.

As we grow old, we often become less adaptable yet have to face many changes. Issues of retirement, separation from society, illness, and death are described, as well as how the elderly deal with these issues. Because it is so common among the elderly, special attention is given to dementia. Disability, stigma, and ways of dealing with loss are also described. Despite these many seemingly depressing changes, the great majority of the elderly still cope well with life's problems, leading a fulfilling life.

Review

ADL: Activities of Daily Living
Body schema: sense of self, identifying with one's own body
Chronic suicide: chronic self-destructive behavior
Compliance: following directions especially as given by health care provider for patient health
Confabulation: coverup in which the patient fabricates or makes up events
Dementia: chronic diffuse mental deterioration in a conscious patient, manifest primarily by memory loss, and secondarily by behavioral and emotional changes
Differentiate: make distinct, make separate
Disengagement: process of separating from society
Dyad: a couple, a group of two
Dynamic: rapidly changing, growing, not stagnant
Institutionalization: person who eats, sleeps, and spends working time (or what should be working time), in the same place
Intervention: stepping into health problem issues in order to facilitate change
Neonatal: the 1st four weeks after birth
Parasuicide: mentally allowing death when death need not occur, includes chronic suicide, giving up, and dying of a broken heart
Primary sex characteristics: changes in reproductive organs
Role: part played by an actor in drama or of a person in life
Satiation: being satisfied (usually after eating), sense of having enough
Secondary sex characteristics: changes in shape, body hair, and voice which accompany primary sex development and which occur at puberty
Social mobility: moving between socioeconomic classes within a single generation

1. Describe the effect of parental expectations on the developing infant, toddler, young child, and adolescent.
2. How is differentiation related to body schema?
3. Every third time that four-year-old Andrew writes his name he draws an "M" where the "W" should be. How would you advise his mother to handle this?
4. What are the conflicts for both parents and adolescents which typically arise over differentiation?
5. Make a distinction between the terms differentiation and disengagement.
6. List predictors of successful retirement.
7. List adverse events associated with retirement.

8. What is the disengagement theory?
9. Independence is as important to the elderly as working or parenting is to the young adult. Discuss.
10. What information does the elderly person seldom offer spontaneously?
11. Why do you think many elderly are more afraid of dying alone than of death itself?
12. Why is reminiscing important for the elderly?

Additional Reading

Cummings, E., and Henry, W. E. *Growing Old: The Process of Disengagement.* Basic Books, NY. 1961.

President's Commission for the Study of Ethical Problems in Medicine. *Deciding to Forego Life Sustaining Treatment.* U.S. Government Printing Office. 1983.

Roy, A. *Suicide.* Williams and Wilkins, Baltimore, MD. 1986.

Simon, R., and Pardes, H., Eds., *Understanding Human Behavior in Health and Illness.* Williams & Wilkins, Baltimore, MD. 1981.

U.S. Bureau of the Census, *Statistical Abstract of the United States.* U.S. Government Printing Office, Washington, DC. 1983.

Chapter

6

After reading this chapter, you should be able:
- To define differences between addiction, dependence, habituation, and tolerance.
- To discuss relative causes of alcoholism.
- To recognize the typical symptoms of alcoholism.
- To list the effects of alcoholism.
- To discuss the treatments available for alcoholism.
- To categorize and list substances of abuse.
- To list the physical, economic, and social effects of smoking.
- To discuss ways to help people stop smoking.

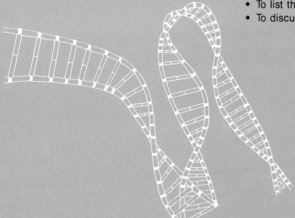

Addiction

In this chapter, we deal primarily with alcoholism as a model for addiction. Alcoholism is a problem that health professionals have to address frequently. Addiction is a special physiological problem with serious psychological consequences. Although down deep addicts know they are addicted, up front they rationalize or deny it. Although it is true that addiction occurs in people with psychological problems, many experts feel that addiction is a biological problem. It can be induced in animals, so there has to be a nonemotional component. Addiction, then, is seen as learned behavior that is physiologically predestined.

Alcoholism

The first order of business in caring for someone who has a significant addiction, of course, is to treat the addiction. The patient must have the support of family and friends in accepting the necessity of abstaining from alcohol. Further, the patient must accept that the drug can never be used again. If she does, she is likely to return to a state of addiction.

It is not easy to convince an alcoholic to stop drinking. In dealing with a nonalcoholic patient, we can address the problem and discuss it with the patient, and usually the patient responds. But normal psychology does not work with alcoholics. Unless pushed hard, the normal alcoholic often stops only after hitting what is called rock bottom. And many addicts die before they reach that point.

Alcoholism can be defined as a chronic consumption of alcohol that continues despite significant interference with a person's physical, economic, or social health. Drinking too much is not alcoholism. What if we learn that a French laborer drinks a liter of wine at work every other day. Is that alcoholism? What if we then learn that 70 percent of French laborers drink this heavily? Are they all alcoholic? Alcoholism could be defined according to each society or each person's group within that society, but this would be clumsy.

The important parts of the definition are the following:
- The person's drinking is having significant ill effects on his or her life.
- The person cannot stop despite the ill effects.
- The amount of alcohol the person consumes relates not to any absolute quantity but to significant ill effects.

In the United States, two-thirds of all adults drink; 20 percent of men and 10 percent of women drink heavily. Up to 10 percent of men and 3 percent of women are alcoholics. The alcoholism rate in women seems to be increasing. Further, women seem to become alcoholic later in life and are more likely to postpone treatment. Also, the alcoholic woman is more likely to be a closet drinker (someone who drinks secretly rather than socially).

Alcoholism is an important disease. Fifty percent of all fatal car and pedestrian accidents are associated with alcohol. Alcohol increases the incidence of heart disease, certain cancers, and pneumonia. Cirrhosis only develops in approximately 8 percent of all alcoholics, but it is number nine on the list of causes of death in all people.

What is Addiction?

To understand what addiction is, become familiar with the following definitions:

Addiction is physical dependence on a substance.

Physical dependence causes a physical withdrawal syndrome (for example, convulsions, fever, hallucinations). With physical dependence, there is an actual physiological "need" for the drug.

Habituation is psychological dependence on a substance.

Psychological dependence causes a psychological withdrawal syndrome only; for example, anxiety (and its symptoms, like a fast pulse), insomnia, or an irresistible urge to take more of a drug.

Tolerance is when a patient needs higher doses of a drug to have the same physical effect. That is, the more a person uses a drug, the more of it he or she needs to experience the same high.

An addictive drug is associated with physical and psychological dependence and tolerance. Examples include narcotics, alcohol, and sedatives.

A habit-forming drug causes psychological dependence, but involves no tolerance dependence. An example is marijuana.

The Causes of Alcoholism

Alcoholism has several causes, and much has been written about all of them. At the top of the list probably comes an inherited predisposition to alcoholism. Whether personality traits or genetic traits cause alcoholism and whether personality is a cause or an effect in alcoholism remain subjects of continuing debate. Societal pressure also has an important impact on alcoholism.

Genetic Theories of Alcoholism. One study looked at 55 men from alcoholic biological fathers who had been adopted in infancy. By their late 20s, 18 percent were alcoholic (interestingly, their brothers who stayed with their biological fathers had a similar rate). By contrast, 5 percent of 78 adopted men from nonalcoholic parents were alcoholic. Although it involved a rather small sample, this study suggests that alcoholism is inherited rather than cultivated.

According to a study done in 1977, 50 percent of alcoholic men have alcoholic fathers, 30 percent have alcoholic brothers, 6 percent have alcoholic mothers, and 3 percent have alcoholic sisters. Anyone who works with alcoholics cannot help but conclude that alcoholism appears to be an inherited disease, especially in men.

In another study of nearly 1800 Swedish adoptees, two types of alcoholism seemed to emerge. Type 1 was the young person who begins drinking seriously in the teen years. They are called *male-limited types.* They were almost all male and became severe alcoholics before the age of 25. About 25% of all alcoholics are Type 1. The Type 1 alcoholics had bad work habits and police records; many had been in jail one or more times. This finding suggests that teenagers and children may become addicted very fast. Having an alcoholic parent was an important factor.

The Type 2 alcoholics were called *milieu limited.* Of all alcoholics, 75% are Type 2. These individuals drank heavily after age 25, but they had good work and police records. They often stopped drinking successfully.

According to the genetic theory of alcoholism, the patient starts drinking for the same reason that nonalcoholics do. But the person who becomes an alcoholic may experience more pleasurable effects, loss of control, alcoholic blackouts (loss of memory while drunk), and greater tolerance right from the beginning. These are early constitutional manifestations of alcoholism that lead ultimately to addiction. Sometimes the children of alcoholics see the devastation of alcoholism and become teetotalers. But their own children, who carry the gene but do not see the devastation, become alcoholic. This has been called the **skip phenomenon**.

The following example supports the genetic theory of alcoholism and also accounts for differing "racial" influences of alcoholism. Jews seem to have a high resistance to alcoholism, with rates of about one percent, and their alcoholism starts late in life. Jews have consumed alcohol since antiquity. Northern Europeans started drinking alcohol over the last 1,500 years, have medium resistance, and their alcoholism begins in middle age. North American Indians and Eskimos have been exposed to alcohol for only 200 to 300 years, have alcoholism rates up to 80 percent, and have an early age of onset of alcoholism. Those with an inherited predisposition to alcoholism at an early age often do not have a family, so the gene eventually dies out. These differences suggest that groups most recently exposed to alcohol are constitutionally more prone to alcoholism.

Psychological Theories of Alcoholism.   Psychological testing of alcoholics frequently reveals a number of common psychological traits: denial, aggression, depression, regression, low self-esteem, and paranoid thinking. Although a group of traits alone may not cause alcoholism, in a genetically predisposed person it may.

Other psychological factors can play a part in alcoholism. If a person has difficulty socializing and alcohol has a disinhibiting effect on her, she will tend to drink whenever she socializes. Similarly, if a patient becomes depressed but finds that his mood is elevated by alcohol, he probably will continue to consume it because he has discovered a drug that works. He feels better and continues to medicate himself with alcohol.

Cultural Theories of Alcoholism. It is easy to dismiss cultural explanations for alcoholism as racism when applied to a culture and prejudice when applied to an individual. Nevertheless, differing cultural incidences of alcoholism are real. American Indians and Eskimos have a high alcoholism rate, Irish lower, English lower, Jews and Chinese lowest.

Some subcultures — persons in the armed forces, bartenders, salesmen, and entertainers, for instance — have higher rates of alcoholism. Availability of alcohol definitely seems to have an effect. The fact that bartenders have a higher alcoholism rate suggests that availability of alcohol increases the chance of alcoholism. Likewise, in certain subcultures (the armed forces, for example), drinking is viewed less repressively, which may facilitate the development of alcoholism.

As another example, in Portugal, 15 percent of the population lives by making or selling wine. It would be difficult to imagine antagonism toward drinking in such a country.

In summary, the causes of alcoholism appear to be a genetic tendency with varying internal (psychological traits) or external (cultural pressure) factors.

The Diagnosis of Alcoholism

How does a psychologist, counselor, social worker, or other concerned health care worker know whether a client is alcoholic?

Because denial is so common and so pervasive as part of the disease of alcoholism, it has diagnostic value. How a person answers the questions "Do you drink?" or "How much do you drink?" is highly important. If the person's answer is straight, she or he probably is not an alcoholic. Straight answers are answers like these:

"I take three highballs after dinner."
"I am a teetotaler."
"Oh, I probably have four beers with my friends on Friday
nights, and maybe an occasional glass of wine otherwise."

These are up-front answers. The patient has nothing to hide.

As a health practitioner, you need to watch for answers that contain an element of denial. Such answers will sound vague, unfinished, defensive, or paranoid. Examples include the following:

"I only drink beer."
"I only drink on weekends."
"Oh, I can hold my liquor alright."
"I don't drink so much now."
"I gave it up."

Answers like these suggest that the patient has something to hide. Note that alcoholics often say, "I gave it up" to cover the fact that they have stopped drinking only a few days ago.

It is significant if the patient's answers seem to provoke you to ask another question. All denying-type answers seem to make you wonder a bit. Asking another question, such as "What do you mean by . . ." often will produce a revealing response. For instance, asking "What do you mean when you say you only drink beer?" may elicit the reply, "Well, I never touch whiskey. I used to, but I don't anymore." Here the message from the patient is: I can't be an alcoholic because I have stopped the hard stuff. You should be thinking just the opposite. This is not proof-positive, but it gives you a clue to focus on.

The alcoholic patient who admits to having a drinking problem is uncommon. Most will deny that they have a problem, so you must depend on other clues. Often the patient's spouse will tell you. Or the patient may smell of alcohol at 10:00 a.m., and, when asked about it, say that she had a couple of beers the night before. Two beers, of course, would only linger a few hours on the breath.

The lives of alcoholics are commonly characterized by marital problems, sexual problems, drunken driving, and problems at work — which are some of those social, economic, and physical consequences of alcoholism that are part of the definition. A red flag should go up in your mind whenever you hear a patient talk about the following:

* Marital problems, divorce, separation.
* Impotence, sexual problems, sexual abuse.
* Being arrested for drunken driving.
* Violence or emotional or physical abuse.
* Being laid off, losing a job, not doing well at work, not getting along with the boss.
* Bankruptcy, business failure.
* Difficulties with the children, poor school performance.

The list of the potential problems of alcoholics is infinite and could almost be duplicated by stopping lots of people on the street and asking them what they think is the worst personal catastrophe that could possibly befall them.

The Effects of Alcoholism

Psychological Effects of Alcoholism.   Defensiveness is another common trait of alcoholics. Emotional augmentation refers to a lowered threshold for action if you are concerned about something. For example, a man on the run from the police may think that every phone call or knock on the door is the police. Likewise, when drinking, an alcoholic husband may react with more than usual anger to any comments by his wife. Emotional augmentation seems to be provoked by alcohol. The wife, upset by the anger, may respond with even more anger. A vicious circle can be set up unless the wife learns to moderate her responses continuously (something that sounds easy but in practice is very difficult!).

A major effect of alcoholism is that alcohol dominates the alcoholic's life. Thoughts of when, where, and how to get more booze take precedence over everything else, including family, business, economic concerns, and health. Alcohol is more important than food, family, friends, and even self-respect.

The psychological changes that occur in alcoholism have been divided into first-, second-, and third-order symptoms.

First-order symptoms are neuropsychological disturbances caused by drinking in an addictive personality. An addictive personality is one who easily becomes physically dependent on substances when exposed to them. Examples include loss of control, blackouts (memory defects during drinking), anguish, and emotional augmentation.

Second-order symptoms represent the psychological reactions of the patient to first-order symptoms. Examples include denial, rationalization, deterioration of self-image, depression, and regression to more child-like behavior (for example, dependent and self-centered behavior). Also, someone who is drunk most of the time between the ages of 20 and 40 will not possess the emotional maturity of a 40-year-old if he or she sobers up at 40. Maturity will be delayed and will be more like that of a 20-year-old.

Third-order symptoms are those that result from the interpretations of friends, therapists, and society. The symptoms include shame, guilt, and conflict from the idea that psychological defects rather than addiction cause alcoholism. This belief, in turn, leads to primitive behavior by the alcoholic, either against himself/herself or against others, including hostility. Yet alcoholics **seek** negative labels from friends and provoke fights with their spouse to have an excuse for taking their next drink.

The Physical Effects of Alcoholism. There are numerous physical effects of alcoholism. They include:

- A red face and goose flesh on the neck.
- A high incidence of cancer of the gastrointestinal tract, pancreas, liver, stomach, head, neck and lungs (because of associated smoking), and bladder.
- Pneumonia.
- Cirrhosis (a serious, progressive scarring of liver tissue).
- An increased incidence of heart disease.
- Neuropathy (nerves stop working, causing distortion of sensation in the legs, impotence, or imbalance).
- Inflammation of the intestines with vomiting, diarrhea, and internal hemorrhage; also acute pancreatitis, acute hepatitis, and peptic ulcers.
- Trauma from accidents.

Fifty percent of fatal car accidents and more than 50 percent of fatal pedestrian accidents are associated with alcohol. Likewise, 70 percent of fatal drownings, 83 percent of fatal fires (usually from cigarettes), and 44 percent of fatal industrial accidents are associated with alcohol. And fatal accidents are only the tip of the iceberg. Rib fractures are common enough in alcoholics that patients in whom alcoholism is suspected are routinely checked for rib injury in a hospital setting.

Fetal alcohol syndrome occurs in babies of mothers who drink excessively during pregnancy. The syndrome occurs in up to 30 percent of the babies of alcoholic mothers. The effects of the syndrome include mental retardation and congenital abnormalities.

Suicide and homicide are also common among alcoholics.

Alcoholics also suffer from Wernicke-Korsakoff's syndrome, which can cause irreversible brain damage. This syndrome is a toxic psychosis caused by thiamine deficiency, which is caused by alcohol abuse. Memory loss and double vision are prominent. Patients who have Wernicke-Korsakoff's syndrome often confabulate, as do the victims of senile dementia.

Withdrawal from alcohol produces another set of physical effects. The best known is **delirium tremens**, or D.T.'s, which only occurs in about one percent of alcoholics, making it quite uncommon. The mortality rate of D.T.'s is 15 percent.

The usual withdrawal syndrome consists of signs of autonomic hyperactivity (fast pulse, high blood pressure, sweating, fever), anxiety, insomnia, tremor (the shakes), incoordination, and muscle jerking (myoclonus). Some alcoholics develop epileptic seizures (rum fits), hallucinations, delusions, confusion, or delirium upon withdrawal.

The Treatment of Alcoholism

There are many schools of thought on how to treat alcoholics. Some health professionals tell patients to stop drinking because of the threat to physical health and prescribe drugs to help their patients stop. Some encourage alcoholics to talk about their problems. Others work chiefly to try to motivate the patient to enter a treatment program. Professionals in inpatient treatment centers think alcoholics need to be coerced (that is, forced) into treatment and that they will become motivated during but not before treatment. Often the spouse and family will precipitate a crisis, forcing the patient to enter the program. These varying approaches hold one goal in common: to get the alcoholic off alcohol.

Identifying the Patient. It is because physicians are left to identify alcoholics, that so many go untreated. The identification of alcoholism should also be the concern of psychologists, mental health workers, counselors, social workers, physician's assistants, and nurses. Most spouses know if their partners have drinking problems. Some deny it because they also have a drinking problem. Some health workers may deny it because the patient is middle class, is likable, or is an upstanding member of the community. Or the health worker may have a drinking problem, too.

You must accept the fact that it can feel intrusive or embarrassing to ask a patient about drinking. Sometimes a patient will react negatively or say something like, "Are you accusing me of being an alcoholic?" A good response would be, "No, I was just wondering whether alcohol had ever been a problem for you." It is all too easy to fall into the trap of glossing over the subject.

Forcing Treatment. If a patient openly admits the problem and agrees to stop drinking, he must be persuaded to obtain help, usually through an inpatient treatment program or through Alcoholics Anonymous (AA). If a patient refuses help ("I can do it by myself!") or denies that she drinks ("I drink but I'm not an alcoholic."), her spouse, friends, or family must be persuaded to force treatment.

A common scenario in a hospital might involve a middle-aged businessman admitted because he is vomiting blood. His wife mentions something about alcohol, but no one picks up on it. When a nurse reviews the patient's history, she notes that the patient's father was an alcoholic and that the patient has been admitted to the emergency room three times in the past four years, once with a large burn and twice with fractures. Despite his denials, the chances that this patient is alcoholic are probably 98 percent. The nurse asks the patient's wife whether he drinks. She replies that they are nearly bankrupt, their business is going downhill, and she has threatened to leave him because of his drinking, but he will not stop. The nurse has made a major breakthrough simply by asking one question. The nurse here has been instrumental in identifying the alcoholic. This information should then be relayed to the physician. If the physician appears reluctant to do anything, a consultation with the hospital's alcohol counselor might be suggested.

Some alcoholics stop drinking on their own, but many need coercion. The coercion itself is usually left to those health workers skilled at it, often alcohol counselors, psychologists, physicians, or mental health workers. The way in which this might be accomplished is as follows.

The patient's wife might be willing to tell her husband (and mean it sincerely) that she will leave him if he does not agree to enter a treatment program. If the nurse or another health care worker can sympathize with and support the patient's wife, it may facilitate getting help for the alcoholic patient.

It is difficult to leave someone you love, and it is difficult to throw a teenager out of the house because he is abusing drugs. But such actions may be the only thing that works.

When a patient will not agree to enter a treatment program, a physician must be asked to confront the patient with medical evidence of how alcohol is damaging his body. Most physicians are willing to do this. Alternatively, a work associate or maybe everyone involved with the patient may succeed in changing the patient's mind. Other possibilities are using the skillful presentation of a questionnaire such as the Michigan Alcoholism Screening Test (MAST), or getting volunteers from AA to talk to the patient.

Coercion is useless, of course, if the patient is intoxicated. Often alcoholics first seek treatment because of a court order following an automobile accident or a driving while intoxicated (DWI) citation. In this situation, alcoholics frequently do not follow through with treatment. Rather than actually participating in the program, the patient may only seek proof of attendance to satisfy various authorities.

The most appropriate referral for an alcoholic is usually to an alcohol counselor in a hospital or to an AA group out of a hospital. If the patient refuses an alcohol counselor, mental health worker, or physician, one usually leaves the door open for the patient and spouse to return or call any time, because a crisis may be just what is needed to force treatment.

What we have described is a direct approach to managing alcoholism. Psychology is hardly delved into; the patient is addicted, it is ruining his or her life, the patient simply has to stop drinking. Other possible approaches to treating alcoholism include psychotherapy, social psychology, drug treatment, rehabilitation, and spiritual help.

Psychotherapy. As previously discussed, psychotherapy initially must be directed at overcoming denial by calling on the alcoholic's spouse, physician, and perhaps co-workers or through special tests. Denial, however, often recurs during treatment and has to be dealt with on an ongoing basis.

Intensive psychotherapy frequently brings too many anxieties to the surface too rapidly, which can cause the alcoholic to start drinking again. Instead, what is often used is supportive psychotherapy that involves here and now approaches such as Gestalt therapy, psychodrama, or transactional analysis. These approaches explore why the patient drinks, the consequences of past drinking, and the consequences of continued drinking. They focus on denial.

An alcoholic patient often is already receiving psychotherapy for an underlying personality disorder, but the therapist may not be aware of the extent of the patient's drinking.

As a health care provider, you must accept that an alcoholic patient can be both angry and dependent at the same time. If you feel angry with a patient, you may give him or her an excuse to drink again. The alcoholic uses anger as an excuse. Psychoanalytic thinking has likened the alcoholic to an infant. Alcoholics are still seeking the security of the bottle and may have immature or arrested personalities. A surprising number of alcoholics remain psychologically dependent on their mothers.

Social Psychology. Group therapy creates a group or social network that is anti-alcohol rather than pro-alcohol. AA is a special example of group therapy. AA was started in 1935 by an alcoholic stockbroker and an alcoholic physician. The only requirement for membership is a desire to stay sober and help other alcoholics achieve sobriety. AA also insists that the alcoholic accept the fact that she/he is an alcoholic. Other aspects of AA include:

- The motto, One Day at a Time, encourages the alcoholic to think of staying sober only for today. The motto discourages the alcoholic from starting to drink again because the thought of staying sober forever is too hard to accept; but for today, it is possible.
- Invoking the help of God, not for the sake of a religious conversion, but as a way of appealing to a higher, spiritual force.
- Discouraging what the group calls "stinking thinking," or the tendency of alcoholics to use denial or rationalization to explain things.

Alanon is a sister organization for partners of alcoholics to help them handle their alcoholic. Alateen is a similar organization for the children of alcoholics. Adult Children of Alcoholics (ACOA) is a recently created group that supports the grown children of alcoholics, who generally continue to feel the pain of their upbringing.

Family therapy is another type of group psychology. Unlike AA and its sister organizations, family therapy treats the family unit together as a whole rather than separately. Often all members of the family of an alcoholic suffer from the disintegration of their relationships. In fact, the threat that the spouse will leave is often what finally motivates the alcoholic to stop drinking.

The therapeutic community is another kind of social psychology. The community offers a group in which the alcoholic lives, replacing his or her own family or other social network. The Salvation Army is one example of a therapeutic community.

Drug Treatment. Using sedatives during acute withdrawal is common in hospitals. Sedatives diminish withdrawal symptoms like agitation, insomnia, hallucinations, and tremor. Giving sedatives to an outpatient is a two-edged sword, however. On the one hand, sedatives may reduce withdrawal symptoms, make life more comfortable, and help the alcoholic sleep. On the other hand, the alcoholic may become addicted to sedatives. Further, taking sedatives clouds thinking and can interfere with vigilance in staying sober. Sedatives also can mask the issues that the alcoholic must deal with in order to stay sober.

Vitamins are commonly used with alcoholics. Wernicke-Korsakoff's syndrome, one of the dreaded complications of alcoholism, can be prevented by administering thiamine. Alcoholics frequently obtain most of their calories from alcohol. A diet that is deficient in certain vitamins accounts for some of the physical effects of alcohol.

Disulfiram—trade name *Antabuse*—is a medication that causes no symptoms when taken alone, but causes severe side effects when taken with alcohol. A patient who drinks while taking *Antabuse* feels flushed, turns red, feels as though she/he will explode, and feels very nauseated. Although *Antabuse* therapy is appropriate for some patients, it does not cure alcoholism. It simply makes the patient feel terrible if he/she drinks (a form of behavior modification that focuses on punishment). If a patient is feeling desperate enough for a drink, she or he may simply wait for the last *Antabuse* to wear off before drinking. Not uncommonly, a patient will drink despite the medication, sometimes with severe consequences.

Some psychiatrists prescribe antidepressants if they think a patient is suffering from both alcoholism and endogenous depression.

The problem with drug therapies (except for vitamins) is that they give the patient a crutch outside his/her own inner determination to stop drinking. This crutch may displace the alcoholic's determination to stop drinking.

Rehabilitation. If an alcoholic's social network consists mainly of other alcoholics or addicts, the therapies we have discussed so far will be of little help. An alcoholic in this situation needs motivation not only to stop drinking but also to change his social network. He needs a place to live and money to live on. Initially, he may be on welfare, but eventually he will need a job and perhaps some education to perform that job. A halfway house, for example, may provide the new community that such a patient needs.

Spiritual Help. AA itself has a spiritual side to it. For patients with strong religious beliefs, spiritual help may be instrumental in motivating them to stop drinking. They trust their lives to a higher power.

Once an alcholic has stopped drinking, it may take six months to two years for her personality and anxiety level to return to normal. She may then have to deal with the damage that her alcoholism caused her business or professional life, her family, her friends, and her health. Furthermore, she must accept that she can never drink socially again. A social drinker can use alcohol; an alcoholic cannot.

Other Recreational Drugs

The general principles of addiction are similar whether we are talking about alcohol or other addictive drugs. Differing degrees of social disgrace or social approval are associated with different drugs. Also, there is no simple addiction gene that you either have or do not have. Addiction depends on many factors, and addictiveness varies from drug to drug.

Alcohol and heroin are two different extremes of recreational drugs. Heroin kills a large number of addicts early on. In contrast, alcohol claims a far smaller proportion of addicts and claims them much later on in their drug-taking careers.

Low doses of sedative/hypnotics promote relaxation; high doses induce confusion or sleep; even higher doses may produce coma, and, if enough is consumed, death may result from paralysis of the lower brainstem, which controls the respiratory system. Sedative/hypnotics include alcohol, the antianxiety agents, and a wide variety of other drugs.

Any combination of the sedative/hypnotics has the potential to be lethal. This is called the **additive effect**. Drinking combined with taking diazepam (*Valium*) or a barbiturate puts the user at a high level dose because of the combined effect of these drugs. The additive effect accounts for many accidental deaths each year.

There are a large number of recreational drugs available. A brief list of the substances commonly abused follows:

Narcotic Analgesics

Narcotic analgesics are powerful pain relieving agents. Users describe a warm, euphoric rush. (The body also produces its own morphine-like substances, which are called endorphins.) Examples of narcotics are morphine, opium, heroin and the opioids, meperidine (*Demerol*), propoxyphene (*Darvon*), oxycodone (*Percodan*), and methadone.

Sedative/Hypnotics

Sedative/hypnotics produce a calming effect without pain relief. Examples include benzodiazepines (*Valium, Librium*), barbiturates (phenobarbital, *Amytal*), methaqualone (*Quaalude*), bromides, meprobamate, chloral hydrate, alcohol, and general anesthetic agents. Toluene, the agent glue sniffers look for, is also related to general anesthetics. Withdrawal from sedative/hypnotics is **more severe** than withdrawal from narcotic analgesics. This means that convulsing to death is more likely during withdrawal from alcohol or barbiturates than during withdrawal from heroin.

Addictions

Alcohol
Narcotic analgesics
  morphine
  opium
  heroin
  meperidine
  propoxyphene
  oxycodone
  methadone
Sedatives/Hypnotics
  benzodiazepines
    (Librium, Valium)
  barbiturates
    (phenobarbital, *Amytal*)
  methaqualone
    (Quaalude)
  bromides
  meprobamate
Stimulants
  cocaine/crack
  amphetamines
  Ritalin
  caffeine
Hallucinogens
  LSD
  mescaline
  marijuana
  PCP
Smoking

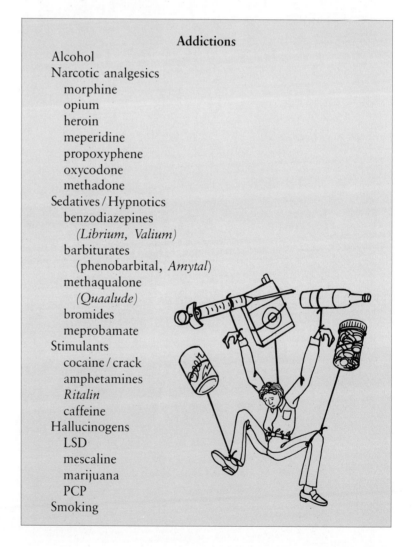

Stimulants

Stimulants produce mood elevation and increased psychomotor activity. Examples are cocaine, "crack," amphetamines, *Ritalin* (methylphenidate), and caffeine. Stimulants tend to be habituating rather than addicting. Cocaine, however, seems to have some addictive tendency.

Hallucinogens

Examples of **major hallucinogens** are LSD and mescaline. These drugs cause hallucinations and delusions. The psychological effects are perceptual, with motor impairment and strong changes in emotions. During a "trip," a user may think that he can fly and jump out of a window. Sometimes major hallucinogens can induce a permanent psychosis.

Examples of **minor hallucinogens** are THC and cannabis (or marijuana). These drugs have a sedative/hypnotic effect with a **reverse tolerance** phenomenon. Long-term users need less and less to feel higher and higher. Even heavy users may withdraw from marijuana without suffering a withdrawal syndrome.

Phencyclidine (PCP) or angel dust is a dangerous anesthetic that elicits psychotic behavior and fatal paralysis. PCP is actually a cross between a sedative and a hallucinogen.

Sedativism

Sedativism means addiction to sedatives. The significance of addiction to sedative drugs is that cross tolerance often comes into play. Cross tolerance means that with continued use of a drug, more has to be used to obtain the same effect. The more you take, the more you need. This is a biological, not a psychological, phenomenon. It is caused by both induction of enzymes in the liver, which metabolize the drug faster, and by tissue resistance to the effects of the drug. Alcohol, for instance, can be metabolized up to four times faster depending on the degree of induction of liver enzymes. Alcoholics can walk around with a blood alcohol level that might be fatal for a nonalcoholic, although an alcoholic can go rapidly from the walking state to coma and death if abuse is continuous.

An alcoholic who receives a general anesthetic may need much higher doses than a nonalcoholic. An alcoholic may be unaffected by a dose of 100 mg of *Librium*, whereas a nonalcoholic might be drowsy after 10 mg. This is cross tolerance.

A patient who is addicted to one sedative must be treated differently from a nonaddicted person when it comes to taking another sedative in the group. This is another reason why tranquilizers should not be freely prescribed for alcoholics. Some people assume that addiction to one drug in a group means that a person will become addicted to another way in the same group. This is probably not true in all cases, but it is not a good idea to take the chance. One exception to this rule is that alcoholics should not be asked to stop smoking within two years of stopping alcohol—it just seems to be too much. It may take up to two years before withdrawal anxiety from alcohol finally subsides. The crutch of smoking is so common in alcoholism that asking a patient to stop smoking may be the last straw that starts the patient drinking again.

People who have addictive personalities often use multiple drugs, not only sedatives but also drugs within other groups (for example, psychedelics, stimulants, and narcotics).

The dry drunk is a phenomenon in which the individual behaves as though drunk, although no alcohol has been consumed. Behavior may be irrational, angry, erratic, or moody. Dry drunks are an effect of alcoholism and often such episodes occur especially in the first few months after withdrawal from alcohol.

The cause of dry drunks is a matter of conjecture. These may be a "flashback" phenomenon. There may be emotional withdrawal from alcohol or a chemical change in the brain. Dry drunk behavior needs treatment. AA and psychotherapy confront this behavior and helps to make the withdrawing alcoholic more positive and less negative. Alcoholics may not know how to behave sober, and dry drunk behavior may be the only way they know to interact with sober people.

The three most common addictive substances in our culture are alcohol, sedatives, and tobacco. Caffeine is a commonly used psychoactive drug, but it seldom causes a major health problem.

There are three important concepts associated with sedativism:

- A person who has an addictive personality frequently uses more than one drug, including nonsedatives. There is a significant association between sedativism and eating disorders.
- Cross tolerance exists between the various drugs within the sedative group.
- A patient who is addicted to one member of the sedative group of drugs must be watched carefully when exposed to another drug in that group.

Smoking is the single largest cause of preventable death and ill health in the United States today. It is the most common addiction, and it is an enormous problem.

Tobacco dependence is a continued consumption of tobacco which the patient cannot control, despite significant physical, economic, or social side effects. One difference between tobacco dependence and alcoholism is that the economic side effects of smoking are not immediately apparent (except for spending a dollar or more for every pack of cigarettes). Also, the physical side effects of smoking are usually late serious health problems like cancer, heart attacks, and emphysema. Often at this late stage the patient's perception is "If I'm going to die from cancer, at least don't take my cigarettes away." Smokers do not perceive anticipated physical problems as a reason not to smoke.

The social consequences of smoking (for example, pressure from loved ones, having to go to smoking areas, higher insurance rates) remain the largest reason why people do or do not smoke. In a society where about one-third of the citizens smoke, it is difficult to say it is unacceptable behavior. We believe that this attitude—that smoking is acceptable behavior—is the reason that smoking is not perceived as a significant addiction like heroin. In the following pages, we offer support for changing this perception.

The Physical Effects of Smoking

Withdrawal from smoking causes craving, anxiety, insomnia, impaired attention, a preoccupation with the actions associated with smoking, headaches, and gastrointestinal disturbances. Research shows that even when people smoke low nicotine cigarettes, they smoke to maintain their serum nicotine levels. They do this, for instance, by increasing the number of cigarettes they smoke or by stopping up the filter holes to raise the nicotine concentrations of the smoke they inhale. There can be no doubt that nicotine is a psychoactive substance.

Cigarettes exert their adverse effects in four main ways:

- Through carbon monoxide levels, which accelerate arteriosclerosis (hardening of the arteries), which can cause heart attacks, strokes, and gangrene.
- Through nicotine, which, via its psychoactive effects, reinforces and habituates the user to smoking.

- Through irritants in tar that may cause chronic lung disease (emphysema and bronchitis or cancer).
- Through passive smoking: for example, standing in the same room with someone who is smoking. The health of the babies of pregnant smokers also is jeopardized through passive smoking.

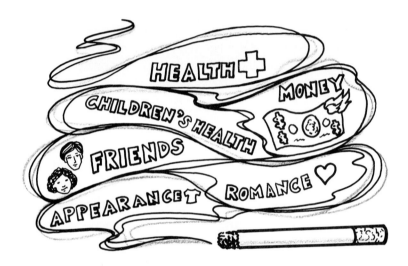

There are some two million deaths in the United States each year. Of these deaths, approximately 400,000 are caused directly by smoking (see Figure 6.1). Thirty percent of deaths from cancer and 90 percent of deaths from chronic lung disease are caused directly by smoking. On top of this are the smoking-related deaths from strokes (smokers have a 20–50 percent greater incidence of stroke than nonsmokers), gangrene (over 90 percent of gangrene victims smoke), aortic aneurysm, and peptic ulcers.

Cancers with a proven higher incidence in smokers include cancer of the lip, tongue, tonsil, mouth, head, neck, larynx, lung, esophagus, bladder, kidney, pancreas, stomach, and cervix. In addition, smoking accelerates facial wrinkling, periodontal (gum) disease, risk of death from being on the contraceptive pill, stillbirth, and neonatal (newborn) death.

For every one of those 400,000 people who die every year from smoking, there are many more who suffer (patients on respirators, persons repeatedly admitted with pneumonia, and those who are chronically short of breath). Statistically, each cigarette a person smokes shortens the smoker's life by five minutes. A woman who lives an average length life and who starts smoking when she is 20 and smokes one pack a day shortens her life by five years.

Passive smoking involves sidestream smoke and mainstream smoke. **Sidestream smoke** comes from the end of the cigarette and constitutes 85 percent of a room's pollution. Sidestream smoke contains 10–15 percent carbon monoxide. (This percentage is the amount present in the smoke itself, not in the room.) **Mainstream smoke** is smoke that has been exhaled by the smoker; it accounts for the other 15 percent of a room's pollution. Such smoke contains only 5 percent carbon monoxide.

The passive smoking may affect the fetus by causing low birth weight (200 grams less on the average). Some of the many consequences of low birth weight include neonatal death, stillbirth, and intellectual handicap (math performance has been proven to be lower in primary school children whose mothers smoked during pregnancy).

The children of smokers have more bronchitis, pneumonia, asthma (70 percent more hospitalizations for asthma), and middle ear problems, are shorter in stature, and have a higher incidence of sudden infant death syndrome. Women whose husbands smoke get 10–20 percent more cancer of the lung. In terms of health risk, spending eight hours at work with people who smoke is probably equivalent to smoking several cigarettes a day.

A quarter of all fires in which people die are caused by smoking. A question that needs to be asked in such cases is who smoked and who died in those fires.

Figure 6.1 Smoking related deaths in U.S. (1983 U.S. Census figures).

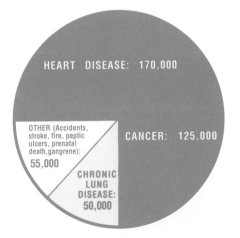

HEART DISEASE: 170,000

OTHER (Accidents, stroke, fire, peptic ulcers, prenatal death, gangrene): 55,000

CANCER: 125,000

CHRONIC LUNG DISEASE: 50,000

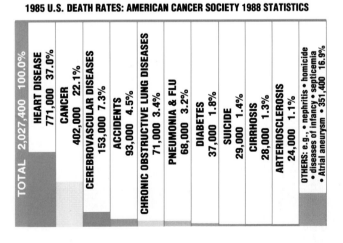

1985 U.S. DEATH RATES: AMERICAN CANCER SOCIETY 1988 STATISTICS

TOTAL 2,027,400 100.0%
HEART DISEASE 771,000 37.0%
CANCER 402,000 22.1%
CEREBROVASCULAR DISEASES 153,000 7.3%
ACCIDENTS 93,000 4.5%
CHRONIC OBSTRUCTIVE LUNG DISEASES 71,000 3.4%
PNEUMONIA & FLU 68,000 3.2%
DIABETES 37,000 1.8%
SUICIDE 29,000 1.4%
CIRRHOSIS 28,000 1.3%
ARTERIOSCLEROSIS 24,000 1.1%
OTHERS: e.g., • nephritis • homicide • diseases of infancy • septicemia • Atrial aneurysm • 351,400 16.9%

The Economic Effects of Smoking

Smoking costs the consumer $16 billion a year in health costs and $37 billion a year in lost productivity and earnings. Those who smoke spend $25 billion a year on tobacco products. Added together, smoking costs America approximately $78 billion a year. This amounts to $340 per capita or, for an average family with two or three children, this costs $1,360 to $1,700 per year. Who pays this money? We all pay through a lower standard of living because of increased health costs and decreased productivity. We also pay through employee health premiums. Everyone pays $100 per person more in insurance to cover those who smoke. Industry pays $300 to $800 per employee in lost productivity, sickness, disability, and accidents for those who smoke. We all pay more taxes to cover health and disability costs for those who smoke.

The Social Effects of Smoking

One study showed that smoking is the number one turnoff in blind dates, coming in ahead of obesity. According to 1983 census figures (the latest available), 35 percent of men and 29 percent of women smoke in the United States. Ninety percent of those who smoke would like not to smoke. Perhaps part of the reason is that the social effects of smoking are unpleasant. Friends may not invite you to their house, they may say embarrassing things about smoking, using words like *smelly*, *disgusting*, *dirty*, or *filthy*. Smoking is prohibited in many public places. In restaurants, nearby diners may ask you to put out your cigarette. Your spouse may apply similar pressure, and so may your children. Insurance sellers tell you that your premiums will be less if you don't smoke. And this goes for life insurance, fire, health, auto, homeowner, and disability policies.

Why Do People Smoke?

Despite all these reasons, people continue to smoke. It should be obvious that people in this circumstance are not just "being sociable" or exhibiting normal behavior. No, they are addicted to smoking.

Social pressure, particularly from teenage or young adult peers, is a common reason to start smoking. Teenagers are told by their peers and by cigarette advertisements that smoking is adult and sexy, normal and fun. With a teenager's intense desire for peer approval and conformity, it is not difficult to see how it starts.

Gradually, secondary psychological factors become important. The patient becomes conditioned by the smell and taste of cigarettes and by the stimulation of smoke at the back of the throat (called bronchial eroticism). Keeping their weight down is another reason some cite for smoking. In fact, the vast majority who cite this reason are smokers who quit smoking for a time but started again because they gained so much weight. The physical activity of smoking offers a ritual that carries with it a sense of security. Some smokers even describe smoking as "like a friend." The inhaling and exhaling may be relaxing.

Finally, when the pharmacologic effects begin, what started as a social act becomes an addiction. Continuing to smoke reinforces the habit, and the smoker avoids withdrawal symptoms by taking more nicotine.

How Can We Help Patients to Stop Smoking?

Identifying the smoker, of course, is easy. Because there is less shame associated with smoking, there is less denial. But there is no use telling a smoker that her habit is dirty and causes lung cancer. Her response is sure to be something like, "Maybe it's not clean, but it's not bad and I enjoy it" or "I won't get lung cancer, only one in eight gets lung cancer" (which amounts to playing Russian roulette).

As with the alcoholic, you, as a health practitioner, need to confront smokers with the most pertinent reasons why they are suffering physically, economically, or socially. You are in an ideal position to identify health areas that should be of concern to a patient. You should explore anything remotely connected with smoking that you think your patient may be sensitive to. A common way to present health problems is to go over with the smoker:

- Lung function tests or chest X-rays that show evidence of emphysema.
- Histories in the patient's own family of any disease connected with smoking (for example, cancer of the lung).
- Risk factors for heart disease; for example, a borderline blood pressure, a borderline cholesterol level, or a history of heart disease in the patient's family.
- Morbidity associated with chronic lung disease

As a hospital nurse, exercise physiologist, nurse practitioner, physical therapist, respiratory technician or dietitian, you would be the ideal person to demonstrate the presence of a real physical problem or concern. Say, for example, that during your contact with a patient the topic of smoking has not come up but you can tell by his breath that he smokes. At this point, you should ask if he has ever thought he would like to be able to give up smoking. If you sense even a glimmer of interest, you could ask whether he would like to stop smoking now. If you cannot find a physical problem or cannot think of even a remote risk factor, you should still ask the patient if he wants to stop smoking. You can answer his response with your own authority: "I think you should stop smoking." If the patient agrees, you can begin to discuss the details.

Like the alcoholic, the smoker finds it difficult to quit. Few will quit because of the advice of a health professional, but you still have an obligation to offer help. Your offer may come at a time when outside factors are encouraging the smoker to quit. Your suggestion may be that last little push the smoker needs. Remember that the patient needs to be sold on the idea. Less than 5 percent of patients approach a health professional asking for help to stop smoking; 95 percent need persuasion. Remember, too, that most patients have been pressured already by their spouses, children, friends, or workmates. They already are at least a little afraid of the consequences, and they have been exposed to at least a little of the social antagonism toward smoking.

Specific techniques for stopping smoking include the following:

- **Smoking cessation clinics.** Patients who find it extremely difficult to quit are good candidates for this approach. Clinics involve combinations of lectures, money deposits refundable only after a period of abstinence, aversion therapy designed to make smoking seem less appealing (for example, having to smoke five cigarettes an hour for two hours or having to smoke while holding a cigarette between the little and ring fingers), and desensitization (for example, timed regular cigarettes regardless of urge to smoke). Initial success rates are around 23–90 percent, but fall to 20–40 percent after one year. Most smokers need more than one try before they succeed.
- **Hypnotherapy, acupuncture, progressive filters.**
- **Literature.** Literature offers the self-motivated patient various techniques to try alone (for example, cold turkey, progressive reduction).
- **Nicotine gum.** This technique can be quite successful, but patients need a lot of instruction on how to use it. The nicotine in the gum eases physical withdrawal. Success rates are similar to those of smoking cessation clinics.

Some enlightened companies offer financial incentives to employees who quit smoking. Aware of the $300–$800 per employee cost of smoking, such a company may offer smokers something like

$1,000 to stop smoking for, say, a year. In the long run and for long-term employees, such companies save money.

Smoking prevention is equally important. Among students who are exposed to smoking prevention teaching, the smoking rate is 15–50 percent less than among those who are not exposed. An important reason to present to young people as incentive for never smoking is that the children of parents who smoke are very likely to copy their parents. A person who smokes jeopardizes not only his own future but also the futures of his children.

As health care providers, we must think constructively about our approach to this subject. If smoking is the number one preventable cause of ill health and death in the United States, we must, in our professional settings, be vigorously anti-smoking. If, as an individual however, your attitude becomes discriminatory and prejudiced rather than sympathetic, your efforts will be counterproductive. The patient will sense your antagonism and deny, rationalize, and avoid the situation rather than work with you.

In the same vein, you should think about your attitudes toward smoking in social settings. Ridiculing smokers in public or private, or implying that they are not welcome if they smoke, seldom helps anyone. Your smoking friends will deny, rationalize, or avoid you. Ideally, you should use your friendships to motivate people to stop smoking. And, if you value human life, you should certainly try to set an example yourself by not smoking. If you still smoke, contact one of the following resources for information on how to quit:

National Interagency Council on Smoking and Health
419 Park Avenue South, Suite 1301
New York, New York 10016

Schick Laboratories
1901 Avenue of the Stars, Suite 1530
Los Angeles, California 90067

SmokeEnders
Memorial Parkway
Phillipsburg, New Jersey 08864

Office of Cancer Communications
National Cancer Institute
National Institutes of Health
Bethesda, Maryland 20205
(800) 638-6694
(800) 492-6600 in Maryland

A Few More Compulsions!

Just as a matter of interest, here is a list of some other compulsions:

- Compulsion to work: workaholic.
- Compulsion to eat: bulimic.
- Compulsion to starve: anorexic.
- Compulsion to purge, or vomit, to lose weight: bulimarexic.
- Compulsion to exercise: kinetaholic (also known as Jones' syndrome).
- Compulsion to gamble: compulsive gambler.
- Compulsion to steal: kleptomaniac.

Chapter Summary

This chapter discusses the concept of addiction. Smoking is the commonest preventable cause of death in the U.S. today. Alcoholism affects up to 10% of all men and 3% of all women. The drug culture is yet another area of major concern. Clearly, addiction is an important issue. By addressing the core problems—the effects of addiction and the common defense mechanisms (notably denial)—we can help guide addicts to abstinence. But more importantly we can help those around us never start.

We discuss the causes of addiction—genetic, psychological, and cultural factors. The diagnosis of alcoholism is not always easy to make, and it is commonly missed. The effects of alcoholism, both psychological and physical, are listed as well as first-, second-, and third-order symptoms. It is often necessary to force treatment for alcoholism.

Again the physical, economic, and social effects of smoking are discussed, and the questions of why we smoke and how to stop smoking are addressed.

Review

ACOA: Adult Child Of an Alcoholic

Addiction: physical dependence on a substance

Alcoholism: chronic consumption of alcohol, that continues despite significant interference with a person's physical, economic, or social health

Habituation: psychological dependence on a substance

Physical dependence: addiction to substance leading to a physical withdrawal syndrome

Psychological dependence: addiction to a substance leading to a psychological withdrawal syndrome

Sedativism: addiction to sedatives, the significance being that cross-tolerance often comes into play

Tobacco dependence: continued consumption of tobacco which the patient cannot control, despite significant physical, economic, or social side effects

Tolerance: phenomenon in which patients require higher doses of a drug to have the same physical effect

1. Why is it difficult to define alcoholism, what are the important ingredients in its definition?
2. List cultural and occupational associations with alcoholism.
3. List first-, second-, and third-order symptoms of alcoholism.
4. List the physical consequences of alcoholism.
5. List the diseases associated with smoking.
6. How much does smoking cost society and what percentage of men and women still smoke?
7. How should we react in our personal lives to smokers around us?

Additional Reading

Fielding, J.E. *Smoking, Health Effects and Control.* American Cancer Society. 1986.

Mendelson, J.H. and Mello, N.K. *The Diagnosis and Treatment of Alcoholism.* McGraw Hill, NY. 1985.

Milan, J.R. and Ketcham, K. *Under the Influence. A Guide to the Myths and Realities of Alcoholism.* Madrona Publishers Inc., Seattle, WA. 1981.

U.S. Department of Health and Human Services. *The Smoking Digest.* National Cancer Institute and National Institutes of Health, Bethesda, MD. Published yearly.

Chapter

7

After reading this chapter, you should be able:
- To describe the use of the term client versus patient.
- To examine the role of counseling as essential to wellness.
- To describe the relationship of genetic programming, environmental conditions, and lifestyle factors to physical and mental health.
- To demonstrate skill at developing strategies which will maintain wellness.
- To understand the uniqueness of individual client's personal reward/ punishment systems.
- To better motivate clients toward compliance.

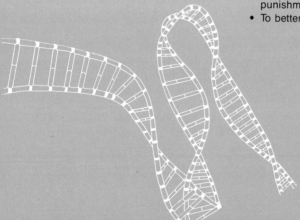

Counseling in Prevention

The Role of Counseling
in Prevention

How can counseling skills be used to maintain wellness or prevent human suffering and disease? To answer this complex question, we need to look at the causes of loss of wellness. When we become unwell the source of our problem can be traced to one or more of the following considerations: genetic programming, environmental conditions, or lifestyle factors.

Counseling and Physical Health

In this chapter, we frequently switch from using the word patient to using the word client. Although most health professionals think in terms of a patient / professional relationship, the context of *preventive* thinking somewhat alters this relationship because the customer of preventive health care is well. Patient, which denotes a loss of wellness, is no longer appropriate.

Many diseases, or weaknesses that predispose us to disease, are inherited, i.e., **genetic programming**. Heart disease, high blood pressure, diabetes, and many lesser known conditions are at least in part inherited. One recent study determined that if your parent dies of a specific form of colon cancer, you have a 50 / 50 chance of developing that cancer. This finding makes a fairly convincing argument that cancer also can be genetically determined.

Many diseases can be caused by factors, **environmental conditions**, in the world around us. The quality of our air and water are among the most obvious concerns. Noise pollution, and overcrowding also influence the potential for adding disease to our lives. As concerned citizens of this planet, we all are alert for causes of permanent damage to our environment. The strong protests against nuclear power plants and the concern over the disposal of hazardous wastes are further evidence of the way we are beginning to value our environment. Some scientists believe it is already too late to prevent damage from the thinning of the ozone layer. Without sufficient ozone protecting us from the sun's ultraviolet rays, there will be many more victims of skin cancer.

Other major environmental concerns are voiced about the tragedies at Love Canal and at Woburn, Massachusetts, where children playing on a former hazardous dump site have been the victims of a high number of leukemias. In 1986, Chernobel, U.S.S.R., was the site of the world's largest nuclear power accident. Thousands of Russians were affected, and vegetation and animal life throughout Europe were contaminated. The world may not yet know all of the consequences of this catastrophe. The varied uses of asbestos have resulted in health problems for many persons. Certainly there is convincing evidence that the environment brings about a significant proportion of the disease we know today.

Most of the diseases people have can be at least partially traced to their **lifestyle factors**. As discussed in Chapter 6, cigarette smoking is the largest preventable cause of death in the United States today. Drinking alcohol; abusing other drugs; having high fat, high salt, and high sugar diets; and leading sedentary (inactive) lives are all detrimental to health. Lifestyle issues also include how much sleep we get, how much television we watch, and how well we deal with stress. Some lifestyles even involve direct and overt assaults on health. Two examples would be race car drivers and teenagers who frequently get involved in street fights.

In the last few years the public has become increasingly convinced of the importance of healthy lifestyles. Jogging, walking, cycling, and other forms of aerobic exercise have increased. At the same time, sales of red meat have decreased, indicating another change in lifestyle among Americans. The incidence of heart disease has also been declining in recent years. This decline probably is due to the combined effect of less smoking, better eating, more exercise, and more aggressive treatment of blood pressure and serum cholesterol.

The Role of Counseling for Prevention with Genetic Programming

Counseling can have a direct impact on disease prevention through genetic counseling. In its earliest days, genetic counseling was primarily limited to working with couples who had already produced a child with a genetically linked birth defect. Such counseling provided information to the couples about their chances of having a healthy offspring. Couples then weighed this information against their desire to have more children or their ability to cope with another child with a disability and made an informed decision. These decisions generally were made prior to conceiving another child.

Amniocentesis became available to the general public about 10 years ago. This test is an invasive procedure that involves removing amniotic fluid from the pregnant woman. The needle of a syringe is directed through the abdominal wall into the fluid that surrounds the growing baby. This fluid contains both maternal and fetal cells. When these cells are cultured, the existence of certain genetic diseases can be determined. Most prominent among these diseases are Down's syndrome (mongolism) and spina bifida. Amniocentesis is now recommended for women who are expecting to deliver after the age of 37 or who have a family history of these abnormalities. It can also be used to detect a number of other diseases.

Counseling initially plays a role in informing a couple about amniocentesis. The risks and benefits must be carefully explained to prospective users. Encouraging a couple to have this test may prevent the birth of a child who could not be accepted by the couple and whose quality of life would be severely limited. If a fetus should test positive for one of these problems, counseling would then play a key role in determining the final outcome of the pregnancy.

Neither Down's syndrome nor spina bifida affects each unborn child the same way. That is, some Down's syndrome children are only mildly retarded and have the potential for nearly normal lives, whereas others suffer severe mental retardation, severely shortened lives, and a host of physiological limitations. Parents need to know what they are up against. In all likelihood, what would their baby be like? What, if any, chance does their baby have of being normal? What community and medical support would be available? What decisions do most people in their position make? What impact does a Down's syndrome baby have on the rest of the family? (The impact of a Down's syndrome baby on the family is usually enormous. Sometimes it is helpful for the couple to meet a parent with a Down's syndrome child.)

The health professional who counsels such a couple must help them to deal with the answers to these questions. Many of the answers are not easy to face. Most couples faced with a positive test for Down's syndrome choose to have an abortion. It is not necessarily true that couples who would not consider abortion would not have elected to have the test initially. Some couples may test in order to prepare themselves. Others test without allowing themselves to think about a negative outcome until it is reality. In any event, a health practitioner

Counseling in Prevention

with good counseling skills can play a valuable role in assisting the couple to make the decision that is best for their family.

Counseling with genetic diseases may best be used for preventive strategies. A large number of genetic diseases might be decreased or postponed through counseling that ties in lifestyle issues. For example, people with a strong family history of cancer or heart disease would be facing more risk than the average person if they choose to smoke. Those with diabetes in their families might postpone the onset of the disease by limiting weight gain. Many diseases have known risk factors that the health care provider will seek out and examine.

If a man comes from a family in which every male has died from a heart attack before age 60, he may seek counseling to avoid this fate. Such counseling would involve getting a whole perspective on the patient. The genetic problem might warrant further investigation to determine whether other genetic factors were contributing to the heart disease. Such risk factors could include hypertension, diabetes, or high cholesterol blood levels.

Once the genetic factors were clear, the health professional would look at environmental conditions. Is this man exposed to any substance that has the potential for causing heart disease? Since he comes from a family with such a high incidence of heart disease, this question would focus especially on any environmental conditions he might hold in common with his afflicted ancestors. For example, the health worker would take a close look at the work environment if the man, his great–grandfather, and all the deceased male members of his family had worked in the same place.

Lifestyle factors may offer the greatest potential for increased longevity. The man in our example, who is at high genetic risk for heart disease, can do much to control his risk if he avoids becoming overweight, avoids cigarettes, limits his use of alcohol, controls high blood pressure, gets 20–30 minutes of aerobic exercise four times a week, lowers his cholesterol and sodium intake through diet, and realistically controls the stress in his daily life. Aerobic exercise involves moving without great resistance while making the heart muscle work; walking, jogging, and swimming are examples. Anaerobic exercise involves significant resistance; weight lifting and rowing are examples. Controlling stress is discussed later in this chapter.

The above example illustrates that a person who is primarily at risk for a disease via one pathway can prevent or postpone that disease through attention to the other pathways (avoiding suspect chemicals in the work environment and adopting a lifestyle that includes diet, exercise, limiting abusive substances, and medical control of blood pressure when needed).

Genetic counseling can serve to prevent health problems in two additional ways. First, **genetic counseling can help people live with impending health problems** or determine their need for doing so. Some genetic diseases, for instance, strike a high percentage of offspring. An example is Huntington's disease which affects 50 percent of all children born to one affected parent (Figure 7.1). Because the disease does not become evident until the victim is already 30–50 years old, parents do not know for certain that they are carrying the disease until it strikes them. And usually it strikes **after** they have already had their own children, setting up a new generation of potential victims.

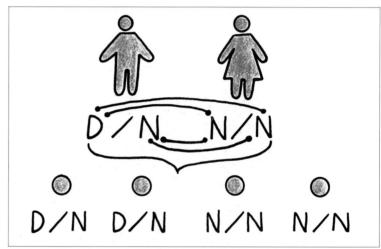

Figure 7.1 Dominant inheritance: With a faulty dominant gene such as Huntington's (D), each child's chance of receiving the faulty gene is 50%. Each child also has a 50% chance of receiving two normal (N) genes.

Huntington's disease affects the central nervous system progressively, eventually causing dementia, involuntary movements, and death. Currently there is no known treatment. Potential victims may first discover they are ill when they begin to fall or stumble for no reason.

There are now tests to determine whether a person will be a victim of Huntington's. A genetic counselor or counseling health professional can help the person who is living under this threat to know what the future will bring. Understanding what the future will be like can help Huntington's victims make decisions about parenting.

Living and waiting for the symptoms of such a disease to begin sounds like torture. Yet many of those who could now have the test and know their fate refuse to do so. They continue to wish to live in hope rather than face a possible horrible truth. They also continue to bear children believing it is their right and the real meaning of life. Although such responses are understandable, they place an obvious burden on the genetic counselor, who not only is unable to help the individual but also sees the problem extending into future generations.

Second, **genetic counseling can help individuals accept themselves.** Many people have been victims of social pressure to become perfect. Especially victimized are the overweight. People who are naturally overweight due to hereditary factors need to understand the reasons for their heaviness. Torturous diets and expensive fads will never offer good health to a person who is genetically programmed to be overweight. The only thing that weight reduction regimens do for such people is make them anxious and doubtful of their self-worth. Counseling must inform and support those who are fighting against heredity for, except in small modified instances, they can never win.

The Role of Counseling for Prevention with Environmental Conditions

Genetic programming has a well-developed role for a genetic counselor, but there is no environmental counselor per se. Health or sanitation officers, environmental engineers, occupational health clinic personnel, company nurses, solid and hazardous waste disposal experts, and employees of the Occupational Safety and Health Agency (OSHA) probably fill the most recognizable roles in this category. Certainly environmental protection agencies and groups rely on the expertise of these trained specialists. All too often, however, private citizens have been the ones who have smoked out major environmental hazards.

The chemicals that seeped into the ground at Love Canal, New York, until the mid-1970's, what agent orange did to the trees and environment of Vietnam and to the people who worked around it and what chemicals leaking into wells all over this country have set up are part of the potential legacy of death for generations to come. Yet in most of these situations, the government, the chemical plants, and the gas and manufacturing companies have not come forward to admit responsibility for long-term environmental damage. Indeed, they seem rather to hide and bluff their way through accusations of wrong until they are forced to correct a chemical horror.

Union Carbide is one of the few companies that has had to take some responsibility for its actions. When Carbide's insecticide gas dioxin was accidentally emitted into the atmosphere of Bhopal, India, 2,000 persons died instantly and thousands of others were permanently injured. Yet, even in the face of this catastrophe, Virginians who live near a similar Union Carbide plant in the United States have been told that such a tragedy could never happen to them.

It took decades and hundreds of hours of litigation before asbestos was declared carcinogenic, even though the asbestos workers who were dying from lung cancer were certain of it. To some companies and groups, avoiding financial liability appears to be more significant than saving human lives.

As a health professional, there may be times when you can use your counseling skills to alert individuals to dangers in their environment.

The Role of Counseling for Prevention with Lifestyle Factors

Why can Bill eat enormous quantities of food and never gain weight while Craig watches his diet constantly and still gains? Why can Ellen work two jobs and then go out dancing and drinking while Marcia has trouble feeling well-rested after eight hours of sleep? Chances are that genetic programming is a key factor. But what would happen to Marcia if she had to work both of Ellen's jobs? What would happen to Ellen if she had to get eight hours of sleep every night? Chances are these alterations in lifestyle would bring about dramatic changes in each person's physical and mental health.

Although much of who we are is what our ancestors were, the remainder is influenced heavily by the lives we **choose** to live. And, because lifestyle involves a high element of choice, most of the advice or counseling health professionals give revolves around lifestyle factors. As already noted, we may be able to postpone, avoid, or even alter the course of diseases for which we are genetically programmed **if** we significantly compensate with a healthy lifestyle.

Much has been written about the unhealthy lifestyle changes in our entire culture. When we were a more agrarian society, rigorous exercise was a part of daily life. Even city folks got regular exercise before the automobile was introduced. Today's sedentary lifestyle is blamed for high disease risk. Every period in history has offered unique risk factors, however. We often ignore the risk factors that dominated the old ways of life. These included death due to the complications of burning (people relied on wood), childbirth, and farm accidents.

Counseling in Prevention

We are currently faced with one of the biggest risks to public health in the history of modern medicine. A deadly virus, known as AIDS (Acquired Immune Deficiency Syndrome) is being spread through lifestyle practices.

Seventy percent of AIDS patients are homosexual males. This figure may change rapidly however as the incidence of AIDS increases in intravenous drug users and heterosexuals who have intimate contact with either bisexuals or drug users. A small percentage of persons with AIDS are hemophiliacs or other blood product users, mainly those who had blood transfusions from 1978–1985. Infected mothers may also pass the virus to unborn babies.

For a variety of reasons, those who carry the AIDS virus may ignore or be ignorant of the risks which they generate for others. Some AIDS carriers experience no signs or symptoms of the disease. These individuals may not have had a blood test which is a necessary part of diagnosis. They may practice sex or share intravenous needles without knowing that they are passing on a deadly virus.

The best advice for those who have been practicing homosexuals within the last 8–10 years, those who share needles, or those who have multiple sex partners is to be tested even if they have no symptoms. This advice is especially difficult to impart as many of the AIDS carriers are outside of the mainstream of American life. They may not be able to read; if literate, they may never see a newspaper or listen to the news. An intravenous drug habit is often a full time occupation. The only successes, albeit limited, with IV drug users have come from direct educational approaches: handing out condoms and clean syringes.

Another problem is that of the individual who has tested positive for the HIV (also known as HTLV III) virus (AIDS). This blood test, available since March 1985, detects antibodies to the AIDS virus. Such persons may have no symptoms or only moderate symptoms such as fever, tiredness, and swollen glands (known as ARC, that is AIDS Related Complex) or the uncontrollable infections and diseases of active AIDS.

A positive HIV test does not necessarily mean that an individual will get AIDS (although very recent evidence shows that *increasing* proportions of those with positive tests *do* eventually develop the disease). An antibody test simply indicates that an individual has been *exposed* to the virus. The ambiguity of this test presents a problem for many. Should they have the test when symptom-free only to learn the worst and worry perhaps for years, perhaps forever, as to when the disease will hit them?

If we could empathize with the possible victims of Huntington's disease when they chose to live their lives without knowing whether or not they were carriers, perhaps we can understand the feeling of the potential AIDS patient not to want testing. Until an *antigen* test is approved (a test which shows the presence of the virus itself), the current AIDS test leaves too much room for speculation.

Yet it is hard for most health professionals to argue against testing even with our current limitations. While the victim of Huntington's disease remains ignorant, he or she may unknowingly pass the gene on to offspring. But their numbers are limited by comparison to the AIDS patient's potential victims. The unknowing AIDS carrier may infect hundreds of others who then infect others who then infect others. The potential mathematical progression of the disease is terrifying.

There are also the tragic cases of prostitutes and those addicted to sex who cannot or will not limit their sexual activities despite a positive AIDS test. These individuals are a true threat to public safety. In a few instances, these individuals have been quarantined and jailed.

There is also the consideration that constitutional law appears to provide for the rights to public safety over the rights of an individual for confidentiality. In other words, the law appears to favor protecting the general welfare (of many) even when that may infringe on the constitutional rights of one. However, it must be proven that the individual will inflict harm to the public and be proven that restrictive means are necessary. As a nation, we are in serious debate over individual rights of confidentiality versus the need for public safety.

When the AIDS patient appears to be behaving in a responsible and serious manner, confidentiality is easier to interpret. Recall the stigma of homosexuality which we discussed in the adolescence section of Chapter 5. That stigma, combined with the national hysteria over this deadly disease itself, make confidentiality extremely important. AIDS patients are losing health and life. How can we feed a system which would also cost them their livelihoods and friendships as well. It appears that the antidiscriminatory statutes such as the Federal Rehabilitation Act of 1973 (antidiscrimination of the handicapped) are far from sufficient protection for AIDS prejudice.

Intravenous drug use which spreads blood contaminated with the virus, and rectal and vaginal intercourse currently are the only *proven* methods of spreading the AIDS virus. As you read the motivation section of this chapter, think of how you might increase the compliance of AIDS victims and potential victims with practices of safe sex and safe needle use. Think how you might advise high risk individuals about testing.

The role of counseling for prevention relies on making the client aware of the risk factors that exist today, providing the client with information that will permit a change to take place and actively working to motivate the client to adopt a healthier lifestyle. This strategy, called AIM, for awareness, information, and motivation, is described in the last section of this chapter.

The accompanying box lists some of the risk factors that influence health in today's society. Before going on to the next section, see whether you can think of any others.

Lifestyle factors that influence health risk

Amount of sleep	Use of leisure time
Marital status	Hobbies and interests
Number of family members	Occupation
Attitude toward health care	Living environment
Exercise	Smoking
Job stress	Number of sexual partners
Eating habits	Use of caffeine
Drinking habits	Religious beliefs and practices
Use of recreational drugs	Hours on the road

Considerations of genetics, environment, and lifestyle are also meaningful when we focus on what influences mental health.

Counseling and Mental Health

Genetic Programming and Mental Health

Determining the relationship of heredity to mental health is not an easy task. First, if we define mental illness as distinguishable from physical illness, we nearly eliminate the possibility of a genetic link to mental disease since such a link would mean the disease could be defined as physical. For example, alcoholism is classified as a mental illness. If a chromosome were discovered that passed the disease on, we would then be looking at an apparent physical condition. Currently it appears that a genetic weakness or tendency toward alcoholism does run in families. Environmental and lifestyle factors then figure prominently in disease onset.

The second factor that makes genetic links to mental illness difficult to determine is the overlap or contamination of environmental factors. Consider this example:

Young Tom has been raised in the presence of chronic alcohol abuse. Every time his mom and dad are unhappy, they open a bottle to drown their sorrows. There are few days when they do not turn to alcohol.

When Tom enters high school his life isn't going smoothly. He finds his schoolwork difficult, he is tired of his part-time job, and his teachers are unsympathetic. His friends think it is great fun to get drunk in the restrooms and then go to class. Soon drinking becomes a way of life for Tom.

Did he learn to drink because his mom and dad demonstrated that booze was the best way to cope? Are his friends primarily responsible for Tom's problems? Did he inherit a program for alcoholism that was physically determined to take effect as soon as he took his first drink? Or are there other considerations that must be examined?

Schizophrenia has been the subject of much etiological research (research that looks for causes). One major question has been whether a schizophrenic who has one or two schizophrenic parents inherits the condition or develops mental illness because of her/his environment. For many years the hazards of being raised by mentally disturbed people were believed to be the cause of second-generation mental illness. Then a reasonably large sample of twins and siblings was studied. These children had at least one schizophrenic parent. Half of them were raised by or around the schizophrenic; the other half were raised in homes free of any clear signs of mental illness.

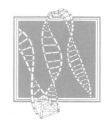

The incidence of second-generation schizophrenia remained consistent. That is, the children of one schizophrenic had a higher incidence (10 percent) of schizophrenia than did the population as a whole (1 percent). Further, whether they were raised with their family of origin or in a schizophrenia-free environment, the percentage of victims remained the same. Finally, there was a higher incidence of schizophrenia among the children who had two schizophrenic parents than among those who had only one schizophrenic parent. This study makes a fairly convincing case for the influence of heredity on some forms of mental illness. Of course, schizophrenia emerges in families with no **known** previous history of schizophrenia. Also, even when both parents are schizophrenic, not all offspring are similarly afflicted. These exceptions may indicate that heredity alone is not a sufficient explanation.

How does such information help when counseling for prevention? Well, just as the potential victims of heart disease, diabetes, or cancer might wish to understand their risk factors, so do the potential victims of alcoholism, schizophrenia, and manic depression. Taken to the healthy extreme, the child of alcoholics who wishes to be certain of never becoming alcoholic, might never drink alcohol. Or the cautious individual with an alcoholic background would be alert to possible signs within herself so that she could seek treatment before a problem got out of hand.

The children of schizophrenics and manic depressives might recognize a need for lifelong medication, if they fall victim to their heredity. Awareness and information are essential to accepting the need for prolonged medication. In many cases the medication may allow for near-normal functioning. In the past, victims of these afflictions tended to deny their mental illness and self-medicate with alcohol, which always leads to disastrous consequences that take a heavy toll on both victims and their families.

The more aware a person is about a genetic tendency for mental illness, the more effective counseling may be in other areas. For example, people who are at high risk for mental illness would do well to learn good coping strategies for stress, choose an occupation that best accommodates their individual needs, and develop the kind of support groups that will most promote their ability to function.

Environmental Conditions and Mental Health

The possibility of an environmental link to mental illness focuses on the notion that mental illness can be "learned" through repeated exposure to a mentally ill parent. The relationship of a disturbed environment to the onset of illness has been fairly well accepted by mental health experts. Patients with all degrees of psychological impairment are virtually **expected** to reveal a traumatic past. A difficult family life, blaming problems on mother, and complaints of having received no love are common revelations in psychotherapy. Few people would argue that an abused child has no reason for emotional difficulties. The degree of emotional difficulty appears to depend on the severity of abuse. The book *Sybil* reveals a life of maternal torture of a child. As a defense against this brutality, Sybil developed some 17 separate and distinct personalities, most of whom did not know one another. Closing her life off in little boxes was the only way Sybil survived. Yet years later, when she was no longer being tortured, continued psychotherapy freed her enough so that she became nearly normal and could face life with just one personality.

If mental illness is learned as a response to environmental stress, it may be unlearned when the stress is eliminated or reduced. Unfortunately, many people do not see their own responses to stress as inappropriate. Abused children tend to abuse their own children. One reason is a psychological phenomenon that makes those who were the passive victims of an act need to repeat that act on someone else. Children who were helpless in the face of abuse may get "revenge" through their own children.

Other abused children truly have "learned" that the only way to control children is with harsh physical punishment. They have probably also learned that kids are good punching bags for handling frustrations. No one demonstrated any other options for coping with stress. A boss tells them off at work and they hurry home to punish somebody.

Still other abused children react differently. Perhaps they had at least one significant adult role model who was not brutal, or perhaps they have a special inner awareness. In any case, they recognize fully that they themselves were misused by their parents. Further, they are determined not to treat their own children as they were treated. Such individuals struggle to make good the wish not to repeat history. If they have dealt with their anger and other psychological scars, it is possible that they will not abuse their kids. But, if they have difficulty coping with life in general and if they refuse the notion of psychotherapy, they are likely to repeat the pattern of child abuse.

An essential point here is that early recognition of potential emotional problems warrants early treatment. Counseling that helps the young adult resolve parental conflicts and close off the past prevents that individual from perpetuating the abuse. "Fix yourself before you have your kids so your kids will have a better chance" is a good slogan for counseling prevention.

Environmental considerations for mental health can also be broad in scope. For example, overcrowding and noise pollution have their own impact on mental health. Studies with rats have shown that overcrowding can make animals paranoid. Competition for space and guarding against and fearing neighbors are all part of paranoia. We can easily transfer this knowledge from rats to human beings. Just think of the number of locks most inner city people have on their doors. The kind of trust that is the norm in a rural community has been totally conditioned out of those who live in large urban areas. Finding an environment that offers enough stimulation to be energizing without generating unmanageable stress is an important consideration for good mental health.

Social/familial support during illness is also an environmental consideration. As discussed in the final section of this chapter, such support is the cornerstone of motivation.

Lifestyle Factors and Mental Health

Stress is undoubtedly the most significant word in our lifestyle vocabulary. It is a word that means different things to different people. Some people cannot be happy until the stress goes out of their lives. Others accept stress as natural, cope with it well, and even thrive on reasonable amounts of it. How many times have you heard people say that they work better under pressure? The hands of a potter must apply just the correct amount of pressure for a piece of art; too much pressure and the pot collapses.

Stress, anxiety, and depression are generally considered negative feelings. To a great extent they have common roots. Certainly no human being goes through life without experiencing some degree of these emotional states. What is important to understand is how and why these feelings become mental illness or serious problems.

An individual who feels stressed can choose either a good coping strategy or a poor one. Good coping strategies would be physical exercise as a release for stress or simply dealing directly with the source of the problem. Examples of poor coping would be denying that anything is wrong, calling in sick to "punish" the boss, or over-using alcohol or other drugs.

Poor coping usually comes from a sense of inadequacy or a loss of self-efficacy (belief in self). Subjects will say to themselves "Oh, I can't handle this" or "I'll show them if they think they can put me down."

The most self-defeating of internal messages is the one that says, "This is hopeless, I can't change a thing, I just want to get drunk (stoned, high) and forget it all." As noted in Chapter 6, substance abuse is not only physically damaging but also difficult to break free from. Yet there is social pressure to drink and to take other forms of drugs and as a culture we both condone and encourage turning to drugs for comfort. Our teenagers use drugs to fill loneliness, to conform, to prove themselves, to blow away reality. The faster and cheaper a drug is, the more teenagers will accept it. The current crack epidemic is one example.

Another aspect of stress or social pressure is the all-consuming quest for perfection. Those who accept the notion that being thin is essential — and most who do are females between 12 and 24 years old — will take any drug that will help them lose weight. Speed, ipecac, diuretics, and laxatives have all been abused by people who want to be thin.

Review the coping skills in Figure 7.2. Plug other stressors into the square on the left. For instance, try pressure to take drugs, pressure to smoke, pressure to have sex, or financial pressure. Then list poor and good ways of coping with these stressors.

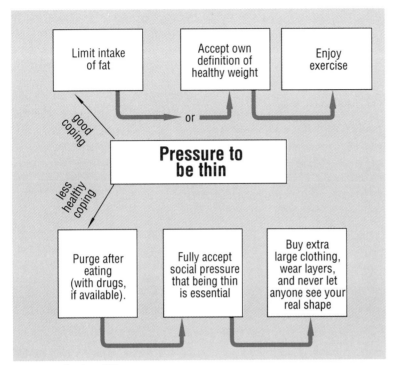

Figure 7.2 Coping skills.

The more we mask what bothers us in life, the more difficult coping becomes. Drugs are a big part of our culture. Some groups in our society accept them; others frown on them. Certainly health professionals would have to wish for a culture that relied less on self-medicating. To the extent that we, as a society, use drugs, we put ourselves in jeopardy for creating more mental illness.

The divorce rate in the United States has been high for the last two decades. In certain areas of the country, new marriages have only a 50% chance of survival. Many divorces affect young children, which affects lifestyle. When lifestyle involves frequent divorce, the negative consequences of divorce demonstrate an additional lifestyle problem.

Too much affluence appears to breed mental health problems just as too little money does. In both situations, the eventual downfall is likely to be the same. Children who have been overindulged frequently turn to drugs as a way of getting their kicks. Children who have been raised in poverty turn to drugs as an escape from a harsh and unrewarding world.

Lifestyle affects mental as well as physical health. Symptoms can be the cause or the effect of lifestyle problems. For example, sleeplessness often indicates emotional disturbance. And if sleeplessness occurs for a prolonged period of time, it can also lead to physical health problems. A lifestyle that pushes a person to "party" or work with little rest sets the stage for both mental and physical health to deteriorate.

Balance or harmony probably provides the individual with the best chance for good mental health: a balance between work and play; a sense of freedom yet a sense of responsibility; meaningful connections with other human beings especially in primary relationships; and above all a belief in one's own basic goodness. When lifestyles encourage us to act in ways that conflict with such a balance or when we do things we do not believe are right, we disturb the balance.

To the extent that lifestyle is choice, we choose risks to our health. If we buy into a quest for the biggest home in the neighborhood and the most trips abroad, then we **invite** extraordinary pressure. We may end up with the biggest house and the shortest life or the biggest house and the least happiness. Or, if we fail to attain such a competitive goal, we may end up with a deep sense of failure.

Counseling Strategies for Prevention

Earlier in this chapter we mentioned a counseling strategy called AIM (awareness, information, and motivation). This strategy relies on the basic scientific knowledge that all health care relies on. How it differs significantly is in its emphasis on **motivation**. Although your knowledge as a health practitioner is essential to providing service, it is not sufficient. In fact, the health professional who has only knowledge will fail. Counseling skills are a necessary part of success. You cannot succeed if you do not learn **what** will motivate your clients and then learn **how** to motivate them.

Counseling, of course, is a scientific process, and no counselor needs to be more of a scientist than does the health care provider who counsels toward prevention. AIM relies on a scientific process to analyze all significant aspects of each individual client. The awareness and information aspects of this process depend on a thorough understanding of the client's genetic, environmental, and lifestyle factors.

Awareness

As scientists, health professionals are aware of the underlying causes of many diseases. But we must transmit our understanding of risk factors to our clients, and we must do so in language that our clients can understand.

As a counselor, your first job is to see what the client's history is. (You should use the counseling model described in Chapters 1 and 2 as you question a client using open-ended questions whenever possible.) In general, you will seek the following information:

Previous History. Where did you grow up? What did your parents do? Where did you go to school? How well did you do in school socially and intellectually? What jobs have you held? What hospitalizations and operations have you had? What serious diseases have you had?

Family History. How many brothers and sisters do you have? What serious diseases do your siblings, parents, children, or grandparents have? Does your family have any history of depression, suicide, overweight, high blood pressure, alcoholism, drug taking, or bizarre behavior?

Personal, Social, and Psychiatric History. Describe any counseling you have had before or any hospitalization for mental health problems. Do you smoke, drink, or take drugs? Where do you live? What are your living conditions? Where do you work and what hours do you work? Does your spouse work? How many children do you have? What problems do you have with your children, friends, or family? What financial or sexual problems do you have? Who do you have your primary relationship with? How much do you exercise? How many hours do you drive a day? What causes stress in your life? What do you normally eat?

Ideally, several health practitioners would act as a team to study the client's family disease / health profile carefully. The same care, of course, would be given to the client's health status. The review of the client's history would focus intensely on lifestyle factors including diet and exercise.

After such a review, you would be aware of the most likely threats to this client's wellness. Your next step would be to describe these risk factors to your client in language that she or he could understand.

Conveying what you found back to your client is a crucial point and one that is often ignored in ordinary health care settings. Many health professionals, especially physicians, take a thorough family history, but few convey anything to the client. For example, a physician may see several overlapping medical problems in close relatives. These problems might make the physician think the client is a good candidate for a stroke. But, unless the client has **developed** stroke risk factors it is unlikely that the physician will mention the risk. One justification for this approach is that we should not frighten someone about symptoms they may never develop. But the point of preventive counseling is to tell the client **before** symptoms develop.

This issue comes down to whether we regard the health professional or the patient as responsible for the patient's health. If we believe that the health professional is ultimately responsible for the patient's health, then we would follow the traditional medical model, which is to gather important information about each client and use it when or if necessary.

The preventive model, however, places responsibility for the patient's health **on the patient**. Information regarding the patient's family background, current health status, and future forecasts are to be given to the patient / client. Then the client can decide how seriously to take this information.

A healthy 30-year-old who is told he has a relatively high risk factor for heart attack may, in fact, want to ignore this threat until symptoms develop. But what if he doesn't? What if he conscientiously wants to modify his diet and increase his exercise because he is now aware of this particular risk to him? This client may know what the risk factors for heart attack are. He may even see a pattern within his own family. But, until a health professional works with him as an individual while looking at all his familial risk factors, he may not see his own destiny. Awareness spells out for a healthy client what he or she needs to be most aware of.

The reason health professionals study long hours, read extensively, and conduct research is to broaden their information base. Health professionals also consult with one another to further increase the scope of their information base.

Information

Giving appropriate information follows awareness in the responsible counseling process. The client who is told that she is at risk for a heart attack also needs to be told what she can do about that risk. Awareness alone would be cruel. Awareness coupled with information allows the client to see both the problem and its potential solution. To be optimally helpful, the health practitioner must convey enough information and the right information. Handing the person at high risk a pamphlet on how to avoid heart attack might be helpful, but it would be insufficient. Rather, the prevention counselor needs to delve into the client's current lifestyle. Holding up a model of perfection and advising the client to mimic it is too easy.

The helpful health care provider will need to know what constraints the client faces in trying to change her behavior and so improve her health. If, for example, exercise is highly important for this client, the health provider will need to explore what gets in the way of exercising. How does this client stop herself from getting exercise? Chances are that she will say she does not have time to exercise. Traditionally, the health practitioner would go through the client's daily schedule with her and help her see how she could budget the exercise in. This might still be helpful, but with indepth information, precisely helpful advice can be offered.

The health professional might first ask what exercising means to the client. Does it perhaps mean jogging five miles followed by a shower and a change of clothes? What if the client could gain all the conditioning response she needs for a healthy body from four 20–30 minute brisk walks per week? Doesn't that free up time? Doesn't it also eliminate the need for showering and changing clothes, thus allowing more flexibility? And doesn't it sound like a small sacrifice for continued good health?

Information follows awareness. It provides the client with options for helping to maintain health in the face of risk. Also, since it takes into account the special needs of the individual client, it is the **best information** for that individual.

Motivation

In the past, awareness — especially in the face of developing health problems — was believed to be a sufficient motivational force to get some people to change their behavior. If people knew they would become increasingly unwell unless they followed certain instructions, surely they would do what they should. Information that approached the client at his or her own level or took particular needs into account was seen as a further advance. Maybe everyone couldn't keep their weight at the right level for optimal health, but couldn't everyone adjust their diets to eliminate high fats or heavy salts? The answer was — and is — **no**. Even together, awareness and information have left a tremendous gap in compliance. That gap is called motivation.

Motivation can be defined as an inner drive that forces the individual toward action. If survival is instinctive, the quest for wellness would appear to be motivational in and of itself. But the vast history of patient noncompliance tells us we must look beyond awareness of risks.

We usually assume that individuals who seek health care are at least somewhat motivated. But from the outside, it is difficult to know how motivated a patient is. A real understanding of motivation can only be gained on an individual basis. That is, what motivates one individual to act may in fact stop another from acting. Consider this example.

> Helen Wilson has cared for her invalid mother-in-law for seven years. She continued to find the daily tasks of caring for her mother-in-law to be tedious, difficult, boring, and generally unrewarding.
>
> Helen is then diagnosed as having high blood pressure. Her physician prescribes exercise, diet changes, and rest, and mentions that Helen may have to both take medication and change her lifestyle if she cannot lower her blood pressure through these methods. If Helen believes that prolonged high blood pressure may lead to the removal of her mother-in-law from her home, what is she likely to be motivated to do?

This example may seem contrived, but it is a reasonable example of what actually happens. Recall our discussion of illness behavior in Chapter 3. For some individuals and for some families, the illness itself becomes reward. And, if illness is a reward, then wellness is a punishment. If you are a student of logic, this becomes the only plausible explanation for noncompliance. That is, **the disease itself is rewarding**. Further, we might surmise that **the patient finds some aspect of compliance more difficult than the problem itself**.

A basic key to behavior modification is determining what the reward is. A classic example is the child who wants parental attention. Little Jesse's parents are often too busy and preoccupied with other matters to pay much attention to him. So Jesse throws his dinner on the kitchen floor. His parents, who do not like to have food wasted and their meals disrupted, spank him. Has Jesse been punished or rewarded? If you think he has been punished, recall what he was trying to get. Bear in mind, too, that rewarding negative behavior only serves to increase it.

Health professionals who want to motivate a patient are frequently successful when they find the right reward to modify the patient's behavior. But the key to success lies in distinguishing punishment from reward. Here is another example.

> Gretchen, 37, is married and has two young adolescent children. Gretchen has a long history of frequent hospitalizations due to anorexia nervosa. At times she has held her own emotionally and done well enough with her weight to be out of danger. Then, virtually overnight, she falls apart emotionally and drops 15 pounds in a matter of days. When this happens, Gretchen must be hospitalized.
>
> This pattern, which Gretchen has repeated for 10 years now, has the health professionals who care for her baffled. They reason that a woman who wants to get well and enjoy her young family will struggle hard to keep her weight up and avoid hospitalization. They see **time with her family as Gretchen's reward for good eating**.

But what has been the reward for Gretchen? Hospitalization has been the reward. Peace and quiet have been the reward. **Time away from a demanding, hectic, often unpleasant family life has been the reward.** This reward has motivated Gretchen to starve herself. Years before, Gretchen learned that people did not bother her or expect too much from her when she was ill, especially when she was in the hospital. But she is no longer on a bizarre quest for thinness. She now uses anorexia to cope with too much environmental stress. She starves to gain her reward: a peaceful environment.

Once hospitalization was determined to be Gretchen's goal, her anorexia was virtually cured. All the health professional had to do was promise Gretchen that she could be hospitalized upon request. Anytime the stress became too much for Gretchen she could be hospitalized — without weight loss. Instead of having to starve herself, Gretchen could be rewarded at a normal weight.

Contingency-management procedures and **token economies** are often-used strategies in successful behavior modification programs.

With contingency-management systems, patients frequently are required to deposit money. Contingent upon attending group sessions or changing a behavior, the patient gets the money back. In one particularly affluent group, participants were paid $250 for every five pounds they lost. This system frequently works, at least in the short run, because most people feel rewarded when they earn money and punished when they lose it.

A **token economy**, which is generally used with an inpatient population, is even more individually tailored. Tokens are given as rewards for adopting desirable behaviors. The patient can then exchange tokens for a privilege or desirable commodity. For example, the patient who earns two tokens for cleaning his room each day may, after five days, exchange them for a privilege like smoking alone on the hospital grounds, which costs 10 tokens. This is a more sophisticated form of behavior modification than contingency management because the tokens are exchanged for a reward of the patient's choice. If a specific reward such as smoking rights were offered for good behavior, some patients would not consider this a reward. Tokens allow everyone to choose what will be rewarding to them.

Theories other than behavior modification influence our thinking on motivation. One such important theory is the theory of **cognitive dissonance**. According to this theory, the human mind is always seeking to simplify and reconcile information. The mind is seeking a state of harmony or consonance. Consider the example of trying to decide which of two products to buy. While we struggle to decide between product X and product Y, our minds are in a state of disharmony or dissonance. Once we actually purchase product Y, we quickly think about all its good characteristics. We justify or rationalize why we were right to buy it. Further, we see all the flaws in product X and feel justified in not having bought it. This allows the mind to return to a state of harmony. It also helps to explain why many individuals have fierce brand loyalty.

Counseling in Prevention

Transferred to motivational theory, cognitive dissonance can explain something about campaigns waged to change human behavior. Fear is a tactic often used by those who want to encourage people to quit smoking. Many clearly link smoking with cancer. But most smokers will deny the truthfulness of this link. They will say that they do not fear cancer. People who have a tremendous fear of cancer will most likely have quit smoking on their own or will never have smoked because tremendous fear creates a state of dissonance. To overcome this fear, those who are concerned about cancer cannot smoke or the dissonance would be too great.

For those who do smoke, a cancer fear campaign simply increases their resistance. They cannot both smoke and live in fear, so they deny the message of the campaign. They may even increase their smoking to prove to themselves that they are not afraid. This then returns them to a state of harmony, regardless of what it does to their lungs. In this example, what is expected to be the motivator — fear — actually prevents the smoker from making any positive health change.

A final concept essential to understanding motivational theory is the concept of **antagonists** to motivation. To understand this idea, we can look at the victims of chronic illness. (An antagonist is something that opposes something else.)

Initially, Jim, a diabetic patient, seemed highly motivated to comply with his diet, exercise, and insulin regimens. Frequently, however, he suffered mild insulin reactions due to the tight control he kept. When he complained about these reactions, the health care provider assured him that they were a necessary part of good management for the sake of his future health. But insulin reactions continued to make Jim feel frail and unwell.

Then Jim realized that the limitations of his diet had made him somewhat of a social burden. He was no longer invited to dinner very often, which was demoralizing. Jim decided to take his chances on what the future might bring and go ahead and run his life with higher blood sugars. His physical feelings improved along with his social life.

How could we, as health professionals, intervene to return this man to a level of safer compliance? Indeed, should we intervene? Can we expect victims of chronic health problems to make extensive sacrifices in the present to avoid a possible punishment in the future? (We may have these expectations, but we must recognize that our chances for success are undoubtedly limited.) This is certainly a case for our best counseling skills.

Not enough work has been done in the area of motivation and compliance. Recent work suggests that screening may yield a profile of patients who are most likely to comply with preventive regimens. Perhaps by concentrating efforts on patients who are most likely to succeed there will be an increased number of successes and a cost benefit to society.

Screening for success involves evaluating for risk factors, individual skills, history, and social factors. The profile for a successful patient is many-faceted. Genetic, environmental, and lifestyle factors must be evaluated. The individual's commitment to success or change is imperative. Finally, the individual's history of successes, ability to comprehend a complex problem, and ability to treat himself/herself must be evaluated.

Generally, a patient who has family responsibilities and support is a good candidate for success. Getting or staying well because there are people who need and love you appears to be a good motivator. Patients in mid-life generally comply best. Adolescent patients quickly tire of or ignore protocols aimed at a distant gain when they are asked to make sacrifices in the present. Other older patients comply well because the threat of physical illness is so near.

Good mental health and at least average intelligence are also important to success. But the factor that is the most difficult to measure and predict — inner motivation — is undoubtedly the key ingredient for success.

Although the principle of screening may be supportable, applying it is not. In practice, few programs would turn a candidate away because she or he appeared to be a poor risk. The ethical dilemma raised is, given limited resources, do we have the right to give less time to people because they are likely to waste it and give that time to someone who is likely to make good use of it? What is needed in this area is further understanding of what motivation really is.

This chapter begins with a discussion of the preventive or wellness perspective of a "client" rather than a "patient". It then proceeds to demonstrate the importance of counseling skills to maintaining wellness. Both mental and physical health are viewed in terms of risk factors which counseling may mediate. These risk factors are viewed in three major categories: genetic programming, environmental conditions, and lifestyle factors.

The final section of this chapter reviewed a counseling strategy called AIM. AIM stands for Awareness, Information, and Motivation.

Information related to genetics, environment, and lifestyle is used to increase the client's awareness of risk factors. Information is then given in ways which the client can understand. This places the major responsibility for wellness and success on the individual client rather than primarily on the health care provider. Finally, we reviewed motivational theories and strategies as follows:

- What actually is the reward? A prominent theme for success is analyzing the client sufficiently to know what actually constitutes a reward for them.
- Behavior modification techniques like contingency management and token economies may also assist with motivation.
- The theory of cognitive dissonance shows us that denial is used to avoid conflict. Sometimes this denial gets in the way of motivation.
- Last, we need to understand better the potential for success as it exists in the individual.

Review

Aerobic exercise: requires increased or heavy breathing

Agrarian: focused on agriculture, farming

Amniocentesis: medical procedure in which amniotic fluid is removed from abdomen of pregnant women. Tests run on this fluid indicate certain health characteristics of the fetus.

Anaerobic exercise: does *not* require increased breathing

Antagonists: opponents, against good

Contingency management: specific rewards given or withheld contingent or dependent upon specific behavioral changes

Dissonance: lack of harmony

Down's syndrome: common type of congenital mental retardation which can be moderate to severe; patients have oriental-like features with a generally dwarfed build

Environmental conditions: the world around us

Etiology: cause

Genetic programming: inherited characteristics carried by our genes

Lifestyle factors: how we choose to live

Motivation: drive toward a particular action

Sedentary: inactive

Self-efficacy: belief in self

1. Compare the risk factors of an agrarian society to our current risk factors. Which society would you rather live in and why? Which society had (has) the longest life expectancy? Try looking at these risk factors by gender differences between agrarian and today. What differences do you see?
2. Discuss the difficulties of motivating an AIDS victim to comply with safe sex practices.
3. You are a health care provider treating an AIDS patient. What would you say to the spouse of this patient when you are asked for the patient's diagnosis?
4. A neighbor has been dating a friend of yours. She approaches you and says: "The only problem with dating these days is fear of AIDS. Your friend Steve is straight, isn't he?" You know Steve is bisexual. How do you respond?
5. Based on our discussion in this chapter, what do you think causes mental illness?

Auchincloss, Louis. *Sybil.* Houghton Mifflin, Boston, MA. 1952.

Green, Hannah. *I Never Promised You a Rose Garden.* Holt, Rinehart & Winston, New York, NY. 1964.

Kerr, C. *Postgraduate Medicine.* Aids and the Issue of Confidentiality. 81, 8, 95-111. 1987.

Koop, C.E. *Surgeon General's Report on Acquired Immune Deficiency Syndrome.* U.S. Public Health Service. Washington, D.C. 1987.

Levine, C. *Hastings Center Report Special Supplement.* AIDS: Public Health and Civil Liberties. 15-23. December, 1986.

Matthews, G. and Neslund, V. *Journal of the American Medical Association.* The Initial Impact of AIDS on Public Health Law in the United States. 344-351. 1986-87.

Reich, Charles A. *The Greening of America: How the Youth Revolution is Trying to Make America Livable.* Random House, New York, NY. 1970.

Shute, N. *On the Beach.* W. Morrow, New York, NY. 1957.

Smialek, J., and Lambros, A. *The New Physician.* Reporting AIDS on Death Certificates. 11. May-June, 1987.

Winstons, M. *Hastings Center Report.* AIDS and a Duty to Protect. 22-23. February, 1987.

Telephone Hotlines (Toll Free)

PHS AIDS Hotline
800-342-AIDS
800-342-2437

National Sexually Transmitted Diseases Hotline/
American Social Health
Association 800-227-8922

National Gay Task Force
AIDS Information Hotline
800-221-7044
(212) 807-6016 (NY State)

Information Sources

*U.S. Public Health Service
Public Affairs Office*
Hubert H. Humphrey
Building, Room 725-H
200 Independence Avenue, S.W.
Washington, D.C. 20201
Phone: (202) 245-6867

*Local Red Cross or
American Red Cross
AIDS Education Office*
1730 D Street, N.W.
Washington, D.C. 20006
Phone: (202) 737-8300

Chapter

8

After reading this chapter, you should be able:
- To recognize the role of education in promoting wellness in individuals and within the community.
- To describe the role of education in promoting compliance with therapeutic regimens.
- To teach patients about their diseases and treatment.
- To involve the client/patient in the treatment process including goal setting.
- To incorporate education into all stages of treatment.
- To describe the educational techniques of participation, relevancy, collaboration, reinforcement, credibility, and individualization.
- To describe the principles of learning.

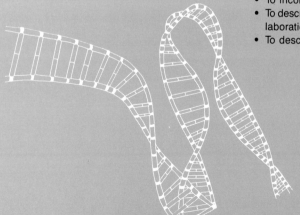

Health Education: A Tool for Practice and Prevention

This chapter focuses on how you can use your teaching skills to help your patients get better sooner, prevent disease and disability, and enhance their health.

Health education, which is teaching patients about their disease and how it is treated, is a time-honored approach to patient care. Most physicians and health professionals are involved in health education to some degree. Certain medical specialists such as pediatricians, obstetricians, internists, family practitioners, and psychiatrists place considerable emphasis on health education. Nurses, nurse practitioners, dietitians, physician assistants, and medical and nursing assistants also emphasize education as an integral part of the treatment process.

Although many practitioners value education, some have considered diagnosis and treatment to be the main tasks of medicine. In some instances, education is used only when treatment fails or has been less than satisfactory. But education should not be the final stage of treatment; it should be the first step in providing help and guidance to the patient.

The Role and Value of Teaching in Clinical Practice

Priscilla D. Douglas, the author of this chapter, is currently a professor in the School of Allied Health Professions, University of Connecticut, where she also is director of the graduate program. A registered dietitian, she holds B.S. and M.S. degrees in nutrition and a Ph.D in higher education administration. She is currently editor of the *Journal of Health Promotion* and is active in the American Dietetic Association and the American Society for Allied Health Professions.

Two definitions that support the primacy and priority of education in treatment are:

- Patient education is a process by which the health professional guides patients to expand their awareness of alternatives and options for gaining control of their health.
- Patient education can be defined as planned change done in a systematic way and used to facilitate voluntary adaption of behavior conducive to health.

There are two types of patient education, one for improving compliance with therapeutic regimens and the other for improving compliance with preventive regimens. For patients who are being treated for medical problems, education may mean providing information on using certain medications and helping with special dietary restrictions. Education for disease prevention suggests that health providers can keep disease or disability from happening and implies that health practitioners have a responsibility to improve the quality of their patients' lives. For example, many of the physical problems seen in the elderly are the result of lifestyle excesses such as smoking, unhealthy eating, and excessive alcohol consumption. To ensure a relatively active and productive old age, education aimed at these abuses and stressing individual decision making must start early.

Educating patients about their health is cost effective and provides for continuity of care. Treating a client with medications to control a problem may have little long-term benefit if the individual has not learned other strategies. For instance, a patient with hypertension may be very good about taking medications, but if not educated about the importance of reducing dietary salt, losing weight, and increasing exercise, fewer long-term benefits will accrue.

The educational process makes both patient and provider accountable. Information is shared, first by the provider on what choices the patient has regarding a health problem and later by the patient, who describes concerns and expectations. Both have a responsibility for deciding on a treatment plan that is workable and achievable.

Education personalizes care and affirms that the client is unique and special because it is designed to meet each individual's wants, needs, and goals. This process goes beyond the practice of handing out booklets and pamphlets that are expected to meet the needs of each individual, but in actuality are limited in use and effectiveness.

Teaching about health necessitates verbal communication between the client and provider, fosters rapport, and furnishes an opportunity to tailor the educational message to the patient's needs. Because behavioral change is implicit in education, personalized and achievable goals must be agreed upon. Through achieving these goals or changing behavior, the client feels valued and strengthens the sense of self-worth.

One recent study demonstrated the value of health education and its strong link to compliance, patient-provider accountability, personalized treatment, and client-self-worth through goal achievement. In this study, which was designed to improve compliance with diabetic regimens, compliance was improved by individualizing the diet to the patient's lifestyle; making sure that the patient felt like a member of the team; addressing the patient's concerns, especially around issues of weight and diet prescription; setting goals that were realistic and achievable; sharing knowledge on the disease and its treatment; and providing feedback on a regular basis.

Education for health promotion and disease prevention unrelated to a current medical problem is a new concept in health care. It calls for an expanded educational role for health providers and a transition from educating about disease to educating about health and how to achieve it. Those health professionals who first participated in prevention efforts often had both a personal commitment to health and a philosophical concern for the long-term well-being of their clients.

More recently, increased numbers of health professionals have seen the need not only to educate their patients about illness but also to optimize their patients' health and wellness. In a recent study, dietitians, nurse midwives, physician assistants, and dental hygienists identified important roles for themselves in health promotion and preventive services to their clients and the community. They wanted to see health promotion become a major focus of practice and saw themselves assuming greater responsibility for appraising their clients' behavioral risk factors.

Health professionals are participating in primary prevention through such large-scale studies as the Multiple Risk Factor Intervention Trial (MRFIT). In this study, middle-aged men determined to be at risk for coronary heart disease were randomly placed in either a special intervention (SI) group or in a group that was treated through the usual sources of medical care (UC). The SI group decreased their intake of dietary cholesterol by 40 percent, decreased saturated fatty acids by one-third, and had a mean weight loss of 3.5 pounds for years 1, 3, and 6. Intervention included nutritional counseling and extensive educational programs on nutrition, smoking, and hypertension.

The men in the UC group showed some improvement in dietary intake over time, although the magnitude was not as great as for those in the SI group. For instance, there was a decrease in total energy intake which was reflected in a mean wieght loss of 0.5 lbs for years 1, 3, and 6 and small reductions in the intake of total fat, saturated fat, and dietary cholesterol for the UC men. The researchers have explained these self-induced changes by saying that peoples' eating habits in the United States changed over the 10-year study and influenced the food choices of those subjects (UC) not receiving intervention.

Because intervention made it possible to reduce risk factors associated with coronary heart disease, it appears that intervention, in general, works and that health professionals will continue to play a significant role in "preventing" disease.

Health professionals also need to expand their client base to the community and assume their rightful role as community health educators. Education skills learned as health providers in a one on one setting can be used in group settings as well. Valuable health information needs to reach the laity. More and more hospitals that see the need to expand their services are using community outreach as both an education service and a marketing tool. In order for hospitals to retain their position as the focus of community health care, hospital administrators must adapt a health promotion mentality.

Teaching about health or illness is an important, if not vital, role for the health care provider. Educating clients about their health problems may improve compliance, provide long-term benefits, and be cost effective. Patients who are taught about health and disease appear more able to take charge of their health. As more health care providers view wellness intervention as a logical extension of their more traditional role, the need for educational skills will become even more essential.

Incorporating Health Teaching into Practice

Patient education is generally assumed to be part of a nurse's job responsibility. This is also true for the clinical dietitian, whose primary function is to teach about normal nutrition and needed dietary changes. Other health care providers such as physical, speech, and occupational therapists, physician assistants, dentists, dental hygienists, respiratory technicians and pharmacists readily incorporate teaching into practice. Many professional practice acts state that patient education is part of professional responsibility.

Leaders in some professional associations, such as the American Society of Allied Health Professions and the American Pharmaceutical Association, have suggested that health professionals devote more time to educating their clients. An example of this increased emphasis on education as a part of practice, is the current practice of adding 10 cents to the professional fee of each prescription when educational services are provided by the pharmacist.

Today, leaders in the health care field believe that professionals in every primary health care setting should be expected to provide their clients or patients with systematic educational programs. These leaders emphasize that the educational process should be systematic, designed for specific health settings, and offered to both the well and the ill.

To be able to educate your clients, you need to understand behavioral and educational techniques and the basic principles that promote the learning process. Remember that education often depends on more than one learning experience and on multiple approaches that take place over time. You will enhance the learning process for your clients if you follow the basic principles of participation, relevancy, collaboration, reinforcement, credibility, and individualization.

Health Education: A Tool for Practice and Prevention

CHAPTER 8

Participation

Participation by the learner is essential. Clients learn by doing or internalizing new information. Encouraging active participation in the learning process increases the chance that learning will take place.

Examples of active participation include having your patients paraphrase what you have said, summarize important points, and describe how they plan to use new information.

Relevancy

Teaching must be relevant to the learner's needs and must take into consideration the person's social, cultural, ethnic, racial, and economic background. Cultural blindness on your part may foster misunderstanding and create barriers to learning. Once you have identified a patient's needs, you must try to understand where he or she is coming from. The patient may wish to comply and meet health goals but may need help in arriving at suitable strategies. The more removed you are from a client sociologically, culturally, and economically, the harder it will be for you to understand what your client says or does.

> At first, the dentist felt scorn for Kate, a middle-aged woman with dirty teeth. But once the dentist took the time to ask some questions, it became apparent that apathy and disinterest were not the cause of Kate's poor oral hygiene. Kate had severe arthritis of the hand, which made it impossible for her to hold and use a conventional toothbrush. Once the dentist understood the situation, she was able to fashion a suitable cleaning instrument by applying a bicycle grip to the handle of a regular toothbrush so Kate could again brush her teeth. This client wanted to comply, but she needed help in developing an appropriate strategy.

Collaboration

In most cases, you and your patients should be partners in the education process. You should establish learning goals and decide together what needs to happen in order for the client to get better. Remember that education should be an interactive process.

To make the regimen understandable, you and the patient should develop specific goals. Because most regimens include multiple tasks such as taking medication, modifying eating habits, and making lifestyle changes, you will want to set priorities and start with behaviors that the client can handle reasonably well.

Reinforcement

Learning takes time. Your patient needs reinforcement as he or she tries to develop. Remember that old behaviors have probably been in existence for years and establishing new behaviors takes time.

Reinforcement should be immediate and timely, especially when a regimen is first being introduced. Praising behaviors that result in a desired good is an example of a simple but effective technique. A smile, a pat on the back, or a few simple words of encouragement and approval go a long way.

Credibility

Your credibility as a health professional and your ability to establish trust and rapport affect how your clients learn. Being professionally confident, but not authoritarian or judgmental, facilitates the educational process. Your patient should feel relaxed, not anxious, and you should inspire confidence with your knowledge. You can increase your credibility by modeling good or appropriate health behavior. A nurse who has yellow-stained fingers will have a hard time convincing a patient to give up smoking.

Individualization

Every plan for learning must be designed for the client. Take into consideration differences in learning speed and efficiency. All of us learn in different ways, but in general we learn by doing. Age, multiple illnesses, and anxiety can all have a negative impact on learning.

Learning is more efficient and effective when the client perceives that what she or he is expected to learn or do is relevant. Developing a patient contract that is totally individualized is one strategy. Pregnant women have been encouraged to contract to abstain from alcohol and drugs during their pregnancies and to follow exercise and dietary recommendations. In this case, contracting enhances prenatal care and ensures a relatively healthy pregnancy and baby.

The Basics of Learning

There are three steps to follow in providing effective and efficient learning. First, you must assess your client by finding out who she is, what she knows, and what her expectations are. You will need to consider your client's educational level, literacy level, wellness, type of illness, and cycle of treatment. Try to explore with your patient his beliefs about health and his perceptions of what caused his current problem. You also need to assess your patient's readiness for learning and identify what she wants to learn first.

Next, you must set the stage for learning by creating a positive environment and maintaining a friendly and supportive attitude. Use language that your client understands. If you have to use a technical term, first define it in simple to understand language. Keep communication open throughout the teaching process. Strive for an environment of mutual trust and humaneness.

Finally, you must organize the learning experience so it goes from the simple to the more complex. Plan experiences that influence attitudes, develop skills, and increase knowledge. For example, teaching a diabetic patient about his new diet without instructing him in the use of insulin and without providing him with some motivation would be inadequate. Also, it would provide for neither an attitudinal change nor skill development.

Some individuals learn best by listening (auditory learning), some by seeing (visual learning), and some by doing or physically manipulating textures, shapes, and outlines (kinesthetic learning). To compensate for differences in learning style, you should use a combination of teaching methods that incorporates them all.

Once you have set the stage for learning, there are five practical principles that you can use to improve comprehension, recall, and compliance. These principles are logical and utilize a common sense approach to teaching. Mastering them requires skill and planning. The five principles are the principles of brevity, primacy, readability, repetition, and specificity.

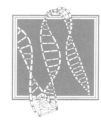

The **principle of brevity** states that information should be brief and to the point. The number of statements a client forgets increases with the number presented, so you should select the most important information, present it clearly, and repeat it as needed. Do not overload your client with unnecessary information. For example, if your patient needs medications, give her explicit instructions about how to use them. Do not complicate your message by offering information about other drugs. If you do, you will interfere with your patient's ability to remember your instructions.

The **principle of primacy** establishes the advantage of information presented first. Research has shown that people have better recall for information that is presented in the first third of the communication or instructional period. In other words, if it is important, say it first.

The **principle of readability** says that written materials must be readable in order to educate. In the United States, approximately 12 million people over the age of 13 cannot read above the fourth grade level. Because so many people have difficulty with reading, you must provide pamphlets and handouts that are designed for clients with limited reading and comprehension skills. For example, a handout that includes a simple diagram and simple explanation would be appropriate for those with poor reading skills.

The **principle of repetition** states that information that is repeated is retained and recalled more readily than information that is not repeated. Remember that few clients can recall information or directions that have only been offered once. It may be old information for you, but for the client it is new and interesting.

The **principle of specificity** says that the more specific the goal, directions, or information is, the more powerful the learning will be in terms of retention and effect on behavior. The client will remember a goal that is specific and will also find a specific goal easier to achieve.

Recommendations for Practice

Learning Objectives

One planning method you can use to help ensure success for teaching and learning is to establish objectives and goals. In patient education literature, goals are defined as long-term global statements such as improving one's health, losing weight, taking medication, and exercising regularly. Behavioral objectives are short-term precise statements of what the client or patient will be able to achieve after learning has taken place. The more precise the objective is in terms of defining what the behavior is to be, the easier it will be for you and for your client to know when the expected outcome has been achieved.

Examples of behavioral objectives are:

- To lose one pound per week for the next four weeks.
- To take own blood pressure accurately.

The most desirable behavioral objectives are written to include how learning will take place. The conditions under which learning will take place are now described for the second objective above.

This objective could be rewritten to say:

- Given the opportunity to view an instructional film on blood pressure and to practice under the supervision of a nurse, the client will be able to take his/her own blood pressure accurately.

Contractual Management

Another method used for planning educational outcomes is a contractual system in which rules regarding some health behavior or goal are specified. The contractual statements are positive and clear, and the client usually decides on the rewards or punishments. This method allows a client to gain control over her life and to develop a sense of success and independence by fulfilling the contract. When specific rewards are identified, a contract also provides some incentive for realizing goals.

Contracting has been used with some success in treating obesity and alcoholism, and it has been used as a preventive strategy to improve blood pressure control. In one study, patients chose their own blood pressure intervention (medication compliance, weight loss, or stress management). Inexpensive reinforcements were provided as part of the contracts. An example of a reinforcement would be depositing money in a jar each time the medication is taken and then later using that money for a luxury item. In this case, using contracts was successful in helping patients lower their blood pressure and lose weight.

Instructional Aids

You should use a variety of instructional materials and you should design your materials with the differing attention spans and interests of your clients in mind. You also need to consider the interests and cultural and ethnic backgrounds of your clients and your own skill in using materials. You can prepare or purchase audio-visual aids, audio-cassettes, and handouts. Most health care settings have communication departments that can offer assistance in preparing materials.

Demonstrating new skills, reviewing handouts with your client, and encouraging clients to paraphrase written materials are important aspects of the teaching-learning process. You also should help your clients integrate new learning into their lifestyles by anticipating what their new behavior might mean to others in their lives. For example, a client who is learning about weight reduction must become aware that some friends or relatives might not want to see her slim down and may sabotage her best efforts. A significant part of learning entails identifying interrelationships and the relevancy of the new behavior.

Evaluation

Evaluation can help you judge whether your client is achieving goals in a timely fashion, decide whether new strategies need to be developed or old ones revised, and help you measure your effectiveness as a teacher. You need to evaluate both throughout the process (formative evaluation) and at the end of a project or period (summative evaluation).

One way to handle formative evaluation is to develop a series of questions designed to show whether your client is making progress toward her objective. Calling your client on the telephone or providing opportunities for feedback are examples of formative evaluation. If your client has met her objective, then the evaluation is positive. You can judge your effectiveness as a teacher by determining how well your clients accomplish their goals and through the feedback your clients provide.

Compliance and Motivation

Getting patients to comply with medical regimens is sometimes difficult. The word *compliance* suggests conformity, so *cooperation* may be a more appropriate synonym in the context of this chapter.

As health care providers, we want our clients to stay well. And staying well frequently requires sustained therapy and compliance with established regimens. Research has shown that compliance can be substantially improved by setting goals and rewarding each improvement through encouragement and praise. Reducing the complexity of a regimen is likely to be most effective in improving compliance when it is coupled with educational efforts to increase a client's knowledge and comprehension. Tailoring treatment to the client's daily routine may also promote compliance. Success in gaining compliance appears to be linked to the teaching-learning principles and strategies already discussed. Some people think that compliance will cease to be an issue when health professionals become successful teachers and integrate sound learning and behavioral techniques into clinical practice.

Motivation is also an important force in learning. Assessing a client's potential for change and ultimate success is discussed in Chapter 7. Characteristics such as good mental health, average intelligence, family support, and a sense of responsibility to others have been linked to taking control of ones health and developing a healthy lifestyle.

Developing counseling skills that incorporate motivational strategies and theories is an important part of teaching and learning. As a health practitioner you must develop appropriate motivational skills and then learn how to apply them individually to each client or patient in illness or health. The real challenge is not only to educate patients fully about their illness, but also to optimize their health and wellness by using motivational and compliance assessment techniques.

Chapter Summary

Client education is a vital component of medical care and treatment. It ensures that the client acquires the knowledge and skills needed to change behavior, attitudes, and values. Client education is also cost effective, provides for professional accountability, meets the client's needs for personalized care, supports the client's concept of personal worth, and expands the role of the health professional to include health promotion and disease prevention. Client education seeks to employ the most up-to-date theories on teaching and learning. It emphasizes basic components of the learning process, including specifying learning outcomes at the onset of instruction and by evaluating client progress and objectives met.

Client education is a fundamental part of practice for both the beginning health professional and for the 10-year veteran. Do it well and both you and your clients will be enriched beyond measure.

Review

Accrue: increase, to be added
Auditory: related to hearing
Formative: done while in process, to build upon
Interactive: participation/involvement comes from more than one side
Kinesthetic: having to do with motion
Laity: nonprofessionals
Primacy: coming first
Summative: done at the end, as a summary
Visual: related to seeing

1. List the pros and cons of involving the patient/client in establishing the goals of treatment.
2. How would a paramedic/social worker/family planning worker or lab technician use education techniques with clients?

3. Think of your home community. What type of educational programs might best benefit this community's maintenance of wellness?

Additional Reading

Cotanch, P. H. 1984. Health Promotion in Hospitals. In *Behavioral Health*, edited by J. D. Matarazoo, et al. New York: John Wiley and Sons.

Douglas, P. D. 1986. Practice Implications of Health Promotion and Disease Prevention in Allied Health. *J. Allied Health* 15: 323-327.

Eckerling, L., and M. B. Kohrs, 1984. Research on Compliance and Diabetic Regimens: Applications to Practice. *J. Am. Diet. Assoc.* 84: 805-809.

Fox, C. 1987. Increasing Patient Compliance in Cardiac Rehabilitation Centers. *Card. Mangmt.* Feb./March: 31-38.

Gorder, D.D. et al. 1986. Dietary Intake in the Multiple Risk Factor Intervention Trial (MRFIT): Nutrient and Food Group Changes over 6 years. *J. Am. Diet. Assoc.* 86: 744-751.

Green, L. W., et al. 1980. *Health Education Planning.* Palo Alto: Mayfield Publishing Co.

Grubb, A. 1981. Roles, Relevance, Cost of Hospital Education and Training Debated. *Hospitals.* 75-79.

Hamburg, M. V. 1986. Health Education: A Tool for Preventive Care in Allied Health. *J. Allied Health.* 15: 305-308.

Havenstein, D. J., M. R. Schiller and R. S. Hurley. 1987. Motivational Techniques of Dietitians Counseling Individuals with Type II Diabetes. *J. Am. Diet. Assoc.* 87: 37-47.

Hogue, C. C. 1979. Nursing and Compliance. In *Compliance in Health Care.* R. B. Haynes, D. W. Taylor, and D. L. Sackett. Baltimore: The Johns Hopkins University Press.

Holcomb, J. D., P. D. Mullen, and C. E. Fasser. 1985. Health Behaviors and Beliefs of Four Allied Health Professionals Regarding Health Promotion and Disease Prevention. *J. Allied Health.* 14: 373-385.

Kirscht, J. P., and I. M. Rosenstock. 1982. Patient's Problems in Following Recommendations of Health Experts. In *Health Psychology*, edited by G. C. Stone, F. Cohen, and N. E. Adler. San Francisco: Jossey-Bass.

Mattern, W. D., D. Weinholtz, and C. P. Freidman. 1983. The Attending Physician as Teacher. *New England J. Med.* 308: 1129-1132.

National Commission on Allied Health Education. 1980. *The Future of Allied Health Education.* San Francisco: Jossey-Bass.

Phillips, J. A. and F. P. Hekelmau. 1983. The Role of the Nurse as a Teacher: A Position Paper. *Nephrology Nurse.* Sept/Oct.: 42-46.

Steckel, S. B., and M. A. Swain. 1977. Contracting with Patients to Improve Compliance. *J. Am. Hosp. Assoc.* 51: 81-84.

Totson, D. 1975. The Right to Know: Public Education for Health. *J. Med. Ed.* 50: 117-123.

Zifferblatt, S. M. 1975. Increasing Patient Compliance Through the Applied Analysis of Behavior. *Prev. Med.* 4: 173-182.

Chapter

9

After reading this chapter, you should be able:
- To contrast inter- and intradisciplinary communication.
- To discuss the difference in roles of consultant, collaborator, and referral source.
- To understand the use of the word "network."
- To list different kinds of interdisciplinary communication, together with advantages and disadvantages of each.
- To discuss different examples of role sharing.
- To decide when it would be in the patient's best interest for you to share roles.
- To understand the functioning of teams.

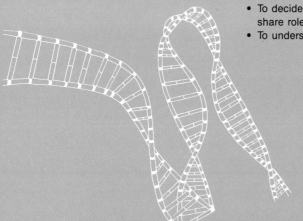

Interdisciplinary Communication

A role can be defined as all the behaviors expected from a person who occupies a particular position and status in a social pattern. In considering what is expected of us as health professionals, we will examine changing roles, communication roles, who defines roles, and the specific roles of consultant, collaborator, and referral source.

Your Roles as a
Health Professional

Changing Roles

The role of yesteryear is not the role of today. Society changes, technology changes, the law changes, the allied health professional changes. The advent of amniocentesis, for example, changed the genetic counselor's role dramatically. In certain states, the nurse midwife is prohibited by law from independent practice. But, when the law changes, so too will the role of the nurse midwife.

Most health professionals are expanding their roles. Podiatrists, for example, are moving away from the foot and more toward the body mechanics involved with walking and running. They now meet the needs of a society that is interested in jogging.

Health care providers are becoming increasingly involved in management. In days past, they may have been heavily involved in one-on-one patient care, personal care, psychological support, and surgical aftercare. Now they face a different world. The complexities of modern pharmacology, for example, make drug dispensing to hospitalized patients a specialized and critical task. Because lawsuits are so common in our society, health care providers spend a lot of time on documentation. It is now common to find many kinds of nursing specialists in hospitals; for example, pediatric physical therapists, respiratory therapists, occupational therapists, rehabilitation therapists, and cardiac rehabilitation therapists. New problems in society have even created a need for new professionals, such as the medical records specialists.

Inter- and Intradisciplinary Communication

Communication within a team is dealt with later in this chapter. Our topic here is one-on-one communication. An important aspect of your role in such communication is whom you are talking to. From studying Chapter 3, you already know how transactional analysis works. You also need to be aware of the difference between intradisciplinary communication and interdisciplinary communication.

Intradisciplinary communication is communication between members of the same health specialty, for example, when one physical therapist speaks to another. **Interdisciplinary communication** is communication between different health practitioners, for example, when a dietitian speaks to an occupational therapist. The language you speak and the role you assume are affected by whether you are communicating with someone who works within your own discipline and your relative positions within the hierarchy of command.

Who Defines the Role?

Patients usually prefer to get to know one person well and relate to that person for their health needs. But health care is a highly specialized field with multiple areas of expertise, so one health care provider cannot always possess the necessary expertise. As a health practitioner, you must be able to assess when it would be in your patient's best interest for you to share roles with another expert. Here you yourself will be defining your role. Sometimes your role will be defined by your patient and sometimes it will be defined by pure chance or circumstance.

Consider this example. A physical therapist in private practice is seeing a patient for neck pain. The patient, a 55-year-old man, asks about back pain, which he has had for 20 years. Would it be appropriate for the therapist to refer this patient to a physician? The answer is that it depends on the desires of the patient, but the patient probably wants the physical therapist to deal with it. What if this patient were to mention that his mother has just died and then spends 10 minutes talking about it? Now the physical therapist would need to use her own judgment about a mental health referral. She may be the only access point the patient has to the health care system. Referral probably would be made only if the physical therapist thought the grief reaction were becoming pathological.

Sometimes the patient defines your role by talking about psychological problems because you are the health practitioner she or he feels comfortable with or because you just happen to be there at the right time. For this reason, all health care workers need to be aware of crisis intervention therapy.

Crisis intervention therapy involves brief counseling, typically for a few weeks, to resolve a major crisis in a patient's life. Such therapy focuses on environmental modification and decision making rather than on deep psychological issues. Crisis intervention therapy is usually used when the patient's premorbid personality is relatively healthy and when the patient can understand the maladaptive responses that may have been involved in the crisis. Not every situation warrants this type of intervention. The health care provider needs to explore the situation sufficiently to judge whether such brief intervention would be appropriate.

Who else defines your role? Frequently a hospital or clinic has written or unwritten job descriptions for its employees. Applicants often see a written job description before they are employed. Obviously the health professional in private practice is in a far better position to define his or her own role and has more latitude than an employed health professional does.

But a written job description need not contradict your professional activity and ethics within your chosen field.

Your own perception is an important determinant in defining your role. What is the scope of your specialty? How does your specialty fit in with other specialties? What have people in your specialty done historically? Your perceptions after training and while in practice will further mold your own role definition. What are the potentialities of your specialty? What do you feel most comfortable doing? How do you see yourself best relating to other specialties? What meaningful role expansion do you perceive? What are your time constraints?

One further important determinant of your role is liability, which imposes legal restraints on your role. Whereas, for example, obstetric nurses are permitted to deliver babies in some states, in other states it is illegal. When should we refer? How much testing should we do?

How much documentation is necessary? How much explaining is appropriate for each patient? What if the hospital tells you to do something you do not feel comfortable doing? These are the sorts of issues in which liability may determine your role.

The Roles of Consultant, Collaborator, and Referral Source

A **consultant** usually acts as a temporary adviser on current problems. The consultant does not necessarily need to see patients.

Scheduling problems in an X-ray department, for instance, could be discussed with a consultant. An outside or inside consultant could be used. An outside consultant such as a time and motion study expert might make recommendations that would be objective. If the recommendations were rejected, the outside consultant would be unlikely to experience any role conflicts. Alternatively, an inside consultant, for instance the chief of the school of X-ray technology, might be asked for an opinion. This person would be more likely than an outside person to know the personalities involved, to understand the subtleties of how the department functions and to understand the workings of the X-ray department. But it would be harder to reject this person's opinions because they would be the opinions of an insider.

Collaborators are two or more people working together to a common end. They may share or even exchange roles. There is give and take in the relationship.

A **referral source** is someone to whom the health professional turns for material information or to transfer patient care. An example would be a physical therapist referring a patient to an occupational therapist for swallowing problems after a stroke. A referral source is not an adviser and may play a continuing role, which is the opposite of the consultant role.

Sharing Roles

Formal and Informal Teams and Networks

Health care is provided by health care teams that may be quite apparent or hidden. When a person is admitted to the hospital, the health team is apparent, but when a person visits a dentist's office the team is hidden. The dentist may refer a dental problem to a hygienist, periodontist, endodontist, or another specialist or may discuss a problem with a medical doctor. He or she may even admit a patient to the hospital, for example, for anesthesia. The patient is therefore using a hidden network that the dentist can activate at any time.

Almost all health care professionals are part of a network. (Communicating with other network members provides a good opportunity to utilize your communication skills.) If the health care team is apparent and obvious, we call it a **formal network** or **formal team**. Teams may come together physically, as in a patient care conference, for example. Or teams may never actually come together, but use, for instance, the patient's hospital chart for communication between team members. Such an arrangement may be called an **informal team**.

Types of Networks

Sharing roles in health care may be carried out in a number of ways, as illustrated in Figure 9.1

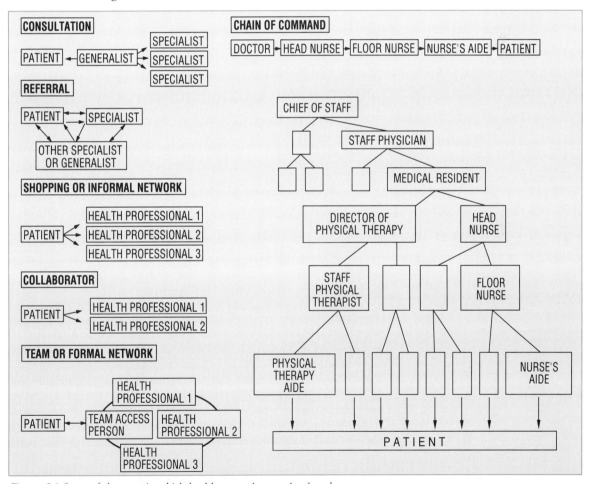

Figure. 9.1 Some of the ways in which health care roles may be shared.

A pyramid, the last example in Figure 9.1, is also a team, but it emphasizes a hierarchy with a formal pecking order. As a health care provider, you should ideally know the area of expertise and role of each person in a pyramid or team and should use each person to the best advantage for each of your patients. Unfortunately, resentments, jealousy, and other human emotions often create conflict within a network. What would you do, for example, if you were a physical therapist and a physician ordered passive range of motion exercises on a limb due to be amputated within a few days? Would you merely carry out the order blindly? Would you call the physician and talk about it? Would you check with other physical therapists in the department?

The Relationship of Allied Health Professionals to Physicians

How do allied health professionals relate to physicians? How autonomous are they? The answer depends on where the health professional is on the continuum of technician to professional. An EKG technician takes a cardiogram when the physician directs. A psychologist, who is on the other end of the continuum, can be an independent professional.

Autonomy is more likely if:

- The professional has a complex expertise.
- The professional is licensed by the state legislature or is an independent practitioner.
- The professional is separately reimbursed by third party payers.
- The professional is not wholly dependent on the physician for liability.

Sharing Expertise Versus Sharing the Burden

The reasons for referral, collaboration, consultation, or networking are many. Usually the reason should be that referral or consultation is best for the patient physically, psychologically, and financially. Sometimes, however, referral is made for the professional's psychological benefit; we call this passing the buck. At other times, it may be made for the patient's psychological benefit. Before such a referral is made, the professional involved needs to examine why the patient is demanding it, what might be done about it, and whether he or she can realistically do anything about the situation. After this exercise, the professional may find that, if a referral is necessary, it may be to a social or mental health worker rather than to a dietitian or physician or physical therapist.

Personality Conflicts and Turf Issues

Personality conflicts are inevitable. Some health professionals are authoritarian, some are casual, some are unprofessional, some are prejudiced, and others are ineffectual. Even though in our roles as health professionals we may strive to set ourselves apart from ordinary human failing, we are still human. Each of us must examine our own strengths and weaknesses and try to discuss conflicts sensitively and professionally.

Turf refers to territorial rights within an area of expertise. If you step outside your area of expertise, you are in danger of stepping on the toes of other health professionals. Someone will be offended. You must be particularly sensitive about turf issues until you know your way around a network in a particular locale. You should take on a role that is consistent with your specialty and tread lightly outside that area until you know the ground better. Alternatively, you can discuss turf issues with others within your network or with an outside mentor. You also should think about how you feel when someone steps on **your** turf.

The most effective way to deal with turf issues and all issues of both formal and informal networks is through use of good communication skills. Focusing on the needs of our peers, paraphrasing, and establishing a rapport help us to function better and enjoy our work.

The Position of the Student in Shared Roles

Although as a student you may feel awkward, you actually have an advantage. As a nonexpert, you have just come from the patient's world. You generally can assume a role of patient advocate and confidante much more easily than a teacher can. You may have much more time to spend with the patient. You may be regarded by the patient as someone who is half health professional and half friend. In assuming this role, you are creating a stepping stone that allows for a gradual shift to the role of fully fledged health professional.

Networks

Networking means marshalling people, systems, agencies, or resources that a specific person needs at a specific time. A system here refers to a segment of society; for example, family or work.

In a business sense, networks often involve computer information and people like business managers, politicians, or others who are good at networking. In a social sense, networks are people in a patient's life who interact with him or her, like family, friends, or business contacts.

An effective networker knows who has the key talents and empowers the user to use these talents. Rather than simply providing a list of resources, the good networker motivates the patient to utilize resources.

In this section we discuss teams. Not all teams meet at set times around a table and deal with printed agendas. In the real world, most health practitioners are part of information teams.

Patients in a hospital usually have multiple health care providers caring for them, often using the physician as case manager or networker. Communication between disciplines is chiefly through the hospital chart, to which health professionals have open access (incidentally, confidentiality may be a problem here).

Outpatients often have a single professional caring for them, so no networking or case manager is required. Communication is by telephone or letter to other professionals, and confidentiality is quite good.

For hospital health professionals the corridor consultation is a common means of communication. As the name implies, this is usually a brief chance meeting with another health professional during which clinical problems are discussed. Proximity certainly is valuable to this form of communication.

Modes of Interdisciplinary Communication

Interdisciplinary communication has always been a problem in the health care field. There is not enough of it, it takes too long, and it is filled with irrelevancies such as filling out forms, listening to what you already know, and so on. Interdisciplinary communication needs to be specific and relevant to a case plan or problem. For instance, a nurse should not just call up a social worker and request a consultation. The social worker needs to know why the patient needs to be seen. Is it for social casework? Is it to arrange a walker at home when the patient leaves the hospital? Or is it because the patient, despite the best efforts of nurse and physician, still seems to deny his heart attack and this denial could jeopardize his chance for a safe recovery?

In general, health practitioners communicate with one another through case conferences; telephone calls; letters, forms, and notes; and the medical record.

Case Conferences. Multiple case conferences improve patient care and time efficiency. As noted earlier, in the ideal world, interdisciplinary communication is best conducted through a case conference. But to assemble six health practitioners for one hour to discuss one patient means that there must be a reasonable expectation that something will come out of the meeting. All too often, however, one health professional will go off on a tangent that wastes everyone's time or another will be more interested in protecting her or his turf than in sharing information.

Generally, then, case conferences are held only when a patient cannot be adequately cared for without them. Case conferences may be held routinely with specific disease states like burns or renal failure. Everyone involved must be highly specific, and everyone must agree on a common focal point. In hospitals, case care conferences often focus on how the patient can best be helped to cope at home.

Telephone Calls.   Like other types of communication, telephone communication must be specific. If the message can reasonably be conveyed another way through a filled-out requisition form, for example, then interruptions during patient care, messages to call back, etc., can be kept to a minimum.

Telephone technique is very important, not only in communicating with health practitioners but also in dealing with patients. If possible, you should answer the telephone within three rings, and preferably after the first ring. Greet the caller and identify your department and yourself; for example, "Good morning, pharmacy, John Reed speaking."

Because the telephone permits no nonverbal cues, it is especially important that you project your attitude (which will be friendly and professional, we hope) over the telephone. It is helpful if you smile while using the telephone. If you make the same facial expressions while listening on the phone as you would during face-to-face communication, your pauses and comments will come at the right time and will be more appropriate.

Being a good listener is even more important on the phone than in face-to-face communication. Because you cannot look the caller in the eye, it is important to use the caller's name.

If you cannot do what the caller asks, be sure to ask what should or can be done; for example, "I'm afraid I can't see your patient tomorrow, but would the next day be all right? Would you like me to call you after I've seen her or should I just write my comments on the chart?"

Letters, Forms, and Notes.   Written communication should be brief and specific. Because letters of referral document the communication in writing, it may actually be less time consuming to write a letter than to try to reach someone on the telephone. Remember that it is unprofessional to make a referral without specific communication as to why the patient has been referred. Both the reason for referral and the answer to that reason should be communicated through accepted channels for every consultation, collaboration, or referral.

The Medical Record. For hospitalized patients the medical record is the major form of interdisciplinary communication. Unfortunately, many physicians do not take the time to document the patient's progress adequately in the chart. On the other hand, nurses' notes are sometimes so lengthy that they discourage good communication. An even more appalling innovation is computer generation of progress notes in narrative form based on punched-in information and superimposed on an excessively wordy base. Such a report may look useful in court, but it is dangerous because it hinders communication. An ideal medical record is clear, concise, brief, legible, and all-accessible in one easily available chart.

Medical records are frequently used in court litigation. What you write and whether it can be read may be pivotal in a malpractice case. Unfortunately, physicians tend to set the worst example by frequently writing illegible and sketchy notes.

Examples of Health Care Teams

The Hospice Team. Hospice care is a relatively new concept that relies heavily on teamwork. The hospice approach emphasizes:

- Continuing care by a group of health practitioners.
- The acceptance of death as imminent (usually patients are accepted in such programs only if death is expected within six months). Symptom relief, not saving life, is stressed. Hospice patients, therefore, always have no code orders in a hospital.
- A lot of time for talking, especially talking related to death and dying.
- The involvement of family and friends whenever possible.
- Maintaining the patient at home whenever possible.

The hospice team is typically composed of a hospice coordinator (usually a nurse or social worker/psychologist), priest or minister, pharmacist, physician hospice director, patient's personal physician, hospital nurse, home nurse, social worker, trained volunteer and psychologist or thanatologist. The patient typically interacts with the team, chiefly through the psychologist/thanatologist, and often through the hospice coordinator or nurse, the patient's private physician, and the home visiting nurse. The pharmacist/home supplies specialist and physician program director may have little direct contact with the patient.

Regular, often weekly, meetings are held, and inpatients and out-patients in the program are monitored. The hospice coordinator or physician program director may be in charge of the meetings, but the patient's personal primary care physician is in charge of the patient's overall care. Like any other team, the hospice team may have shy, overbearing, puffed up, or sensitive members. Decisions are often made by consensus, however, and the decision-making process guides the primary care physician and establishes policy for the workers who have primary patient contact, especially the hospital nurse or home nurse. Relationships between team members are generally open and trusting. Communication after team meetings is usually good.

The Rehabilitation Wardround

The wardround, which represents an informal team, is not necessarily scheduled. It may be "after lunch" or on "Friday mornings usually." The usual team members are the rehabilitation physician (may be an orthopedist, rheumatologist, physiatrist, or neurologist), physical therapists, occupational therapists, the rehabilitation coordination nurse, the floor nurse or charge nurse, the social worker or rehabilitation counselor, and involved patients. The purpose of the wardround is to monitor and give direction to coordinated patient rehabilitation. The patients typically are victims of strokes or auto accidents or are paraplegics or amputees. Dietitians frequently play a vital role with the rehabilitation team.

Anyone may be in charge; it may be the person with the dominant personality or it may vary from patient to patient. The meeting takes place at each patient's bedside. Even though various members of the team do not always show up, the team still functions, and in this respect roles may be shared. Although the rehabilitation nurse coordinator may be considered responsible, team members may regard the rounds more as a forum for exchanging information than as a management technique.

The Hospital Team. Of all the possible teams, perhaps the most important is the hospital team. It represents both a formal health network and an informal health team with people coming and going. There may be several teams within the hospital team. Communication is primarily through the patient's chart. Numerous health professionals may see the patient on a consultant, collaborative, or referral basis, or as members of various teams. The hospital is an instant network for the patient.

Other examples of teams include discharge planning teams, social work teams, cardiac rehabilitation teams, visiting nurse teams, and psychiatric casework teams. The list is almost endless.

Interdisciplinary Communication

CHAPTER 9

Who is in charge?

Logically, it might seem that the responsible person should be in charge, but responsibility can be transferred by appointing a team head. Alternatively, responsibility can lie with the case manager. A team leader heads a team that may be devoted to anything (for example, an infection control committee or care for 10 patients). A case manager handles a single patient only.

Another way of selecting the team leader is to choose a professional who is good at networking. Managers in the business world are selected on the same principle. The best person to be case manager is usually the person who is a good networker by training or aptitude. Such a person knows who has specific skills and where the resources are, and can empower people to use them. This person can manage the show for the patient.

Common case managers are physicians, social workers, nurses, physical therapists, occupational therapists, and psychologists. The case manager could be the patient as long as he or she is not depressed, psychologically disturbed, or psychologically immature, and as long as the patient retains insight. Some patients are best managed by a particular health professional. For example, an indigent unwed pregnant teenager may be managed well by a social worker. A patient with multiple nursing needs, like ostomy, wounds, and home IV therapy, may be most aptly managed by a nurse. A patient with multiple medical problems and recurrent hospitalizations may be best managed by a physician.

Although legally the physician is the patient's case manager in a hospital, this may not always be appropriate. Physicians sometimes discriminate and may not allow other health professionals to play their part.

Outpatients may have anyone as a case manager. The good networker is the ideal person. In practice, it is often a social worker, nurse, psychologist, or physician.

The case manager is the person who is ultimately responsible for the patient's care and who must coordinate all aspects of the patient's health care. If we remember the definition of health as not simply the absence of disease, but a state of complete physical, mental, and social well-being, it is clear that the patient's health encompasses a great deal. The primary emphasis must be on the patient's needs.

What Is a Team?

A team is a group of individuals with a common purpose who communicate, collaborate, and consolidate knowledge. In most cases, there is some outcome beyond intellectual consolidation. A task focus is the outcome toward which the team is working.

Each member of a team has his or her own position. That position entails the individual's personality as well as her or his perspective, team position, and expertise.

The **personality** of a team member may determine the person's ability to produce an effect. The person's power, team position, and flexibility are all reflections of their personality. Whether a person is an introvert or an extrovert, for instance, will affect how the person functions on the team. Personality may be expressed differently in team settings than in private settings. Examples of team personalities include catalyst, facilitator, devil's advocate, and boss.

Team position refers to a person's role. It may be a labeled position (team leader), an assumed position (physical therapist), or an unassumed position (devil's advocate). The generalist is the patient's mouthpiece to others within the team. Sometimes teams are leaderless. Sometimes the patient may be made team leader. The leader is ultimately responsible for how the team functions.

Some people naturally grab power; others are unassuming. Power in a team setting may be appointed or nonappointed. Power refers to the ability to exercise authority, in particular to punish or reward. Powerful people also tend to coerce team members to think as they do. This tendency can become stifling, inhibiting the free flow of ideas and resulting in a team in which all members tend to think alike.

Status refers to a person's position in the network pecking order. Power implies expression of control. Status implies rank, without necessarily expression of power. Each team member has their own status, which affects how other members of the team react to them and their ideas.

Flexibility of personalities and roles in a team is important. If the team leader is absent, it is good if another can easily take the role of leader for that meeting. If there is disagreement, it is ideal if team members can accept the right to disagree without feeling angry or inadequate.

Team members often are appointed on the basis of **expertise** rather than personality. The hospice team, for example, contains a pharmacist, nurse, physician, and so on. The area of expertise may be further defined, for example, by requiring the home care nurse and the hospital floor nurse. The team member's labeled position is often simply the person's area of expertise; for example, pharmacist.

Team members all have their own unique **perspective**, which entails many factors beyond expertise and personality. For example, one X-ray technician may be a 60-year-old religious, widely-traveled father who is new to the community, whereas another X-ray technician may be an atheistic, unmarried 27-year-old local woman. Such differences make each team member unique and special.

Some Requirements for Effective Teaming

A successful team requires much of its members, particularly understanding, willingness, trust, and a focus on the patient as the center of the team's effort. Each team member must understand the roles of team members as well as the strengths and weaknesses of their personalities and their areas of expertise. Each team member must be willing to share some professional responsibilities when it is in the patient's best interest. Team members must trust that:

- Other team members will put the patient's needs over their own.
- The team will still function if one or two team members are absent, and team members will substitute for each other when necessary and safe.
- Other health professionals will take responsibility for their actions.
- Giving and receiving feedback is not an interpersonal battle, but it is necessary to optimal team function.

Finally, team members must focus on the patient as the center of the team's effort. If may be helpful to include the patient as a key member of the team. Doing so will enhance communication, increase control and responsibility for the patient, and decrease ethical dilemmas. If the patient is mentally fit, he or she may even be the ideal team leader.

Chapter Summary

In this section we have focused on examples of the idealized team, rather than on informal teaming. We have discussed the different methods of interdisciplinary communication, who is in charge of the team (team leader) and of the patient (case manager). We have talked about requirements for effective teaming, and how each member's position in a team encompasses personality, perspective, team position, and expertise.

The aspiring health practitioner needs to be skilled not only in communicating with patients but also with other health professionals.

Review

Collaborator: two people working together to a common end for material information or to transfer patient care

Consultant: temporary adviser on current problems

Crisis intervention: brief therapy to resolve a major crisis in a patient's life

Health: Not simply the absence of disease but a state of complete physical, mental, and social well-being

Hierarchy: Rank or order of people or things, each one being below or above another

Interdisciplinary communication: between members of different health specialties

Intradisciplinary communication: between members of the same health specialty

Network: System of channels of actual or potential communication with different people or agencies

1. What is the significance of the difference between inter- and intradisciplinary communication?
2. Describe a network in your school. Is it formal / informal or hidden / revealed?
3. How would you answer a patient who complains that anyone can look in his chart in the hospital and that the information is not confidential?
4. Design a form for interdisciplinary communication to go in a patient's chart. What are the important ingredients of this form?
5. List items of telephone technique which we call good telephone manners.
6. Give an example of a team in which you have been involved. What was your role, who was in charge and what was the purpose of the team? What were the major problems encountered in fulfilling that end?

7. What is a case manager?
8. What is a team leader?
9. List the different factors which characterize a team member's position on a team.

Additional Reading

Brill, N. I. *Teamwork: Working Together in Human Services.* J. B. Lippincott Company, Philadelphia, PA. 1976.

Ducanis, A. J., and Golin, A. K. *The Interdisciplinary Health Care Team — A Handbook.* Aspen Systems Corporation, Germantown, MD. 1979.

Rubin, I. M., Plovnick, M. S., and Fry, R. E. *Improving the Coordination of Care: A Program for Health Team Development.* Ballinger Publishing Co., Cambridge, MA. 1975.

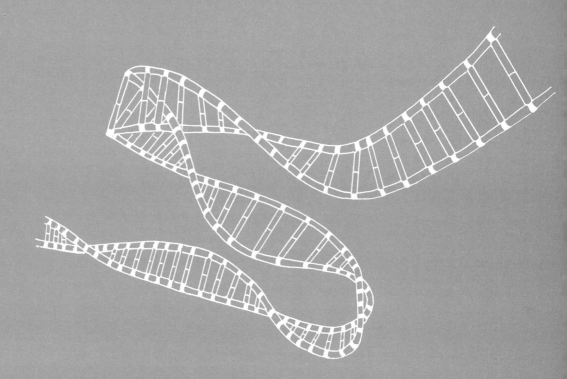

Professional Issues

Chapter
10

After reading this chapter, you should be able:
- To better define the term "ethics."
- To distinguish between an ethical code and a legal one.
- To describe basic responsibilities or ethical principles of a health care provider.
- To better examine concepts such as "evaluation," "objectivity," and "informing."
- To discuss and analyze current ethical dilemmas.

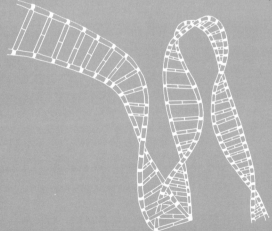

Professional Ethics

The term ethics is difficult to define. We might define ethics as a code of moral behaviors that enable the health care provider to distinguish right from wrong. But whose view of moral behavior would we use? Who would decide right from wrong and in which culture and at which time and place? Although ethical and moral standards are often linked, they are, of necessity, separate entities.

What Are Ethics?

During the 19th century, medical codes were frequently called etiquettes. An etiquette is considered useful because it avoids the problems of defining morality. An etiquette *presumes* an "upright man instructed in the art of healing." *Decorum* is more literally the medical etiquette of the Hippocratic oath. This etiquette chiefly governs the professional contacts of members and defines professional courtesy. Well-intentioned, educated people disagree on many of the issues related to modern health care. Although some moral questions evoke striking moral consensus (for example, whether to legalize rape, terrorism, or child abuse), issues of health care ethics seem always to evoke persistent disagreements (for example, abortion, right-to die, confidentiality in relation to communicable diseases, urine testing.)

The ethics of the American Psychological Association offer a pragmatic view. Here the term *ethics* refers to a set of guidelines for professionals primarily designed to ensure public or consumer safety. A professional claims the right to profess something, and ethical guidelines define the scope of that professing so the public can be

reasonably certain of what the knowledge and practice of a given professional entails. It is important that the patient can trust the health professional. Knowing that a health professional is highly ethical helps the patient's trust to develop. Any violation of ethical principles represents a violation of public trust — a violation of all patients. Such violations also undermine and harm the status of all professionals.

Ethics differ from the law in two major ways. First, an ethical principle tends to be **absolute**. That is, either the health professional did or did not behave in an ethical manner. Legal decisions usually involve a qualifying factor of **degree**. Both torts (civil actions involving harm or injury) and criminal law focus on a degree of negligence or intention to do harm. The more rigid view of professional ethics stems from a value that the public needs to believe in exemplary conduct from health professionals. This is a matter of public trust. The consumer must be able to believe that the health professional acts to protect and enhance the well-being of the consumer, not in any self-serving manner. The **consequences** of legal and ethical violations also differ. Legal convictions generally result in **fines, probation and service, or incarceration**. If a legal conviction is sufficiently serious (a felony, or serious crime, rather than a misdemeanor), professional organizations impose corresponding **sanctions** against the offending member. These sanctions include the possibilities of **reprimand, censure or expulsion, and loss of membership** for the most severe breaches of ethics.

There have been many instances in which acquittal from legal charges did not release the professional from sanctions for unethical behavior. A behavior or practice can, therefore, be legally acceptable but professionally unethical.

For behavior judged to be inappropriate but not clearly unethical, members can be sanctioned through a variety of methods. Consider the following example:

> A physical therapist in private practice has been regularly treating a patient who cannot pay for services. This patient is also a carpenter. The physical therapist suggests that the patient work off some of his debt by putting an addition on the therapist's home. The carpenter agrees but makes some building errors that result in major roof leaks and additional expenses for the therapist. When the carpenter comes in for treatment, the physical therapist has difficulty remaining objective about the patient's care.

This relationship is not unethical, but the health professional is guilty of using poor judgment. In such a case, educative advisory sanctions (cease and desist orders) would constitute typical action from the professional organization. That is, the therapist would be educated about the error in judgment and told to either stop using the carpenter's services or stop treating the carpenter as a patient.

To summarize, our definition of ethics focuses on two principles: concern for the protection of the public and concern for the knowledge and fitness of the health practitioner. It is little wonder that ethics are heavily emphasized on most licensure examinations. A breach of ethics is an embarrassment to all members of a profession and constitutes harm to the public the profession purports to serve.

Overview of Ethical Principles

All health professionals share a common code of ethics. Although wording of various codes may differ slightly from profession to profession, the basic underlying intent does not. For example, the American Physical Therapy Association is just as concerned about the problem of a member sexually abusing a patient as the American Medical Association is — both consider such abuse a tremendous violation of ethics.

The following review of ethical principles was adapted from the *American Psychologist* (1981). It offers a foundation of ethics that is common to all health professionals. This commonality of principles is easy to understand when we accept that all health professional organizations charge their members with basic responsibilities to the public in 10 areas: professional responsibility, competence, moral and legal standards, public statements, confidentiality, welfare of the consumer, professional relationships, assessment techniques, research with human subjects, and care and use of animals.

Professional Responsibility

The principle of responsibility means that health professionals must accept the consequences of their own actions. They must maintain the highest standard of their profession as practitioners, educators, and researchers.

With respect to research, health professionals must never suppress, mislead, or distort their findings. They must choose the subjects they pursue for research carefully and must never accept a research project that could cloud their objectivity or create a conflict of interest. In all instances they must make full disclosure of the limitations of their findings.

As teachers, practitioners, or researchers and in a social context, health professionals must not misuse their influence. Consider the following example:

A man named Theodore D. Sterling, Ph. D., reviewed the American Cancer Society studies linking smoking to lung cancer and published his findings in an article entitled "A Critical Reassessment of the Evidence Bearing on Smoking as a Cause of Lung Cancer" (*American Journal of Public Health,* Sept. 1975, 65:9, pp. 939-953). He concluded that the studies were poorly done, biased, and worthless. He further attempted to convince readers that smoking had **no** influence on lung cancer. Much of Sterling's work was seen as biased. Without reading the document, what opinion do you formulate when we tell you that Sterling's research was funded by the American Tobacco Institute?

Competence

The principle of competence also requires that a high standard of skills be maintained. Health professionals must accurately represent their education, training, specialties, limitations, and boundaries. Duties must be performed in conjunction with careful preparation. If a health professional suffers a health or personal problem (for example, alcoholism or bereavement) that creates conflict with the person's professional effectiveness, she or he must refrain from practicing or must seek help. The person with the problem must seek the help of other professionals to determine what actions he or she needs to take. For example, although some practitioners may be able to work effectively while partially impaired, an objective opinion should be sought to determine the degree of limitation. The following example relates to competence in terms of educational training and boundaries:

An occupational therapist who works in a small general hospital is asked to help fill in for a few weeks while a physical therapist colleague has her baby. The occupational therapist has a strong general knowledge and has often seen physical therapists in action. Would it be ethical for her to teach walking with a prosthetic device? (*Probably not unless the physical therapy staff could prepare and supervise this activity.*)

Moral and Legal Standards

Health care providers must live up to the same standard of moral and legal behavior expected of any other citizen, except when such behavior might compromise their ability to fulfill their professional duties. Health practitioners must be aware of prevailing community standards and must not act in a way that would jeopardize their ability to perform their professional duties. They must always consider the possible impact their actions may have on the public. Further, health professionals must never act to violate or limit the legal or civil rights of others.

A health professional who works in a small private Catholic women's college is troubled by the number of women he sees at the infirmary who know nothing about contraception. In response, he wages an all-out campaign to teach human sexuality and contraception to the students. He places brochures in the infirmary, the dorms, and the hallways of classrooms. He hangs many posters that promote specific contraceptive devices and that feature explicit photos of human anatomy. Many of the students, their parents, and the faculty are offended. Is this health professional guilty of ethical misconduct? (*Yes, the health professional's views are clearly unacceptable when the standard of this community is taken into consideration.*)

Public Statements

Health practitioners may make public statements or advertise their services only to the extent of assisting the public to make informed choices and only within the scope *permitted* by their professional association. Health professionals must accurately represent their own credentials. In no way should they use fear to solicit patients, and, of course, they should make no misleading or false claims about available services or outcomes of treatment. Health professionals should not induce any member of the media to promote them or their services. The name of an individual's professional association should never be used in such a way as to imply endorsement of a product by that association.

A dietitian advertises that services are available for help with weight loss. Credentials, hours, the address, professional affiliations, and fees are listed in a pamphlet. This statement appears at the end of the copy: "If every diet and gimmick has failed, this is the place for you." (*This last statement would represent a breach of ethics because it implies success without any scientific evaluation that would back up such a claim.*)

Confidentiality

The patient has the right to expect that the details of his or her health care will be shared only among those health practitioners who require the information in order to perform their duties. Among some professional groups, patient information can only be shared if the patient gives written consent. In no instance is information about a patient's health to be shared for any non-health-related purpose. Health care providers must always guard the patient's privacy and must not invade that privacy unless they are medically required to do so. Health care workers must also provide reasonable security for records and any written information about patients.

Health professionals who write or lecture about actual cases must have prior written consent or must adequately disguise the case to protect the patient's identity. When professionals work with those who are unable to give informed consent, the best interest of the patient takes precedence.

Health professionals might need to inquire about a patient's sexual contacts from a given point in time should syphilis or AIDS be diagnosed. They do not, however, need to know how many sex partners the patient has ever had nor do they need to inquire about positions or sexual techniques. Such questions betray idle curiosity. Further, should the health professional's best friend live next door to this patient, no overt or covert disclosure of the patient's diagnosis could be made.

Welfare of the Consumer

Health practitioners must act to protect the welfare of their patients. Conflicts may arise between the needs of the patient and those of an institution offering service or between the needs of the patient and health professional. When such conflicts occur, the health professional is responsible for seeing that they are clarified and that all concerned parties are informed.

Health professionals must be aware of their own needs and not use their influence and position to further their needs at the expense of the consumer. Patients are not to be exploited sexually or otherwise.

Before treatment, health care providers inform the consumer about all financial arrangements. Health professionals do not accept financial remuneration for referring patients. When a health care provider believes that a patient is not benefitting or progressing from the services, the provider terminates treatment and refers the patient for appropriate follow-up elsewhere.

> The physical therapy department that John works in continues to accept patients for treatment even after their ultrasound machines have broken down. Therapists offer the patients alternative treatments but feel uneasy because they know they cannot provide the best care. Still, what can John do? The hospital administrator insists that the department not turn away patients who have insurance. (*Clearly, John is bound by ethical standards to explain the treatment limitations to prospective patients. Further, he needs to make it clear to the administration that he will not compromise his treatment standards.*)

Professional Relationships

Health professionals know and understand the competencies of other health professionals. They use available resources to ensure the best possible patient outcomes. Health professionals conduct research within the ethical guidelines and standards of their profession and the institutions for which they work. In the case of publications, health professionals assign credit proportionately with the size of the contribution.

> A patient keeps complaining of persistent morning diarrhea. The health professional maintains that this is the patient's reaction to stress. The patient is treated for stress for 18 months until a conversation between another health professional and the patient reveals the possibility of lactose intolerance. (*The first health professional is bound ethically to know the limitations of treatment and the potentially valuable role of other health professionals. The practitioner failed to act ethically by not calling in a dietitian or physician.*)

Health practitioners do not engage in sexual harassment of either patients or other professionals. When health professionals become aware of ethical violations by other health professionals, they attempt to resolve the problem first informally and then formally if necessary.

A student health professional reports to the clinical supervisor that a clinical professor has continued to ask her for dates even though she has not encouraged him and feels uncomfortable having to repeatedly turn down the advances of someone who must grade her. (*The clinical supervisor speaks to the professor, who readily agrees to stop requesting dates. The matter has been handled informally. Should the professor continue to seek dates with this student, the supervisor would have to make a formal request. It is always preferable to resolve such matters simply and quietly.*)

Assessment Techniques

Health practitioners develop and use only those assessment techniques that meet a high standard. The welfare of the patient is uppermost in considerations related to assessment techniques. Health care providers explain the use, meaning, and validity of all assessments to the patient in understandable language. Further, health providers do not encourage the use of assessment techniques by untrained or unqualified people.

A firm that specializes in the sale of psychological tests frequently makes large volume sales to a health school graduate program. The graduate students then test volunteers and publish the results on such measures as internal/external locus of control, depression, assertiveness, empathy, and self-efficacy. (*The problem here is that the students are not really trained to administer or interpret these tests. The test company is not concerned because it is being well paid for the tests. But the volunteers and the public are being misled into assuming that the test results are valid and meaningful.*)

Research with Human Subjects

Following the horrors of the Tuskegee experiments, in which prisoners from Alabama were intentionally inflicted with syphilis and followed for 30 years without treatment, the then Department of Health, Education, and Welfare established guidelines for human research. These guidelines became law in 1974. Since that time any researcher or institution wishing to receive federal funds has had to comply with these regulations. Because these guidelines also reflect sound ethical practices, health professional organizations have accepted them almost universally.

Health practitioners who wish to conduct research on human subjects must weigh the risks and benefits involved, make arrangements for the issues surrounding prior informed consent, determine whether the research could be conducted without the use of human subjects, and deal with the promises made to subjects.

Risks / Benefits Ratio. If an experiment carries moderate risks with possible major benefits, the risks / benefits ratio is appropriately balanced. An example might be the experimental use of a drug that could cure AIDS. An AIDS victim would gladly risk a side effect, such as loss of hair, for the potential benefit of saving his or her life. But what if the experiment involved injecting volunteers with cancer cells to see how the body's immune system might fight off the cancer? Certainly the ratio here would be heavy on the risk side, and the experiment would offer no obvious benefit. When health professionals are determining what type of research to conduct, a key part of decision making revolves around the risks / benefits ratio. Obviously, the ideal experiment would involve no risk to the human subject and a possible major gain.

Prior Informed Consent. Researchers cannot always adequately judge the benefit of a given experiment. Further, any risk is best judged by those who are going to take the risk. Before an experiment can be conducted, the researcher must gain the written informed consent of the subject or the subject's legal representative. Subjects must be informed of:

- The nature, purpose, and methodology of the research.
- The possible risks and benefits.
- What compensation will be made to them should anything go wrong as a result of the experiment.
- The fact that they can withdraw from the experiment at any time.

In cases in which advanced notice of experimental conditions might render the experiment meaningless, a researcher must consult with experts to change the design in a manner that will permit prior informed consent, or, if this fails, must submit the research proposal for review to gain permission to perform a research deception. The review board of the institution that employs the health professional usually can best determine whether the risks / benefits ratio is worthy of approving a deception.

If a deception is approved, the health professional must:

- Agree to debrief each subject immediately after the experiment has been completed.
- Compensate any subject who has been injured by the deception.
- Withdraw the data of any subject who objects.

Could the Experiment be Done Without Human Subjects?   This question must be one of the first a researcher asks. There are obvious benefits to conducting research on humans if humans are the population that the findings are designed to serve. One of the major criticisms of early cigarette / lung cancer research was that it dealt with the effects of a cigarette smoked by a mouse, not a human.

If an experiment can be conducted validly without using human subjects, this is ideal. If an experiment with human subjects involves little or no risk, it may be labeled *expedited* and given institutional approval with little review. Examples include collection of nail clippings or excreta, tests dealing with normal educational practices, and benign inventories or questionnaires. Research that involves minors or pregnant women, or that entails such activities as exercise or probing psychological inquiry requires full and objective review.

Promises to Subjects.   Only outcomes that are realistic should be mentioned to subjects as potential benefits. Subjects who are asked to volunteer for experiments should make their decisions freely, based on an informed understanding of the experiment. They should not be harrassed, induced, deceived, bribed, or coerced into volunteering. (For example, if a college professor tells students that they must participate in an experiment or flunk the course, the students would have the right to protest this action as coercive.) If rewards, such as copies of the results, are promised to subjects, they should be delivered. If subjects are told that their answers are anonymous, this must be true. If subjects are told that their answers will be kept confidential, they must be kept confidential or they must be disguised beyond any possible recognition.

Care and Use of Animals

Animals should only be used in experiments for a true advancement in knowledge or for the development of human skills. No undue harm should ever be inflicted on an animal. Animals should be cared for humanely. Once it is appropriate to terminate an animal's life, it should be done rapidly and painlessly.

> A researcher who uses rats does not provide food for them on the weekends because it is an inconvenience to the researcher and because the amount of food the rats eat is not essential to the experiment. (*This researcher would be guilty of inhumane treatment. Starving the rats two days each week would cause them discomfort and might cause unnecessarily cruel death.*)

Ethical Concepts Applied in Practice

Although allied health students "become proficient in the technical aspects of their career field, they lack the skills in decision-making related to ethical and moral concerns." If this statement, which was made by a prominent allied health school dean in 1979 is true, we must focus on building the skills to remedy the problem. The fact that studying the absolutes of the basic sciences is so different from studying the complex dilemmas of ethical and moral judgments may contribute to the difficulties students have. In any case, we health professionals must learn to work within the dynamic and complex health care system to form a meaningful value system that works for us. We must borrow from philosophy, logic, and ethics to help develop the thinking of health care providers. The following discussion is based on *A Modular Approach to Ethical Concepts in Health Care* (1979).

Let us consider for a moment the Patient's Bill of Rights. The patient has the right to: respectful care, complete medical information, information requisite for informed consent, refusal of treatment, privacy, confidentiality, response to requests for service, information on other institutions touching on her/his care, refusal of participation in research projects, continuity of care, examination and explanation of financial charges, and knowledge of current hospital regulations.

Can you see the similarities between these rights and the ethical principles we just considered? The patient's right to know the diagnosis and the right to confidentiality and dignity in treatment correspond directly with the principles of assessment techniques, confidentiality, and welfare of the consumer. There apparently is a clear relationship between the professional's ethics and the patient's needs. Unfortunately this relationship is often muddy. In the paragraphs that follow we point out some of the most difficult ethical questions a health care provider must face.

General Questions of Ethics for the Health Practitioner

What constitutes an **evaluation**? How far do health professionals go when evaluating a patient? When do they draw the line on testing? Is this decision based on probability tables, the patient's expressed concerns, cost effectiveness, time effectiveness, a presumed value for the patient's life, the patient's income, or the need to use or not to use some types of equipment? Would the same examinations be performed on two 76-year-old men if one were the President of the United States and the other a street person?

How do we define **objective**? As health practitioners we may think that we evaluate and treat our patients objectively, but we must examine how true this is. Just looking at the questions in the previous paragraph casts doubt on our or any other human being's ability to be objective. The age, social status, disease prognosis, income, gender, family dynamics, and even personality of our patients may affect our ability to be objective. Provided there are some safeguards, being subjective may even be a necessary part of the service we provide. Because we are human beings, our own histories also color our ability to be objective. Yet, strictly speaking, the ethical principles of health professionals are based on an assumption of objectivity.

How **informed** is informed? We believe that the patient has a right to know his or her diagnosis. Do we believe this in every case? Do we, as health care providers, ever give out partial information either to protect the patient from a harsh truth or to persuade the patient that they must comply with our solution? Do we ever justify a deception, such as the use of placebos, if the end result is likely to be improved health?

Most of us would agree that there may be times when a "degree of informed" is sufficient and necessary. But a judgment that wavers from an absolute interpretation of informed is subjective, open to criticism, and potentially unethical.

Ethical Conflicts

There are thousands of ethical dilemmas that health professionals must face. We frequently read about the most dramatic of these conflicts such as right-to-die issues. Recall the Karen Quinlan case, in which court orders were required to remove her from life support equipment.

Health care workers routinely must cope with difficult questions that are filled with both professional and personal conflict. Consider the following example of ethical conflicts, which deal with AIDS, genetic engineering, and transplants.

AIDS. Think of the conflicts that now arise over AIDS. Health practitioners are ethically bound to protect the public and to provide confidentiality of diagnosis. Because AIDS victims are discriminated against and because AIDS is often linked to presumed homosexual activities or intravenous drug use (as discussed in Chapter 7), many of its victims do not want others to know their diagnosis. Thus, an AIDS patient is likely to want his/her diagnosis to be held in confidence. But what about protection of the public? What sexual contacts has the person had while carrying the virus? Is this patient emotionally mature enough to discontinue sexual activity for the sake of others? How would you respond if you knew that poverty often drives an AIDS patient to sell blood?

The confidentiality issue must also be examined in terms of hospital staff. Generally only those who need to know a diagnosis are informed. Hospital records contain this information, however, and the AIDS diagnosis cannot be withheld from records. Also, access to records cannot be different from one patient to another. Otherwise, patients would not be treated with equal confidentiality and suspicion would be drawn to "different" cases. But what happens when the possibility of risk to hospital personnel exists? Should a medical technologist or an assistant be allowed to draw blood from an AIDS patient? Certainly, but they would need to know the diagnosis. What do we say to health care providers who are afraid to work with AIDS patients? Since there is no known cure, can we guarantee their safety? Conflicts around informing the public, remaining objective, and protecting the patient's right of confidentiality are extremely loaded when working with AIDS patients.

Genetic Engineering/Artificial Insemination. What scientists and researchers have seen as breakthroughs, many laypeople have seen as proof of moral decay. "Tampering" with the unborn, promoting pregnancy where "God may not have willed one," determining gender before birth, and aborting an imperfect child are all seen as immoral and horrifying acts by some segments of society. Certainly the potential of genetic engineering raises concerns for the species. For example, do we have the right to develop a baby specification kit whereby would-be parents could take a pill and predict the size, gender, IQ, appearance, and longevity of their child? What ultimate impact would that have on society? Would everyone look alike 30 years from now? Although this possibility may seem far-fetched, scientists must deal with this view of the future.

Transplants. The scientific/medical advances related to the transplantation of human body parts has raised other ethical dilemmas. Not only do we have to decide what constitutes death, as we did with right-to-die issues, but also we have to ask: Who gets the organs when

there are not enough to meet the needs? What is the value or expense of saving a life? Which lives can society afford to save? Is it moral to ask a grieving relative for the organs of their lost loved one? Are artificial devices like the Jarvic heart worth transplanting? What constitutes undue risk or experimentation on a human subject with respect to transplant surgery?

Connie, a young woman with two small children, had suffered severe renal (kidney) failure and was on kidney dialysis three times a week. She felt unwell — tired, lethargic, and bloated — most of the time. She also had to follow a strict diet and severely limit the fluids she drank. It became increasingly difficult for her to function and play a meaningful role in raising her sons. She finally decided to risk kidney transplant.

Because of her weakened health, the only realistic chance Connie had for survival was with a relative-donated organ, which would minimize the chance of her body rejecting the kidney. Connie reported that she was an only child and that her father was her closest living relative other than her tiny sons, whose kidneys would be too small for her body. When her father was interviewed, however, he revealed that Connie had a severely retarded sister who had spent her entire life in an institution. The father was willing to authorize a transplant from his retarded daughter to Connie. There was no way that the retarded daughter could give her consent to the operation.

An organization that protects the rights of the incompetent took issue with this transplant arrangement. They went to court on the retarded daughter's behalf. Connie then went to the institution where her sister lived to help her decide what to do. Although she had been vaguely aware that this sister existed, she had not seen her in over 25 years. What she saw so shocked and saddened her that she refused to pursue taking her sister's kidney. She believed that her sister had suffered so much all through life that she had no right to inflict more suffering for her own gain. Three years later, Connie died of a heart attack following a dialysis treatment.

This case study raises many ethical considerations: How do we gain informed consent from the mentally incompetent? Who has the right to speak for the incompetent? Does a severely ill patient have the right to refuse a lifesaving treatment? What role should the health professional play in this complex drama?

Would your opinion of this case be different if: The surgery (transplant) had taken place and the institutionalized sister had died as a direct result? Connie's body had rejected her sister's kidney? Both women had died as a result of the transplant?

Chapter Summary

This chapter defines ethics as a set of guidelines for professionals that are designed to ensure public safety. The area of ethics encompasses both an understanding of professional responsibilities and an understanding of the professional's limitations. Consequences for a breach of ethics can be imposed by professional organizations. These consequences are different from the punishments typically handed down for legally defined misconduct.

All health professional organizations charge their members with basic responsibilities to the public in 10 areas: professional responsibility, competence, moral and legal standards, public statements, confidentiality, welfare of the consumer, professional relationships, assessment techniques, research with human subjects, and care and use of animals. Understanding these principles can increase the health professional's skill in making ethical judgments. Themes such as prior informed consent and the risks/benefits ratio are key concepts for future health professionals to understand.

A philosophical view of ethical concepts in health care requires that we, as health professionals, question the absolute definition of such constructs as evaluation, objectivity, and informing.

Health professionals currently face many ethical dilemmas. Public safety versus an individual AIDS patient's right to confidentiality, society's views and the possible risks of genetic engineering, and the multiple conflicts of transplant surgery are examples critical to our time.

Absolute: total, all or nothing
Anonymous: without knowledge of name
Benefits vs. risks ratio: weighing relative gain over possible loss
Confidential: kept private
Degree: implies a step in a series
Informed consent: "knowing" permission
Remuneration: compensation, usually financial
Sanctions: giving force or penalty

1. What ethical violations do you believe would be extreme enough to require loss of licensure or the right to practice?
2. Can you think of a health care example in which the health professional might be found guilty of a crime (legally responsible) but *not* in violation of an ethical principle?
3. Can you describe an experiment using human subjects in which a deception might be justified?

Additional Reading

Brahams, D. *Hastings Center Report,* The Hasty British Ban on Commercial Surrogacy. 17(1), 16-19.

Jonsen, A., and Hellegers, A. *Ethics of Health Care,* National Academy of Sciences, Washington, DC.

Levine, C. (Ed.) *Taking Sides,* Dushkin Publishing Co, CT.

Shaw, A. *New England Journal of Medicine,* Dilemmas of Informed Consent in Children, Oct. 25, 885-190.

Smialek, J., and Lambros, Z. *The New Physician,* Reporting AIDS on Death Certificates, May-June 1987.

Wenston, S. Applying Philosophy to Ethical Dilemmas, in *Health Care Ethics,* Anderson and Glesnes-Andersen (Eds.) Aspen Publishing, Rockville, MD.

Yovich, J. *Lancet,* Surrogacy (letter), June 13, 1, 1987.

Chapter

11

After reading this chapter, you should be able:
- To define and to know the signs of various kinds of abuse.
- To list causes of abuse.
- To be able to recognize abused patients.
- To know how to handle cases of abuse.
- To discuss the phenomenon of stigma.
- To list causes and forms of discrimination.
- To describe professional behavior in dealing with emotionally and socially impaired people.

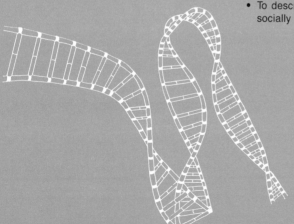

Abuse and Discrimination

Before we begin our discussion, we remind you again that the definition of health is not simply the absence of disease, but a state of total physical, mental, and social well-being.

Abuse

Abuse is the willful infliction of physical or mental pain through acts of commission or omission. Abuse can include deprivation of services necessary to maintain health. **Exploitation** is the process of taking advantage of another. In the case of the elderly, exploitation is using the elder's resources for financial or personal gain. (Although the victim appears to have given consent, there is obvious misuse of their trust or incompetence. Exploitation reflects back to our definition of informed consent and raises the issue of knowing consent.) **Neglect** is the willful infliction of physical or mental pain through acts of omission. Neglect refers particularly to the deprivation of services necessary to maintain health.

Abuse of the Elderly

Abuse of the elderly is denounced in countries where the elderly are revered. In the United States four percent of people over the age of 65 are victims of abuse. This percentage is slightly less than the incidence of child abuse, but it is estimated that only one in six cases of elderly abuse is reported. By contrast, it is estimated that one in three cases of child abuse is reported. As defined above, abuse includes not only active abuse but also passive abuse or neglect as well as exploitation (usually financial in the elderly) and violation of rights.

With the elderly, neglect, which is certainly the most common form of abuse, includes particularly isolation, inattention, and withholding physical or mental care that would undoubtedly be offered to a younger person.

Restraint.   Although persons of any age may have to be in a medical setting, it is most common among the elderly. Is restraining a patient a form of abuse? To answer this question, we must consider primary interests of the patient, and we must take other patients into account. It is reasonable to restrain a patient when there is a risk that the patient may injure himself/herself or others. If, for example, a patient might pull out intravenous lines, try to commit suicide, fall out of bed, or try to hit others, restraint is reasonable.

Reasonable medical restraint usually consists of a material vest with tapes tied to the bed or the back of a chair, and padded siderails on the bed. For a very violent patient — for example, an acute manic or intoxicated patient — a four-point restraint might be used. Such a restraint consists of leather cuffs for the ankles and wrists that anchor the patient to a bed or stretcher. In cases in which a patient simply has to be watched carefully, putting the patient in a chair with a table across the arms and positioning the chair opposite the nursing station might suffice. Although the patient would not be tied down, and traditionally no physician's order would be needed, this arrangement nevertheless would still be a form of restraint. In grey areas such as this, health care providers must weigh the risk to the patient of being unrestrained against the psychological trauma of being restrained.

Restraint may be physical, chemical, or emotional. Chemical restraint, which is using drugs, accomplishes the same end as physical restraint. Strait jackets became virtually extinct with the advent of major tranquilizers in the 1950's. Giving a patient tranquilizing drugs calls for similar consideration as deciding whether to use physical restraint. If, for example, a patient shouts all night long, keeping others awake, and the physician orders that tranquilizers be used on an "as necessary" basis (p.r.n. for *pro re nata*), the nurse has a duty not simply to give p.r.n. sedatives but to ask what the benefit of the sedation is to the patient and to what extent she or he may be violating the individual patient's rights by administering medication. Also, the nurse must balance these two considerations against what is fair to the other patients. The nurse's role is not simply to administer the restraint but to use judgment in deciding whether to administer it. Unfortunately, there seems to be a direct relationship between poverty and long-term chemical restraint. Indigent mental patients may spend decades sedated.

Emotional restraint consists of withholding normal social responsiveness. Walking out on a patient halfway through a sentence, avoiding eye contact with a patient, and shutting a door to quiet a patient's shouting are all forms of emotional restraint. Emotional restraint tends to represent the ordinary subconscious behavior of both family members and health practitioners. It usually is not weighed and considered as physical and chemical restraints are. If emotional restraint is to be used, it should be decided upon in advance and discussed with other professionals. Emotional restraint should not be allowed to be an outlet for the health professional's frustrations.

Recognizing Abuse. The elderly recipient of abuse commonly is female, white, and over 75 years old. Elderly victims commonly suffer from one or more physical or mental impairments and are economically, physically, or mentally dependent. Excessive dependence makes people especially vulnerable to abuse.

The abuser is commonly a female relative of the abused who has served as caretaker for the victim for many years (averaging about 10 years). The abuser is over 50 years old in 75 percent of the cases and is commonly the least socially integrated of the siblings, often being unmarried or unemployed. It is common for abusers of the elderly to have been abused themselves as children. Steinmetz found that one in two adults who were abused as children abused their parents in later years, whereas only one in four hundred adults who were not abused as children abused their parents later. Ninety percent of those who abuse the elderly are clinically depressed. It is common for the abuser to be intoxicated with drugs or alcohol or to be under mental stress during abusive acts.

The home where the victim and the abuser live may have locks on the doors of the bedroom, kitchen, and other room doors and locks on the phone or kitchen cabinets (to restrict communication or food). The home may lack appropriate aids for daily living.

An abused elderly person commonly reacts to his or her situation by:

- becoming depressed.
- presenting multiple medical problems.
- being hypercritical of caregivers or professional attendants.
- regressing to childlike behavior.
- denying any abuse.

The abuser commonly reacts to the health care provider by:
- being hostile toward the victim or the attendant.

- showing excessive concern over the elderly person.
- being obsessed with control or the burdens of caregiving.
- denying any abuse.

The following is a typical example of how abuse of an elderly person develops:

> Marian is the youngest of four daughters. Aged 42, she is still unmarried, although she was engaged until a year ago. Marian's mother has suffered from dementia for the last six years. After a bout with pneumonia and a stay in the hospital, it became obvious that she could not return to her home alone. All Marian's sisters have their own families and naturally turned to Marian to care for their mother. Marian felt guilty. It had only been five years ago that she got her own apartment and she wondered whether her departure contributed to her mother's downhill course.
>
> So her mother came to live in Marian's apartment. Initially things went well, but after several months Marian's fiance, who had begun to see himself as married to two women, broke off the engagement. Marian was heartbroken and angry. She resented having to be a caretaker for her mother and having to eke out a meager income as a psychiatric aide. Soon after her fiance broke their engagement, Marian discovered that a bottle of wine after dinner eased her sorrow. Her mother was beginning to become disturbed at night, waking up several times each night and sometimes wandering out of the house. She behaved better during the day, but at times she was incontinent of both stool and urine. She was also falling down from time to time. Sometimes she would switch on the gas stove and forget to light it.
>
> A month ago, much to the disgust of her sisters and their families, Marian applied to a nursing home to accept her mother. But her mother put on a good show when they visited the social worker at the nursing home. She denied all problems and refused to go to the nursing home.
>
> The following week Marian lost her job for shouting at a patient, and she began to drink more. One afternoon when Marian went out shopping her mother called up her neighbor and claimed she had been abandoned. When the neighbor questioned Marian, Marian got angry and reprimanded her mother. The same thing happened a few days later. When it happened a third time, Marian lost her temper and slapped her mother across the face. Now when she goes out shopping, Marian ties her mother to a chair

and locks her in her room. Increasingly, Marian is resorting to hitting her mother when she is incontinent or disturbs her sleep, and tying her up during the day when she wants to watch television undisturbed.

Management and Legal Issues.   The Elder Abuse Prevention Identification and Treatment Act was passed by Congress in 1985; it was modeled after the Child Abuse Act of 1974. This act defines abuse, exploitation, and neglect.

Usually a case of abuse is identified by a health professional — nurse, physical therapist, occupational therapist, social worker, or physician — who visits the home or sees the patient in a hospital. Each state has different laws, but many states make it mandatory for a number of health care providers, including orderlies and aides, to report abuse. In addition, the law specifically declares any such reporter be immune from civil or criminal liability.

A report of abuse is generally made to the regional ombudsman for the elderly (see box, p. 268). (An ombudsman is an official appointed to investigate complaints of the public against the government.) Usually a form for protective services is filled out at the same time. The ombudsman then becomes responsible for ensuring that the person in question receives adequate protection. If the elder is mentally competent, he or she can refuse services. Typically, however, a visiting nurse follows the patient at home. The nurse provides general support to the caregiver, involves other family members, may arrange a companion to allow the caregiver a rest, and monitors progress. The abuser may require the services of a social worker or psychologist, particularly if she has a history of being abused or if substance abuse, major depression, or poor social integration is involved. There is often a tendency to adopt a hidden prejudice against the abuser, which hinders providing satisfactory care for the elder.

If the situation does not improve, the elder has to be removed from his or her home and from the caregiver. Removal usually involves placement in a skilled nursing facility or intermediate care facility.

If an elderly person refuses care but appears to lack insight, conservatorship proceedings (discussed in the Issues of Impairment section of this chapter) may be initiated.

Spouse Abuse

A common thread running through all types of abuse is a history of abuse. Eighty percent of male spouse abusers have a history of witnessing or experiencing abuse as a child (Roy 1982).

CHILDREN

WIVES

THE ELDERLY

Abuse can occur at any age and in many forms. What can you in your role as a health care provider do to help the abused? . . . the abuser?

There are two chief theories explaining abuse. The **dynamic theory** states that abuse represents repressed rage from receiving abuse, which is now being expressed through more abuse. In medieval times, some kings used a beating boy rather than punish their own children for wrongdoing. Each time the prince did something wrong, the beating boy got the birch. In modern society, the beating boy would be called an abused child. The abused child grows up wanting to take it out on others when anything upsets him. The anger he repressed at being abused he now expresses by abusing others.

The **learning theory** of abuse states that people are socialized to use abuse in their important relationships. In particular, as children they see that assertiveness is usually punished, and they witness that violence is the appropriate way to exert authority. As adults, abused children abuse their spouses or their own children and later may abuse their own parents if the right situation arises.

Denial. As discussed in Chapters 3 and 4, denial is one of many psychological mechanisms for dealing with events or conflicts that our minds cannot handle. Denial is extremely common in all forms of abuse.

Denial also has a psychological effect on the health care provider: it tends to prejudice her or him. If you, as a health practitioner, were to ask a man whether he hit his wife and he broke into tears and confessed, you could at least feel some sympathy. But if the man denied what you knew to be true, you would feel deceived and probably less sympathetic.

It has been estimated that 30 to 50 percent of all wives are physically abused at least once during a marriage. Typically the spouse, usually female, appears with a significant injury, for instance a fractured jaw from being punched in the face. She eventually admits that her husband did it. When her husband is confronted, however, he says they were only playing around or it was the first time it's ever happened. If pressured, he says there is no problem or his wife needs to change or she hit him. Commonly the man is intoxicated during the physical abuse.

Willful infliction of mental pain is also a form of abuse. Mental abuse merges with being "henpecked," a quasi-acceptable form of mental abuse.

Characteristics of Spouse Abusers and Their Relationships. As mentioned above, spouse abusers frequently have been abused themselves. Men who abuse their wives usually are socially isolated. They have few or no friends to talk to. They feel shame and low self-esteem. They are frequently alcoholic. Ceasing to abuse their spouse is only one of many adjustments they need to make.

Because the abuser is socially isolated, his relationship with his wife is usually very intense. She may be the only person he relates to, and he has a tragic problem in expressing that relationship: He finds it difficult to differentiate between himself and his wife. He becomes disappointed, for example, when she does not anticipate his every need, and he may become jealous and paranoid if she relates to other people. With his low self-esteem, social isolation, and inadequate coping mechanisms, violence represents a moment of reward in exerting his power. Following a violent expression of power, he feels not only very guilty but also fears losing his only relationship. The wife also fears loss of the relationship. This fear leads to a period of intensification of the relationship, a honeymoon period, while he atones for his violence because he fears she will leave him. These cycles often repeat themselves. Sometimes increasing violence is necessary to gain the same effect.

Management and Legal Issues. As with the elderly, excessive dependency fosters abuse. Because the abuser needs to control his wife, he tries to foster dependency. He will not allow her to work. He may control all the money. He may not allow her to leave the house unless he knows the reason and he sets the time limits: "make sure you're back in an hour with those groceries, no dilly-dallying." He may move the family to a distant town to intensify his relationship with her and remove her from her social contacts.

Her dependency makes separation difficult. Where could she go if she left? He might come after her and injure her seriously. What would happen to the kids? She cannot leave them alone with him. She cannot provide for them. She has no money, no job, no housing, no social contacts, no coping mechanism, and no willpower left.

It is not surprising, therefore, that both wife and husband deny that abuse has occurred. What must happen is that the threat of exposure must be stepped up to break through the denial. If necessary this may have to be accomplished by having the husband arrested for spouse abuse. Ideal treatment would then be for the husband to go to group therapy sessions with other spouse abusers. Such sessions are both educational and ego-strengthening. The abuser will be accepted into a group of abusers. The therapy will address the issues of shame, jealousy, low self-esteem, and relating only to one person. Violence and power cannot be used in group therapy. For the first time, the abuser may learn about normal relationships.

Meanwhile, the wife may live with her children in a shelter for abused women. Through group work she will be given a chance to develop esteem, willpower, independence, and new coping mechanisms. A goal for her will be to learn to tell her husband what her limits are: "You may never hit me again. If you do, I will file for divorce. No more second chances!" Often the location of the center is secret to avoid the risk of the husband finding her. He may punish his wife (and possibly his children) for bringing shame on him by exposing their intimate secret.

After both spouses have spent some time in counseling apart, they may go through joint counseling if the wife will accept it. Alternatively, they may separate or divorce. If there is significant substance abuse, that must be dealt with before the other issues.

Few laws address spouse abuse specifically. Physical violence may result in arrest for assault and battery. Legally speaking, assault means verbal abuse or threats, whereas battery means physical abuse. The most common advocate for the abused spouse is the social worker or psychologist, who commonly is called to the emergency room to see a patient with significant injuries.

If an abused patient asks what she should do, the **only** safe response a health practitioner can make is to tell her to get to a place of safety. Once a wife has been hit, she is going to be hit again. As health care providers, it is our responsibility to **ensure the victim's physical safety** before we initiate any other services.

In cases of domestic violence, the police are frequently called in by the abused spouse, by neighbors, or by the children. If violence is obvious or if the wife is willing to bring action against her husband, the police can arrrest him. Unfortunately, because she fears later punishment, the wife often denies the abuse or retracts the charge.

Child Abuse

Psychological abuse in children has also been called psychological maltreatment, mental cruelty, and emotional abuse. Such abuse includes rejection, terrorizing, isolation, exploitation, and mis-socializing. Abuse may begin when the child is an infant and may be presented as failure to thrive (when a newborn baby does not put on weight). Sexual abuse of children is also common.

In 1985, there were 1.9 million reported cases of child abuse in the United States, making it the most common form of abuse. Of this total, however, only 750,000 cases were confirmed, which means that over a million cases were unconfirmed. Some studies suggest that about a third of these cases will be reported again. Of the 750,000 confirmed cases, more than half were cases of neglect involving children who were left unsupervised at home. Only 20,000 cases involved serious injuries like burns or fractures. By contrast, there were 113,000 cases of reported sexual abuse in 1985.

Physical acts of commission include multiple fractures, cigarette burns, rope burns, dunking scalds (the child's buttocks and genitalia have been lowered into too-hot water), subdural hematomas (bleeding between the membranes surrounding the brain — almost always a sign of child abuse rather than trauma), torn lips, and multiple bruises. If these injuries are repeated or multiple, if there has been an obvious delay in calling for medical advice, or if there are recurrent complaints about the child's bad behavior, then physical injuries should be suspected as signs of abuse.

Physical acts of omission include starvation of an infant, leaving open fires or open bottles of pills unattended, and similar acts that threaten the child's life or safety.

Mental acts of commission include locking a child in his or her room or in the attic, or recurrent shouting at a child with verbal abuse. This does not mean that children must never be shouted at or punished. For instance, if, despite being told not to, a young child continues to plug in appliances or play with matches, it may be appropriate to smack the child's hand or shout at her. But locking a three-year-old in a dark attic for three hours because he spilled some milk is abuse.

Mental acts of omission include failing to provide adequate love or mental stimulation for the child, although such omission alone seldom is the basis of investigation for abuse.

Sexual abuse may present any form of trauma to the child's genitalia, venereal disease in the child, or urinary symptoms. A child is most unlikely to complain of sexual abuse, usually because the abuser makes threats to prevent the child from telling anyone about their secret or uses his/her relationship to ensure that the abuse remains a secret. Recently, it was reported that only one mother in seven believes her child when the child reports incestuos relations with her father or step-father.

Management and Legal Issues

Child abuse was first labeled the battered child syndrome in 1962. This led to state child abuse and neglect reporting laws, and subsequently to the Federal Child Abuse Prevention and Treatment Act of 1974, which was amended in 1986. Unless individual states comply with this act, they are denied federal funds.

It is illegal not to report a suspected case of child abuse. Not having proof of abuse is not reason enough to remain silent. The report is made to the appropriate child and youth services agency, which assigns a caseworker to investigate. It is the responsibility of the social worker, not the person who reports the abuse, to decide whether the child has been abused. The reporter's only responsibility is to report anything suspicious. The agency will take action if it is actually or reasonably foreseeable that the injury is likely to result in protracted difficulties if the child is left untreated.

As with spouse and elder abuse, the abuser denies abuse, and often the abused denies it too. The child may fear further acts of abuse if he or she tells.

We must not forget that the abuser, as well as the abused, needs help. There is a universal tendency to sympathize with the abused and treat the abuser simply as a criminal. We began this chapter with elder abuse rather than child abuse because elders elicit less sympathy. Indeed, we can easily sympathize with Marian, the woman in our example. In the section on spouse abuse, we dealt with some of the reasons why people become abusers. It is very difficult, however, for most people to sympathize with child abusers. But we must remember that the person who abuses a child has problems too. As we have noted, he or she probably was abused as a child. Substance abuse is often a problem. Child abusers have psychodynamic problems that are similar to those of other abusers. Child and youth service agencies work with the entire family. The option of removing the child from the parents is seen as a last resort.

Sometimes people are wrongly accused of abuse. It is estimated that up to half the reported cases of child abuse are deemed to be unfounded. Such accusations take a toll on the approximately one million families who are reported, possibly falsely, for child abuse. Victims of Child Abuse Laws (VOCAL) is a support group that has sprung up to help such families.

The Liberated Minor.   Children, like adults, have certain rights. For instance, children of any age may own property, whether they acquired it through a gift or legacy or any other means. Children also have a right to be supported by their parents.

Generally speaking, parents exercise almost total authority over their children until they reach the age of majority, which in most states is 18. Beyond the age of majority the child becomes an adult: legally speaking, the young adult is his or her own free agent.

The liberated minor is a child who, because of circumstances, becomes his or her own agent before reaching the age of majority. For example, a boy who gets married in another state at age 16 and returns with a spouse and obtains gainful employment is a liberated minor. This boy's parent could not direct his treatment or be considered by any health professional as his representative. All medical, social, psychological, and legal decisions can be made by the liberated minor in this situation. Parents may also declare a child to be a liberated minor if they can no longer control the child and wish to absolve themselves of legal responsibility.

The minor who, at the age of 13, goes to a physician for treatment of venereal disease or goes to a social worker requesting help with an abortion is legally a liberated minor. Although generally the health professional would be wise to encourage such a child to communicate with her parents, the health professional is not obligated to tell the parent. And from a legal standpoint, the parent is not entitled to know.

Rape

Rape is one form of sexual abuse. Other examples of sexual abuse include sexual harassment, sexual assault and battery, and sexual molestation of children. There are also several different types of rape, including date rape and statutory rape.

Rape is defined legally as penetration, or its reasonable intent, without the subject's consent. Penetration usually means penile penetration beyond the vaginal introitus, or in the case of anal intercourse, beyond the anal sphincter. If a woman has been tied and held at knife point while the perpetrator uses a candlestick rather than his penis to penetrate her, this also meets the definition of rape. To be able to consent, the subject must be of sound mind (not drugged, mentally retarded, or under age).

Sexual intercourse with a girl under the age of 16 is automatically defined as statutory rape because all state statutes say that people under the age of 16 cannot give consent. Sexual intercourse with a girl between the ages of 16 and 18 (the usual age of majority) is not automatically considered rape. At this age a girl is considered a liberated minor and can give consent.

Date rape, or being forced to have sex with someone simply because you have agreed to a date, is said to be extremely common. Unfortunately, this form of rape is rarely reported because the victim may blame herself, feel ashamed, or fear reprisals from a social network that she has in common with the rapist.

State and federal laws about rape change frequently. Some states say that the rapist can only be male; others say both males and females can be rapists. When this textbook was written, all the states except one said that rape can take place between a man and his wife.

Rape is an act of violence, a demonstration of power, and not really a sexual crime. Most rapists actually despise or cannot relate to women.

The Psychological Effects of Rape.   Rape is an act of violence by the rapist and an act of abuse to the victim. Although rape usually entails a single incident, its effects can be as lasting as the effects of child, spouse, or elder abuse. Rape produces both acute trauma and psychologically long-lasting effects. Rape frequently causes a state akin to bereavement, and acute trauma that takes time to get over. The effect of being raped may vary depending on:

- the victim's previous sexual history.
- the victim's support systems.
- how much violence, pain, or mutilation was involved.
- the victim's age.
- the victim's religious beliefs.
- whether the victim knew the rapist.
- the victim's marital status.
- whether the victim has ever been raped before.

It is not surprising that rape victims frequently have subsequent sexual difficulties. The victim may react differently to her sexual partner. Simply associating sex with the violence of rape may create a feeling of panic with each subsequent sexual act. The victim's sexual partner, who can no longer relate in the same way as before, may not know how to behave. The victim, who feels drawn into her own world of sorrow, and her partner, who feels bewildered by the loss of intimacy, have been thrown into a different world. Victim assistance programs that include both individual and group therapy may be very valuable in this regard.

Form of Abuse	State Organization	Local Advocate
Elder	Department of Aging	Regional ombudsman for the elderly
Spouse	State-subsidized regional community mental health service	Battered women's shelter designee
Child	State agency for child and youth services	Local branch assigned case worker
Handicapped	Office for protection and advocacy for the handicapped (mental and physical)	None; each centralized state agency sends a specific person to investigate each case; homes for the mentally retarded may have resident social workers answerable to the state office
Sexual	State sexual assault center	Counselor at local rape crisis center or designee from victim assistance program

Management. Each state has a central regional office for sexual assault that oversees a number of local sexual assault centers.

If a patient reports a rape that occurred several weeks ago, there is unlikely to be documentable physical evidence of injury. Such a patient should be referred to a rape crisis center. If the rape is recent, the patient should be referred to the emergency room, where an established protocol is followed. The procedure is explained to the patient, who must consent to each part. A pelvic examination is performed. Specimens are collected from the patient's vagina for evidence of sperm, from her fingernails for evidence of blood of the rapist, which can be typed, and from her pubic area for pubic hairs of the rapist.

Careful note is made of any lacerations, abrasions, or contusions, both in the genital area and elsewhere on the body. The patient is also screened for venereal disease.

The patient is then photographed to preserve visual evidence of violence in case the patient wants to charge the rapist later. For the patient this is often the most emotionally traumatic part of the proceedings.

If she is willing, the patient makes a statement to the police. Then she is asked whether she wishes to charge the rapist. Finally, the patient is referred to a crisis worker from the local sexual assualt center.

Faced with this ordeal immediately after being raped, it is not surprising that victims frequently refuse to be examined, to be photographed, to be interviewed by the police, or to make a charge. The courts, however, demand physical evidence.

Federal and state laws dealing with all forms of abuse (including abuse of the handicapped, which is discussed later in this chapter) are often quite similar in content. On the state level, these laws are administered through local branches and advocates, as shown in the accompanying box.

Issues of Impairment

This section deals with impairment and discrimination, a subtle form of abuse that is often sanctioned by large segments of society and may even be regarded as normal by some members of society.

Mental Impairment

Incompetence. Mental incompentence is the inability of a patient to make decisions that are in his or her own best interest. A toddler who walks into a fire is incompetent. A demented person who wanders down the middle of the road without regard to traffic is incompetent. An elderly isolated woman who writes checks for life insurance, leaving herself insufficient money to eat, may be incompetent. We say *may* be in this case because we cannot know the workings of every mind. It is possible, for instance, that the visits this woman has from the insurance salesman to collect her insurance checks are the only form of social contact she has. Reflecting back to Maslow's hierarchy of needs in Chapter 3, it would not be surprising if she craved social contact more than food. Perhaps, therefore, we could not define her as incompetent unless she did other things such as piling old newspapers next to an open fire or refusing medical care despite severe symptoms.

Although we must respect eccentricity in a free society, a patient who is living dangerously or is being abused, exploited, or neglected may not be able to recognize what is happening. The probate court appoints two types of conservators (or guardians): one who appropriates and takes charge of an elder's finances and one who takes charge of making decisions about the elder's mental, physical, and social health. The latter type of conservator may also decide whether the elderly person should be institutionalized. Typically, a bank trustee is appointed financial guardian, whereas a relative or state representative is made responsible for the other areas of guardianship. Conservatorship proceedings also require a statement by a physician that the mental capacities of the elder are substantially and permanently impaired.

A competent person may grant to another the power to take charge of any specified decision (power of attorney). By contrast, conservatorship is usually made by a court to transfer authority for decision making from the incompetent person to a competent one.

Such societal intervention is potentially dangerous. Supreme Court Justice Brandeis once warned that "experience should teach us to be most on our guard to protect liberty when the government's purposes are beneficent." We should be careful when infringing on any person's rights, especially when we think we are trying to help them.

Lack of Insight.   Mental competence describes the ability of a patient to make decisions in his or her best interest; insight describes the ability of a patient to understand his or her own problems. A certain degree of intellect is a prerequisite for insight as illustrated in the following diagram:

A patient may therefore be incompetent because of mental retardation or because of a lack of insight. Intelligent people may still lack insight because of emotional, language, cultural, or other reasons. When lack of insight interferes with making decisions of self-interest, the patient may be defined as incompetent.

Patients who typically lack insight are those who suffer from mental retardation, dementia, drug-related impairment, obsessive/compulsive disorders, and schizophrenia. Loss of insight can be difficult to judge in people who are hermits, those who are excessively religious, and those who cannot speak the prevailing language.

Providing informed consent for surgery is only possible in a patient who has enough insight to see his or her problems in perspective. A patient may be legally competent enough to manage her own finances and everyday life but unable to understand the pros and cons of surgery when presented with complex facts in an anxiety-provoking situation. A mastectomy for possible cancer of the breast is an example of such a situation.

Mental Retardation. Almost identical laws at the federal and state level protect the disabled from abuse. Mental and physical handicaps are both handled by the state office for protection and advocacy for handicapped and developmentally disabled persons. It is mandatory to report abuse of the mentally retarded. This is true for physicians, nurses, dentists, dental hygienists, physical therapists, osteopaths, optometrists, podiatrists, psychologists, social workers, teachers, speech pathologists, police officers, and any person paid for caring for persons in any facility serving mentally retarded people, as well as for private citizens. Any person who reports a suspected case of abuse in good faith is immune from civil or criminal liability. Failure to report a case can lead to a fine.

Emotional Impairment

Emotional illness carries a certain stigma. In some ways, certain of those stigmas have been removed by labeling certain illnesses as medical disease. Alcoholism, for instance, is now largely accepted as an illness rather than an evil.

Although emotionally impaired people have the same rights as all citizens, some people ignore the rights of the emotionally impaired. A man who sexually abuses his two-year-old daughter is undoubtedly emotionally or mentally ill. But he also has rights. He has a right to treatment, due process of law, and lack of discrimination. In actual practice, he will be heavily discriminated against, most of all by fellow prisoners, who universally condemn sexual abuse of children. Part of the problem is also the primitive moral or religious view that has impressed on us the idea that sexual abuse is sinful rather than an illness.

The religious rather than scientific view spills over into the whole of emotional illness. This causes deep-rooted feelings in people who then unconsciously discriminate against people who are emotionally ill.

Social Impairment

Social impairment refers to the inability of someone to integrate properly into the society in which they live. Although the impairment may be due to a relatively normal phenomenon like shyness, it may become a matter for discrimination. Social impairment associated with discrimination is stigma, which we discussed briefly in Chapter 3. We all know or have met people who stutter or who are deaf, blind, physically unattractive, homosexual, obese, alcoholic, illiterate, epileptic, or mentally ill. Indeed, we all have our own imperfections and have experienced times of feeling different, particularly as teenagers or in foreign countries. Stigma refers more to the social disgrace connected with a particular attribute than to the attribute itself.

A stigma typically causes psychologic mechanisms to come into play, particularly overcompensation, denial, rationalization, and inversion. It may also lead to depression or low self-esteem. A patient with polio who tries to become an Olympic athlete is overcompensating. A black patient who blames all his failures on skin color is rationalizing. A patient with an amputated arm who, rather than playing it down, goes to great lengths to flaunt her disability is displaying inversion.

A stigma may be socially obvious (for example, stuttering or facial deformity), and the person may be labeled discredited. Or a stigma may be socially hidden (for example, when a person has had a colostomy or has epilepsy), when the person may be labeled discreditable.

The **discredited** are uncertain how others will respond and may become self-conscious. They may compensate through defensiveness or aggression. The normal person may become confused about whether to ignore the stigma, talk about it, or make allowances for it. These problems can lead to strained and uncomfortable relationships. Some discredited persons become very adept at fielding comments, questions, and situations pertaining to the disability.

Although the **discreditable** person can hide the disability, he or she may be forced to reveal the disability at some later date and this may cause conflicts. For example, the person may have to decide when in a relationship to tell the other person that she or he has had a colostomy. Some discreditable people cannot cope with such questions and choose to handle them by becoming socially or geographically mobile. Others may expose their stigma very early in a relationship in order to assume the role of the discredited. Genital herpes is another important example of this.

The stigmatized person can only feel comfortable with intimate contacts such as a parent, spouse, or health professional or with others who share the same stigma. Sharing the stigma with others is a support mechanism that may even be formalized into a support group. In this group the person learns from others how best to handle the outside world, and feels comfortable with fellow sufferers. On the other hand, the group exposes and emphasizes the stigma and the patient may be ashamed of the stigma and the ghetto-like quality of the group. (Kübler-Ross found that anger in the terminally ill against nonsufferers was eased by fellowship in a group.)

Cultural Impairment

Cultural impairment is the inability of a patient to function optimally in society because of cultural attributes. This is also called discrimination. Discrimination is derived from the Latin *discriminare*, which implies drawing lines of distinction **between** things. Discrimination typically involves color, sex, creed, age, and class. Examples include racism, sexism, ageism, class distinction, and religious creedism. Discrimination is in direct opposition to the concepts of civil rights and liberties.

Discrimination is different from prejudice. Prejudice is a prejudgment about an individual. The person who is prejudiced thinks he or she knows all about an individual because of the person's sex, or age, or race, etc. **Prejudice is a belief. Discrimination is an action.** An individual may be prejudiced but unwilling to discriminate because of the penalties involved, or for reasons of conscience. An individual may discriminate even though it violates their own beliefs, for example for peer approval.

Disabled persons suffer from physical or mental handicap, stigma, and discrimination. Without legislation, protection, and advocacy, life for the disabled can be very difficult.

Rehabilitation for any handicap involves four major areas: medical, social, educational, and vocational. Medical rehabilitation involves particularly physical therapists, occupational therapists, and speech therapists. Social and educational rehabilitation often involves psychologists and social workers. All of these health professionals must be familiar with the issues facing the disabled person. These issues include stigma, prejudice, discrimination, lack of insight, and the financial, physical, emotional, medical, sexual, and vocational aspects of disability.

The Bureau of Disability Determination is a federally funded state-run organization that determines whether disabled people will be paid a disability pension. The bureau also can refer a patient to the Department of Vocational Rehabilitation, a branch of the U.S. Department of Health and Human Services, where vocational specialists can enable the patient to become employable again.

It is estimated that there are 16 million disabled persons in the United States. The World Health Organization and the International

Labor Organization have both been extensively involved in advocacy legislation and training for the disabled. Shelter programs such as Goodwill Industries provide training and experience that enable the disabled to make the transition to regular employment.

Handicapped children in school systems have a right to special education. The exceptional child is defined as one who deviates in mental characteristics, sensory abilities, neuromotor or physical characteristics, social behavior, communication abilities, or multiple handicaps. The deviation must be sufficient enough to require special educational services. The Education for All Handicapped Children Act of 1975 ensured that all states provide such special education to all children with handicaps. In many states, parent/pupil/teacher conferences are mandatory. These are attended by the parent, teacher, nurse, a specialized teacher (for example, a remedial reading teacher), and a social worker or psychologist.

Chapter Summary

Abuse is the willful infliction of physical or mental pain by acts of omission or commission. Several examples are presented of elder, spouse, and sexual abuse. All forms of abuse are subjects of various federal and state laws with similar content. Mental impairment may involve incompetence, lack of insight, or mental retardation.

A central theme in abuse is that abused people themselves often become abusers later in life. Abusers therefore also need professional help, as well as the abused. Most abused people are in dependent roles. When the abuse is of sufficient severity to threaten the immediate or future mental or physical health of a person, then the abused patient must be protected.

Mental impairment is commonly thought of as retardation or dementia. However, there are other dimensions in describing mental impairment. People may be emotionally, socially, or culturally impaired; examples of these are given.

Review

Conservatorship: court order giving financial or social guardianship to another person or organization
Discrimination: action based on prejudice
Exploitation: process of taking advantage of another person or thing
Liberated minor: child who because of various circumstances becomes his or her own agent before reaching the age of majority

Mental competence: ability of a patient to make decisions that are in his or her own best interest: 1) to understand what they may be charged with or asked to do, and 2) to be well enough to assist in their own defense

Neglect: infliction of physical or mental pain through acts of commission or omission

Power of attorney: granted by a mentally competent person to another to take charge of any specified decision

Prejudice: belief based on prejudgment about an individual

Rape: penetration, or its reasonable intent, without a subject's consent

Stigma: feeling of social disgrace connected with a social impairment

1. Define abuse, neglect, and exploitation.
2. What does "physical, chemical, or emotional restraint" mean?
3. Why do abused children often grow up to be abusers themselves? Describe the two theories which account for this.
4. "Dependency fosters abuse." Discuss.
5. If an elderly person becomes dangerous, what legal and diagnostic processes must be gone through to deal with this?
6. How is social impairment different from stigma?

Additional Reading

Gardner, K. and V. J. Halamandaris. 1981 *Elder Abuse: A Report by the Select Committee on Aging.* U.S. House of Representatives, 97th Congress, 1st session, Washington, D. C. U.S. Government Printing Office.

Garrison, E. G., 1987. "Psychological Maltreatment of Children." *American Psychologist,* February, pp. 157-159.

Goffman, E. *Stigma.* 1968. Harmondsworth, Penguin Books.

Kempe, C. H., F. Silverman, B. Steele, W. Droegemueller, and H. Silver. 1962. "The Battered Child Syndrome." *JAMA,* 181: 17-24.

Roy, M. 1982. *The Abusive Partner.* New York: Van Nostrand Reinhold.

Steinmetz, S. K. 1978. "Battered Parents." *Society.* 15: 54-55.

Waldo, Michael. 1987. "Also Victims: Understanding and Treating Men Arrested for Spouse Abuse." *Journal of Counseling and Development,* 65: 385-388.

Whitman, D. 1987. "Child Abuse: The Numbers Game." *U.S. News and World Report,* April 27, p. 39-40.

Chapter

12

After reading this chapter, you should be able:
- To identify common malpractice pitfalls.
- To discuss the system of malpractice suits as well as offer social commentary.
- To list ways to prevent malpractice suits.
- To know who is liable for what.
- To know what constitutes malpractice.
- To understand SOAP notes.
- To make a case that the right of practice is a privilege.
- To define and distinguish among the terms licensure, certification, and registration.
- To review the history of the AMA with respect to accreditation.
- To discuss the current licensure system.

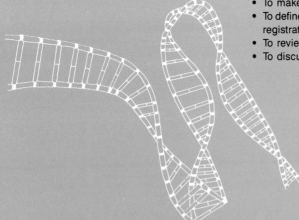

Legal Concerns

What Constitutes Malpractice?

Professional Liability

If an X-ray technologist takes an X-ray of the lumbar spine when an X-ray of the cervical spine was ordered, is this malpractice? No, it is not, because the patient has not suffered actual damage. Rather, it is a maloccurrence, a mistake that resulted in no damage. The two prerequisites for malpractice are **mental or physical harm** and **deviation from the standard of care**.

Mental or physical harm must obviously be significant. A medical malpractice case costs a minimum of $20,000 to take to court. If a mistake is made but no harm results, there is no malpractice. If, for example, the wrong hand is X-rayed, the mental or physical harm is insufficient to qualify as malpractice. If, however, the wrong hand is X-rayed, a malignant bone tumor is missed, and subsequently the patient needs an amputation, then harm has resulted.

Standard of care means what a usual health practitioner would have done in the same situation. Until a few years ago, location was included as part of the standards. Until then a country doctor was not expected to perform to the same standard as the university specialist. But now location is no longer a defense.

A physical therapist who manipulates a patient's neck when the patient has numb legs and recent urinary incontinence is not performing under the usual standard of care. If the patient becomes paraplegic, malpractice has occurred. If a physical therapist performs ultrasound and applies hot pack treatments to a patient with back pain at the physician's request, the usual standards of care have been applied. If this patient were to sue the physical therapist for erroneous treatment of cancer of the spine, the patient's attorney would have a difficult time. The physician is the one who should have made the diagnosis. The usual standard of care does not include a physical therapist diagnosing cancer.

Other standards may be involved in malpractice. The most common malpractice suits involve surgical errors of commission. For example, the operating room technician gets the swab count wrong and leaves a swab in the patient. The patient subsequently develops an intra-abdominal abscess that requires reoperation.

Errors of omission most commonly involve failure to diagnose, especially failure to diagnose cancer. For example, a physician's assistant is told by a patient about rectal bleeding and chooses to withhold the information from the chart or the physician. When the patient is later diagnosed with inoperable bowel cancer, there may be a basis for a suit.

Another error of omission in the United States is lack of informed consent. In a recent English case, a patient became paralyzed after disc surgery to the spine. Although the patient suffered damage, she still needed to show deviation from the usual standard of care. The patient said she was not informed of the risk of paralysis. U.S. courts would label this malpractice, but the English courts did not, instead saying that the physician had a duty to do what any similar physician would have done in the patient's best interest. Lack of information is not part of malpractice in England. In the United States we have a **duty to inform**. Failure to do so, despite intent, is a form of malpractice.

Relationship between Health Professional and Patient. There are a number of themes that are helpful in guiding our thoughts when dealing with legal issues with patients.

Beneficence. We are licensed to practice the health profession of our choice for the benefit of the patient. Our primary duty is to use our professional expertise for the patient's well-being.

Nonmalfeasance. We must weigh the risks and benefits for all courses of action with our patients. Most of the time this value judgment is automatic, but at times decisions require more thought. Then the doctrine of *primum non nocere* applies: **Above all else do no harm**.

Autonomy. Autonomy of the patient means we must respect the patient's right as an individual. An adult of sound mind has a right to make decisions about his or her own life unless there is danger to third parties. Examples of dangers to third parties include infectious disease, denying a spouse income, and homicide. Another issue of patient autonomy is quality of life. Patients have the right to refuse a treatment if it violates their standard of dignity. If, for example, a patient refuses a barium enema (and understands the risks) because it is undignified, this must be respected. The right of a cancer patient to die in peace without invasive or undignified procedures must be respected.

Autonomy of the health professional means that each health professional is morally independent and cannot let others influence her or his decisions. The allied health professions are becoming increasingly independent from physicians. As this autonomy increases, exposure to malpractice also increases. Therefore, all health practitioners must become more aware of malpractice issues.

Justice. A sense of fairness must exist in the relationship between the allied health professional and the patient. Malpractice exists, after all, as a legal recourse or redress for any breach in the relationship between the health professional and the patient.

Justice must also exist in the relationship between society and the patient. For example, a psychologist cannot allow a homicidal patient complete autonomy despite the supposed sanctity of patient confidentiality. If a psychologist believes there is a reasonable risk of violence or death to a person, the psychologist also has a duty toward that victim.

Statutes of Limitation. Each state has a statute of limitation beyond which a malpractice action cannot be brought. Limitations change from time to time as state legislatures adjust their laws. In Connecticut, for example, the statute of limitations is two years from the time of malpractice. But, if a patient did not discover the malpractice within that time because he or she was not told or it went unnoticed, the patient has three years from the time of discovery. A common occurrence is a swab left inside that leads to an infection several years later. If the patient is told what happened at the time it occurs, he has two years to sue. If, however, the patient discovers the swab four years later when symptoms appear, he has three years from that time of discovery to sue.

What if a person who has had a withered arm since birth learns as an adult that it was caused by obstetric malpractice 20 years previously? Can the obstetrician be sued 20 years later? In Connecticut, a child's guardian is responsible for suing within two years of occurrence or three years of discovery. In some other states the child can sue later as an adult. In most cases the obstetrician's insurance company would be responsible for paying. But if the obstetrician had no malpractice insurance, he or she could be sued. If the obstetrician was dead, the estate could be sued. Although a situation like this example is feasible, it is a highly unlikely example.

Issues in the Courtroom

Malpractice suits are not simply the result of negligence or greed. The idea of malpractice suits arose following a period when physicians were seen as all-knowing and godlike. The more patients were made to feel helpless and alienated from their own health care, the more determined they became to fight back where they could get some attention.

Malpractice does occur. Not every health care provider has the patient's best interest at heart, and not every health practitioner is or remains competent. Consumers must have the right to protection through the courts. If a maloccurrence (mistake) takes place and it was caused by an unreasonable action of a health professional, the patient must have recourse.

A court battle is usually an unpleasant experience for both the litigant and the defendant. It is common to wait three to five years for a case to come to court. This can take a heavy toll on the litigant financially. If, for example, a patient cannot work because the wrong limb was amputated, a three-to five-year wait is abusive. From the defendant's point of view, a three-to five-year wait can take a heavy emotional toll.

There are many other blocks to the patient being able to obtain satisfaction from health care professionals: the imposing idea of a court battle, legal technicalities, the difficulty of proving malpractice, and worry over whether they will be shunned by health professionals in the community in which they live.

Deep Pocket Suits Versus Responsibility. It is common practice to name multiple respondents in a medical malpractice suit. One reason is that it is not always easy for attorneys to know in advance exactly who might be involved. Another reason is that awards may be higher where a deep pocket is found. A deep pocket refers to a person or institution with lots of money or high malpractice insurance. Commonly several doctors and a hospital are named when it may be obvious from the start that only one doctor is to blame. Also, the allied health professional commonly is not named because the physician is considered to be "captain of the ship" for hospitalized patients. At present, litigants have no desire to prove a physical therapist or lab technician personally responsible for malpractice because if a hospital or physician is involved, the captain of the ship principle can be used.

Historically, allied health professionals seldom carried malpractice insurance because they were employed by others, especially hospitals or physicians. Only recently have allied health professionals become more autonomous by performing their profession independently. This new autonomy applies, for example, to dietitians, psychologists, social workers, physical and occupational therapists, speech therapists, and audiologists. Obviously, it would be difficult for health professionals such as X-ray technologists or physician's assistants to practice independently.

Although the increased autonomy of many allied health professionals increases their exposure to malpractice, the majority of malpractice suits involve hospital inpatients. In hospitals, allied health professionals only have exposure to malpractice if they are practicing as independent outside contractors. Among hospital-employed health professionals, responsibility, however it is shared, is seen by the courts as the hospital's responsibility. This situation is reflected in the high malpractice insurance that hospitals carry and in the fact that most hospital-employed health practitioners carry low or no malpractice insurance. All other things being equal, the deep pocket is always the pocket that is pursued.

Fair Compensation.   It is not always easy to decide what constitutes fair compensation. In a country where millionaires are still revered, a $1 million award may seem like a bonanza, yet a $5- or $10-million award may be difficult to understand. In determining what is fair compensation, courts consider such issues as economic loss, lump sum versus periodic payments, contingency fees, pain and suffering awards, and punitive damages.

Let us illustrate with the case of a 25-year-old male janitor earning $15,000 a year who has lost a limb because of a surgical mistake. He is unable to continue working. The economic loss of 40 years of lost wages at $15,000 per year is $600,000. This amount may be awarded as a lump sum or as payments of $15,000 per year. The patient may, however, receive disability income from the state. If he has private disability insurance, this should be taken into account, although it is often considered inadmissible evidence. Currently, many states allow lump sum payments, which would give him $600,000. Invested at 10 percent, this award would quadruple his income.

But the patient's attorney may take up to one-third of this amount as a fee for handling the case. Under a contingency fee arrangement, the patient owes the attorney nothing if the case is lost. If the case is won, however, the patient owes the attorney a percentage of the total award. Some states are trying to limit contingency fees.

On top of the $600,000 for the loss of his limb, our patient may also be given a pain and suffering award and a punitive damages award. If he has phantom limb pain (pain where the limb was before the amputation), he may receive an additional award for pain and suffering. There have been attempts in some states to limit pain and suffering awards to, say, less than $500,000.

If the court wants to teach the surgeon a lesson, a punitive damages award may be added. What started as a fair replacement for income lost may end up as a $3 million award, with $1 million going to the attorney. Obviously, no amount of money can replace a lost limb, but the issue of determining fair compensation is a difficult one.

Cost to Society. The other factor in the equation of fair compensation is not how much the defendant gets, but how much society pays. An obstetrician who pays a malpractice premium of $70,000 per year passes a substantial fee increase on to patients. If it costs $2,000 instead of $1,000 for total obstetric care, who pays the extra? We all do, either out of pocket or through our medical insurance premiums or taxes.

Courts also make decisions about patients who are in a persistent vegetative state (prolonged coma). When Karen Quinlan lay in a coma on a ventilator at $600 a day, society was paying that cost, which amounted to almost $250,000 a year.

The cost of malpractice to society also includes the cost of defensive medicine — the extra tests ordered and the extra days in the hospital. A conservative estimate of this cost is 10 percent of the total cost of medical care, which represents many billions of dollars a year.

There has been great concern in the past few years about premiums. Decreasing investment returns for insurance companies along with falling interest rates may have caused part of the rise in premiums. A number of state medical societies have started their own malpractice insurance companies (captive insurance companies), which puts malpractice defense more in the hands of physicians. As a result, there may be less tendency to settle out of court rather than go to court. It is doubtful, however, that captive insurance companies will have that great an effect on costs to society.

Out-of-Court Settlements. As we have discussed, a medical malpractice case may indict multiple health professionals as well as an institution, and may cost a minimum of $20,000 if it goes to court. There is great pressure, therefore, to settle out of court. The average out-of-court settlement is estimated to be about one-third of what a malpractice award would have been. It is little wonder then that insurance companies are anxious to settle out of court. The problem is that cases of dubious merit frequently are settled rather than taken to court. A bird in the hand is worth two in the bush.

The Jury System. The jury system is like a double-edged sword. On the one hand, it puts justice at the level of the common person. On the other hand, the complexity of many cases can make it difficult for an ordinary person to understand. If a social worker appears to have misjudged a patient's suicide risk, is it fair to have untrained people judging the social worker? Explaining the wide perspective of a social worker to a jury during a court case is impossible. Jury members do not have the training to understand every complex issue; they gain much of their perspective from the prosecuting and defending attorneys. Given this situation, appeals to the emotions rather than the intellect are common.

Although both the prosecuting and defending attorneys have to be satisfied with the composition of the jury, who sits on the jury can be controlled to some extent.

Do the courts have the right to satisfy justice in the society/patient relationship, rather than in just the health professional/patient relationship? For instance, if a laboratory technician mislabels a specimen and thereby delays a patient's diagnosis of AIDS, can the courts set an example with a $5 million award? They may, and the case may be appealed, and the appeal may be successful or unsuccessful. It is tempting to say that society will decide, but in practice the courts will decide.

Expert Witnesses. The jury's lack of perspective is answered in part through the use of expert witnesses. Increasingly, however, expert witnesses are seen as "hired guns" who lack impartiality because they are paid by one side rather than by the court.

Expert witnesses not only testify as reference models but also set the standard of care. Health professionals have a duty to use reasonable professional care and to perform within the standards of practice. Standards of practice have traditionally differed between specialists and between communities. For example, the psychologist who specializes in eating disorders might be held more culpable for not recommending hospitalization of an anorectic than would a psychologist who specializes in sexual dysfunction.

Until recently, a laboratory technician who ran a small department in a country hospital was not expected to perform to the same standards as the person at a university teaching hospital. These ideas are now changing, the new thesis being that wherever you may practice you were trained as others were trained and are expected to perform to the same standards. The small country hospital is expected to hire the same staff and perform to the same standard as the hospital in the city.

Preventing Suits

Good Communication.   The old idea that the cause of suits is malpractice must be cast aside. Maloccurrence is needed for a successful suit, but as long as health care exists there will always be maloccurrences. Death, for example, is a maloccurrence and must come to everyone. We must look beyond maloccurrence as the cause of suits. **The most common reason that maloccurrence is taken to court is the lack of a relationship or the breakdown of the relationship between patient and health professional.** Patients seldom sue their counselors because, of all people, the counselor probably has listened most carefully to the patient's problems and has communicated with the patient.

It is important that health practitioners treat their friends and relatives who are patients with the same professionalism as they treat their regular patients. It is simply not true that friends and relatives do not sue. Actually, it is often inadvisable to treat close family members because they frequently end up being overtreated or undertreated, which in itself is poor health care. If, as a health care provider, you do treat your friends and relatives, it is important that you keep records and that you treat these patients in the same setting you treat your regular patients.

An Informed Patient.   Communication is the cornerstone of preventing malpractice suits. A maloccurrence left undiscussed with the patient may result in a successful suit. A maloccurrence discussed is not likely to result in a successful suit.

Although the model of informed consent generally is of an invasive procedure performed by a surgeon, informed consent also must be obtained for procedures such as podiatric surgery, bone marrow examinations by laboratory technicians, and neck manipulation by chiropractors.

Informed consent can only be obtained by the person who is to perform the procedure. If, as a physician's assistant, you are instructed to obtain informed consent for the surgeon, you must establish this fact with the surgeon.

Informed consent requires a description of:

- the procedure.
- any reasonably foreseeable risks of the procedure (Unfortunately, lawsuits have been successful for reasonably unforeseeable maloccurrences).
- alternatives to the procedure.
- benefits of the procedure.

Consent can be given in advance through a durable power of attorney, the designation of the patient's conservator, or in some states, a living will.

Documentation.   A common stance taken by the courts is that if it was not written down, it did not happen. Unfortunately, this stance has led to a deplorable proliferation of hospital charts that make it difficult to find the forest for the trees. But if, for example, a physical therapist writes that the left arm was treated and the patient later sues for right arm pain, the physical therapist's case is probably sound.

Good records are the cornerstone of defense in a malpractice suit. Records should be legible, signed, and dated, and they should document the reasoning that led to significant decisions and to the treatment provided. The ideal way to keep good records is to follow the SOAP (subjective objective assessment plan) format, which is as follows:

S **Subjective** is what the patient says: "I take insulin for diabetes."
O **Objective** is what you observe: Patient has two packs of Oreo cookies and a Burger King wrapper on her bedside stand.
A **Assessment** is how you see the situation: Diabetic non-compliant with diet.
P **Plan** is what you will or did do: Discussed 1,400 calorie ADA diet and gave patient informational brochures.

Rapport. Rapport with the patient may sound like a vague thing, but it is a crucial aspect of treatment, as you recall by reviewing Chapter 2. Listening and smiling and using body language that communicates that you are available may seem like a flimsy way to prevent malpractice, but it is really at the root of the matter. **Maloccurrence usually results in a lawsuit because the patient feels wronged by the health professional.** Your best defense is to maintain a highly professional stance, be available, be a good listener, smile, communicate well, keep your patient informed, show your patient respect, and help your patient to like you. If something does go wrong, the patient with whom you have established rapport is the least likely to prosecute. One patient said about a court appearance, "They never listened to me in the hospital. Now they will have to." Although we want to help health professionals avoid suits, the use of rapport should not, of course, be interpreted as a method for the guilty to avoid justice.

Maintaining confidentiality is absolutely essential to building rapport. A patient is unlikely to sue over a breach of confidentiality alone, but if a maloccurrence should then arise the patient will be much more likely to sue. For example, a physician who tells an acquaintance of a patient that the patient had cancer is unlikely to be sued. But, if the physician failed to diagnose that cancer until it was too late, the patient would be much more likely to sue.

Good Standards of Practice. The essence of malpractice prevention lies in an honest, open, and communicative relationship with our patients. With such a relationship, much litigation could be prevented.

Documenting what we do forces us to review our own actions. If doubt arises, the health professional must discuss it with the patient and must offer an opinion about calling in a consultant. The health professional or the patient may call in the consultant, and the consultation also should be discussed. If, for example, a patient tells the dietitian that her urine sugars have been running high but her doctor said not to change the insulin, then the dietitian must contact the doctor.

Follow-up of the patient adds another dimension to the patient's care. Things may be seen in a different perspective during follow-up. Patients also feel more cared for if there is a follow-up telephone call or appointment. The patient also then has a chance to bring up any residual or hitherto unmentioned gripes, as well as to let the health professional know how treatment is progressing.

Abandonment is more a problem for diagnostic and assessment health professionals like physicians, dentists, and visiting nurses. These health professionals are expected to be reasonably available, and if they terminate care of a patient without making reasonable alternative arrangements for care, the patient can charge them with abandonment.

If, as a health care provider, you are contacted by an attorney about anything other than a worker's compensation or auto accident claim, it is probably safest to contact your own malpractice insurance company or your attorney. Sometimes letters are sent simply as a way of fishing for incriminating information. Other than for a worker's compensation or auto accident claim, you should not respond to telephone calls until you have obtained your own legal advice.

Malpractice is actual damage plus deviation from the standard of care. We can discourage lawsuits and also establish good standards of practice by establishing good communication with our patients, by building rapport with and remaining respectful of our patients, and by documenting all referrals and follow-ups.

The Right to Practice

In this country, the practice of health care is viewed, to a great extent, as a privilege. Health care providers must **earn** the right to practice. Depending on the health care specialty, earning this privilege may be fairly straightforward or quite complex, as reflected in our earlier discussion of health ethics. Ethical standards for health care professionals are guidelines intended to hold health professionals to exemplary standards. Because of these standards, the public can feel safe in placing its trust in the health care professional.

The right to practice is also based on an assumption of the value of the **rights of the patient**. Along with the privilege of being a health care provider comes the **duty** of caring for the patient. When it comes to providing patient care, the health care provider is expected to accept extraordinary responsibility. Health professionals often work continuous shifts 24 hours per day; weekends and holidays must be covered by many health care workers. The needs of the patient must always be accommodated.

Earning the right to practice differs from specialty to specialty and, in some cases, differs from state to state. The first phase of this process is universally a learning stage. For some, this learning involves on-the-job, usually clinic-based training; for others it is a combination of instructional and clinical training with heavy supervision. This latter type of program may span a few months or many years of both academic learning and supervised patient practice. In any case, the goal of the learning stage is to produce a competent health professional.

Legislation and Credentialing

Legal Concerns

The learning stage is, however, only the beginning of access to the health professions. Most health professionals must also deal with certification or licensure exams. Further, individual educational programs must usually be accredited by professional organizations related to the type of training the school, college, or hospital claims to provide.

Accreditation. Accreditation is the term used for the formal approval of an institution or educational program. If a program is judged to be of at least minimal acceptable standard, then accreditation is granted. Standards for accreditation are well-defined. Specific descriptions of these standards are published by the accrediting agencies and updated as necessary. The standards address such issues as the credentials of the teaching faculty, number of hours a specific training program should involve, the curriculum, and the physical needs of a good teaching program. By the time these aspects of education have been delineated, the educational training program has some precise criteria to satisfy which helps ensure standardization.

Accreditation is said to be a voluntary process. That is, no hospital or school is forced to subject itself to review by an outside body. But, without accreditation, a nonprofit hospital or a teaching program might as well not exist. Insurance coverage, government subsidies, and grants are denied to nonaccredited programs. Graduates of nonaccredited teaching programs usually are denied access to the field for which they have trained. As discussed below, being allowed to sit for a licensure exam usually is contingent upon holding a degree or certificate from an accredited educational program. So, although accreditation is a voluntary process, the sanctions against the nonaccredited are in many instances prohibitive.

Who are the Accrediting Agencies? The question of who the accrediting agencies should be has provoked political controversy within the health field for decades. In 1910, Abraham Flexner published a survey entitled "Medical Education in the United States and Canada" under a commission by the Carnegie Foundation. The report criticized many of the medical schools of the day. The American Medical Association (AMA) then took on the responsibility of accrediting these schools and ranking them as A, B, or C, depending on their standards of training. By 1938, only those institutions that had received A rankings still continued to train physicians, even though some of the B and C schools offered reasonable educational programs and provided access to education (especially for women, which was pretty much forbidden in the A schools). In the long run, however, the public wanted doctors who were graduates of A school programs and physicians wanted to be seen as A school material, leading to the rather rapid demise of the other institutions.

Most thinking citizens accepted the need for accreditation. Before the Flexner report there had been no real consistency to the training physicians received. Taken to an extreme, this meant that virtually any group of people could open a school and claim that their graduates were medically trained. The public needed some assurance about what the term *doctor* really represented.

Until quite recently, the Council on Medical Education of the AMA served as the accrediting agency for nearly all health care programs. When nursing programs wanted accreditation, for example, it was the AMA that established their standards, even though there was no accreditation for medical schools at that time. The host of specialties that emerged from nursing were then accredited by the AMA. Most prominent among these were occupational therapy and radiation therapy. Any health specialty that was supervised directly by physicians also received its accreditation through the AMA. These specialties included cytotechnology, medical technology, and medical records. In fact, nearly all of health care education is or was accredited through the AMA.

Although there are good reasons for AMA control of health care education, there are problems as well. As programs like nursing and physical therapy developed and matured, they began to understand their profession and its needs in a distinct manner. As health care became increasingly technical and specialized, it became difficult for physicians to really understand the needs of highly specialized subgroups. Many of the other (nonmedical) health professionals began to resent the control of their educational program by the AMA. They felt unable to claim true professionalism while being controlled by another profession.

Long exhaustive battles were fought between the AMA and other professional associations as they struggled for autonomy. Eventually programs like nursing, pharmacy, physical therapy, and dietetics won the right to accredit their own educational programs. For example, educational training programs in dietetics are now accredited by the American Dietetic Association. For many other health professional groups, accreditation is shared between the group's professional association and the AMA. Many of these groups continue to lobby for total self-management of accreditation.

Accreditation usually involves an on-site inspection of the educational facility by the accrediting team. The team reviews exhaustive reports compiled by those responsible for the teaching program to demonstrate their compliance to the standards. Students and faculty are also questioned by the team to verify critical aspects of the report. It is a time-consuming process for both the accrediting agency and the educational program. Several years are allowed between accreditation visits, but accreditation is not given indefinitely.

Loss of accreditation can occur when site visitors determine that a major portion of the required educational program is absent or deficient. Loss of accreditation also can occur if a significant number of weaknesses exist throughout the educational program. Generally, a previously well-run program with serious problems is granted a probationary status of accreditation or conditional accreditation. Such status gives the institution warning that accreditation will be revoked in X number of years if specific aspects of the program are not brought up to standard. Of course, determining whether the program has been brought up to standard involves another lengthy visitation for inspection and documentation of improvements. A probationary status can cost a program students because some students may not want to risk being enrolled in a program that could lose accreditation. Students who are already enrolled are not at jeopardy, however, because the U.S Department of Education mandates that current students graduate in good standing when accreditation is lost while they are enrolled.

As you can see, a good deal of political power is held by those who control accreditation. It is little wonder that professional organizations like the American Physical Therapy Association struggled with the AMA to gain control of its own educational curriculum.

Licensure.　Licensure is a mechanism designed to assure patients that the care they receive from a professional meets a reasonable standard. Licensure is a function of state governments, so requirements for gaining access to licensure exams can vary somewhat from state to state. Many states will not recognize a license issued by another state if the requirements for licensure are not regarded as equivalent. On the whole, however, most states use a standardized examination process for a given profession. That means that the licensure exam taken by a would-be psychologist in Connecticut is the same as the one a candidate in California takes. Some states even have reciprocal agreements; if you are licensed by one state, certain other states will automatically honor that license (reciprocity). Although most states allow a grace period of practice with an out-of-state license, health professionals must rapidly take and pass the new state's exam.

Generally the candidate health professional who seeks licensure must have graduated in good standing from an accredited educational program and can have no record of conviction of a felony (a serious crime such as murder). Also, letters of recommendation, sometimes called references, may be required from practitioners who already are licensed in that field. Such letters are expected to emphasize the character and ethical behavior of the candidate. In addition, many health professions demand that candidates complete a certain amount of supervised on-the-job training postgraduation before they are permitted to take a licensure exam. To summarize, access to licensure involves:

- Graduation from an accredited educational program.
- Lack of a criminal history.
- Character references.
- Proof of postgraduate training (for specified fields).

Weaknesses in Licensure.   Relicensure, which means continuing to hold a license once it has been attained, has been criticized as too static. Generally the health professional who wishes to keep his or her license simply pays a fee and checks a box claiming not to have been convicted of a felony over the past year. This procedure raises major concerns in the area of professional competency. These concerns are discussed later in this chapter under the comparison of legal and ethical controls.

Another weakness is that licensing mechanisms are usually general. That is, a license offers no legal control for specialty skills. For example, the license for an M.D. reads that the person is a licensed physician and surgeon whether or not he or she has had sufficient training to perform surgery. The right to perform surgery is granted as within the scope of medical practice. A physical therapist could, by virtue of the license, claim to be an expert in neurology when his or her primary emphasis actually is orthopedics. This discrepancy occurs because both neurology and orthopedics are within the scope of physical therapy practice. Later in this chapter we deal with how ethical standards work to control against general misrepresentation.

Certification as a Form of Licensure.   Certain health professionals receive their credentials through **certification** rather than licensure. Certification attests that an individual has attained qualifications for a specified occupation. It differs from licensure in that it does not exclude others from outside professional groups from performing the same tasks. For example, a cytotechnologist is certified as able to perform specified tests. Although this certification is an important credential for the cytotechnologist, other clinical laboratory personnel can perform the same tests because there are no laws prohibiting them from so doing.

Certification for Interprofessional Specialization.   Another assurance mechanism for the training of a professional is the voluntary use of certification. Health professionals may use formal certification procedures beyond licensure to demonstrate their competency in a specialty area. Specialty boards may require candidates to complete educational and clinical training as well as to pass an examination. Such boards generally are linked to professional organizations, not to state licensure bodies. A licensed health professional may then declare that she or he also is certified to do whatever the specialization is and name the certifying body.

Registration. Registration is often used interchangeably with both *licensure* and *certification*. For example, registered nurses and registered dietitians are most appropriately thought of as licensed (nurses in all states are, in fact, licensed). State statutes recognize and protect their scope of practice. In some states only the titles are protected by the term *registered*; the regulation of practice is not. In these states the term *registered* takes on the same meaning as certification. Although certification has the same general intent as licensure, that is, to protect the public from incompetent practitioners, certification and some forms of registration do not have the force of the law behind them as licensing does.

Protecting the Public: A Comparison of Legal and Ethical Controls

A review of Chapter 10 points up that the goals of both ethical principles and legislation overlap considerably. That is, the ethics of today's health care professional must focus on ensuring public safety and protecting the public's trust. The legislation of the health professional's credentials is also aimed at protecting the public. Both legislation and ethical values assume the prominence of the **patient's rights**. Credentialed health practitioners accept a **duty** of serving and caring that puts the needs of the patient before all other considerations. What might once have been understood by virtue of an etiquette is now spelled out in ethical principles and legislated statutes.

As mentioned in Chapter 10, the consequences of violating an ethical principle differ from the consequences of violating a law. Whereas violation of an ethical principle may result in sanctions such as reprimands, re-education, censure, or even expulsion from the profession, violation of the law may result in fines, imprisonment, or loss of licensure.

Although membership in a professional organization offers many benefits, it is not a necessary adjunct to practice. In states where one's profession is protected by licensure, however, loss of license equals loss of livelihood. The legal system carries the potential for more power via punishments than do the sanctions of the professional associations.

Legal and Ethical Controls Working Together. As mentioned earlier in this chapter, one of the weaknesses of licensure is the **static** nature of the license. That is, once a person has earned the privilege of a license, little effort is required to maintain that license. If sending in a renewal fee and checking a box (which states that the person has not been convicted of a felony in the past year) is the full extent of relicensure, how does this really protect the public? What happens to the alcoholic, drug dependent, or otherwise impaired health practitioner? And, what is even more often a risk, what guarantee does the public have of the continued education of their health care provider?

Say, for example, that a health professional entered the field some 20 years ago. Although she may have been bursting with knowledge and skill at that time, we have no way of knowing whether her knowledge and competency have continued to grow. Even with the best intentions of staying current, professionals with hectic and demanding practices can fall behind. It does not take many years of not having time to keep up with the journals to become out-of-date. Medical research and health care technology are advancing too rapidly for any practitioner to be judged fully competent if he or she does not make an effort to learn about new advancements in the field.

What can be done to protect the public from the technically stale professional? One possibility involves legislative directives that would tie relicensure to continuing education coursework. That is, no one would have their license renewed X number of years past examination unless they showed a transcript of relevant or approved courses they had completed during that time. Or, after X number of years, health professionals would be required to retake the state licensure exam. Many states already require that proof of continuing education be demonstrated for relicensure. Physicians and dietitians are two groups that require such updating. The requirement increases public respect for such professionals.

Another avenue of protection for the public exists in the area of ethical principles. Health professionals who are ethical and who are invested in membership within a professional organization must face the issues of responsibility and competency. Inherent in these principles is the tenet that health professionals must take responsibility for maintaining their own professional competency. To do less would be a violation of the public trust. Knowing that the health professional assumes this ethical responsibility helps us to believe that she or he would have great difficulty in ignoring the need for continuing education. Further, the ethical principle of competency helps to guard against the continued practice of an "unhealthy" professional. The alcoholic practitioner and his or her colleagues are duty bound to limit the practice of the impaired.

A second weakness of licensure laws is that they are **too general in defining scope of practice**. This generally leads to too little definition of precisely which specialties a given health professional is credentialed to perform. For example, a nurse primarily skilled in OB/GYN could, by virtue of licensure laws alone, claim to be a psychiatric nurse. Such a claim would be misleading to the public and therefore a violation of trust. One suggestion for controlling this problem has been the notion of a limited license. Such a license would attempt to restrict practice to those with educational training in a specific area related to their general health profession. Although limited licensure has some obvious benefits, it has not become a common practice, undoubtedly because of the complexity of screening and managing such a system and because of fear of the loss of flexibility that general licensure now affords.

Because limited licensure is not currently a reality, the burden of control falls on an assumption of ethical conduct. Once again the principle of competence mandates that the ethical health professional **accurately** represent her or his education, training specialties, limitations, and boundaries and that she or he perform duties in conjunction with careful preparation. Such statements serve as clear guidelines for those who wish to behave in an ethical and upright manner. The professional association is a watchdog in protecting the public from those who might exaggerate their capabilities.

When Controls Fail. As you read the above description of weaknesses in licensure laws, you no doubt became aware of the possibilities for misuse. Misuse might occur through ignorance of a law's intent, although that is no defense. Misuse might also occur if health professionals have not fine tuned their understanding of ethical principles. This is most likely to occur among those who are not active members of a professional association. Finally, misuse may occur among a small segment of health professionals whose intention it is to act fraudulently or with blatant disregard for public welfare.

Sexually seductive behavior by male health professionals with female patients is one of the common examples of disregard for the public good. Although it is possible that female health professionals may be guilty of similar misconduct and that patients may falsely accuse the health professional, this behavior by male health professionals bears further description.

Sexual impropriety with a patient is an obvious breach of ethical principles. A professional association typically expels a member from its ranks for life for such behavior. Legally the offending health professional could be sued. Guilt in this matter could result in paying heavy damage fees to the patient and in **loss of licensure**. Although being expelled from a professional association may be damaging, the health professional is really injured financially through the legal system.

Can the public be protected from such a philandering health professional? Probably not. He need only cross the state border to set up a new practice, ostensibly with a clean slate. If he was not found guilty of a felony, the new state may have no control over granting him a license. He may be licensed and receive the privilege of practicing by taking the new state's licensure exam or he may receive it automatically if the new state has a reciprocal agreement with the old state. Another possibility is that he may hold multiple licenses. Many health professionals do this either as a safeguard against being restrained from practice should they lose one license or simply because they have lived in a number of different states. In any case the problem is the same. States do not have reciprocity of licensure loss unless a felony has been committed. The culprit simply moves to another state. This lack of interfacing between state licensing bodies is a major frustration to those who have been mistreated by health professionals and is also a source of shame for ethical professionals. It remains a problem that needs resolving, although efforts are being made to track and list such persons.

Malpractice requires not only an unexpected event, but also proof that there was deviation from the standard of care and that mental or physical harm resulted. Abuses in the courtroom show how careful we must be to take care in our relationship with the patient. It is this relationship we must work on, not only to prevent malpractice but also because we will make ourselves more professional. The most common cause of suits is a lack of relationship or breakdown of the relationship between patient and health professional. Communication and documentation are the cornerstones of preventing malpractice suits.

The right of practice is a privilege the would-be health professional must earn. Where licensure is involved the scope of practice is legally protected. Only those who have prepared by virtue of educational training, who have not committed a felony, who have good character references, and who have proper clinical training may be licensed. Certification and registration also offer access to professional status and privileges.

Accreditation is a process of approving educational training programs for health professionals. The power inherent in this approval process has made accreditation a historically political tool.

Legal controls like licensure work best in tandem with the ethical controls of the various health professional associations. Weaknesses in each may be compensated for by the other. Still, there remains work to be done as each state struggles to deal appropriately with issues of interstate licensure.

Review

Accreditation: formal approval of an institution or educational program given by an outside agency

Autonomy: respecting patient's rights as an individual/the right to self govern

Beneficence: an act for the patient's well-being

Deep pocket: person or institution with more money

Flexner Report: Abraham Flexner's report on the quality of medical education (1910) which led to accreditation

Maloccurrence: untoward event (not necessarily actionable)

Malpractice: Maloccurrence which is actionable

Nonmaleficence: above all else do no harm

Reciprocal: both giving and taking/mutually beneficial

Static: unmoving, unchanging

Statute of limitation: after a certain period (e.g., five years)

SOAP: Method of record-keeping; acronym stands for Subjective, Objective, Assessment, Plan

1. What are the two prerequisites for malpractice?
2. Give examples of errors of omission and commission as malpractice.
3. What is the duty to inform?
4. Why may allied health professionals assume greater liability for malpractice in the future?
5. List the benefits to society of the current malpractice climate.
6. List the costs to society of the current malpractice climate.
7. What is the most common reason that a maloccurrence is taken to court?
8. How would you *personally* react to news that the school in which you are currently enrolled had just lost its accreditation?
9. Describe what actions you might take and/or your duty to take action when suspecting that a colleague has a drinking problem.
10. It has been suggested that mandating continuing education programs might serve as a means of improving protections of relicensure. Describe the pros and cons of this suggestion.

Advisory Panel on Professional Liability. Report of the Special Task Force on Professional Liability and Insurance. *Journal of the American Medical Association.* 1987. Feb. 13; 257(6): 810-812.

Editorial. "Defensive Medicine: It Costs But Does It Work?" *Journal of the American Medical Association*, 1987, May 22-29, 257 (20): 2801-2.

Inglehart, J.K., *New England Journal of Medicine* "The Professional Liability Crisis." The 1986 Duke Private Sector Conference. 1986, Oct. 23; 315(17): 1105-1108. 1986.

Quam, L. et al. *British Medical Journal.* "Medical Malpractice in Perspective — The American Experience." June 13; 294 (6586): 1529-32, 1987.

Williams, S., and Torrens, P. *Introduction to Health Services.* John Wiley and Sons, New York, NY. 1980.

Chapter

13

After reading this chapter, you should be able:
• To identify the roles of professional organizations.
• To list the benefits of organization membership to the health care providers.
• To demonstrate an understanding of the dynamics of these roles in terms of their impact on the profession, the individual, and society.
• To describe an overview of health care reimbursement mechanisms.
• To define various reimbursement models.

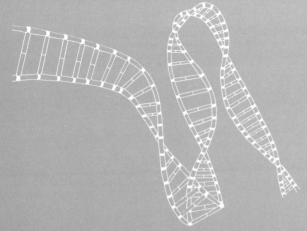

Professional Organizations

Professional organizations play a key role in the health care system. They unite a group of people who are all members of the same health care field. In the case of the American Society of Allied Health Professions, they unite a group of health care professionals and academicians who share common goals and interests.

The Role of Professional Organizations

Membership in professional organizations is voluntary. Members are traditionally required to pay dues to a state or national association or both. In return for dues, members anticipate certain dividends, which may include:

- Identification with other professionals that generally is of a prestigious nature.
- Collective political power as organizations work for the good of their members.
- Surveillance of the environment through maintaining a pro-active eye for the trends in health care and their impact on members so members can work on issues **before** it is too late to change them.
- A service link to members and their primary patient population.

Professional organizations play a role in:

- Developing and disseminating public policy.
- Promoting research.

- Fostering professional development with a view to standards of practice, credentialing, continuing education, and faculty development.
- Recruiting new professionals via advocacy for the profession and attention to manpower, job placement needs, and service to the public.

The strength and power of professional organizations serve to strengthen the position of their members. Collectively, professional organizations exert a tremendous influence on the entire health care system. Many key points in the first section of this chapter are taken from a chapter in *Allied Health Education* written by Glenda D. Price, dean of the School of Allied Health Professions at the University of Connecticut, and Carolyn Del Polito, executive director of the American Society of Allied Health Professions.

Public Policy Role

Political Activity.   Influencing public policy is one of the most vital roles of the professional organization as it continually surveys the health care environment. Its responsibilities involve analyzing legislative activities and disseminating its analysis to its members, to other health care organizations, and to the public. When political action is deemed appropriate the professional organization passes on information directly to policymakers. In fact, most major professional organizations maintain full-time lobbyists on their payrolls. These legislative advocates are familiar with all the laws pertaining to the members of their associations.

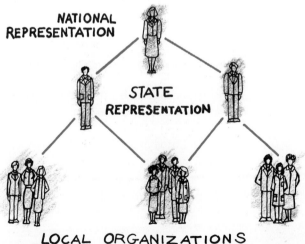

NATIONAL REPRESENTATION

STATE REPRESENTATION

LOCAL ORGANIZATIONS

Lobbyists strive to influence the thinking and voting of members of local, state, and federal policy bodies such as the state legislature and Congress. Professional groups promote or back specific candidates or politicians whom they believe will be sympathetic to the needs of their organization. Just as a professional organization will court a candidate whom it finds favorable, a candidate may woo a professional organization for an endorsement, hoping to receive the votes of its members. Obviously, the larger the organization is the more political power it holds because of the number of votes it commands. This fact alone accounts for the attraction of many to professional organizations. Whereas one health professional's voice alone might never be heard, the collective voice of the professional organization rings loud and clear.

Not only do professional organizations seek to monitor and influence trends in the environment, but they also seek to create them by introducing legislation aimed at protecting and benefiting their members. Since licensure defines and protects the scope of practice, professional organizations whose members are licensed obviously are committed to maintaining and protecting licensure laws. Many organizations whose members are not licensed consistently seek legislation to credential and protect their members.

The professional association serves as a watchdog for the health professional. This watchdog stays alert to protect its master, but it also **serves** the public, partly through disseminating information.

Information Dissemination.   After researching information relevant to its members, the professional association must see that this information reaches those who need it. By disseminating appropriate materials to health professionals, future health professionals, legislators, and health care consumers, the professional organization serves not only its members and future members, but also makes an impact on the climate of health care through legislative bodies and the public. At a time when technology is rapidly changing the parameters of health care, this is a most valuable service. (Review Chapter 10 on ethics for additional discussion.)

Examples of materials developed and supplied by professional associations include: charts of normal infant development, checklists for selecting a long-term health care facility, models for maintaining personal health records, brochures on sexually transmitted diseases, exercises and schedules for fitness programs, nutritional diets and consumption logs, and drug information guides. The possibilities for developing and using such materials are endless.

As technology changes and society evolves, demands for information will continue to be placed on professional organizations. They are in a uniquely resourceful place as they gather information because they are at the forefront of trends, their members are experts, and service to the client population already is one of their goals. Although the primary clients of the professional organizations are the professionals they serve, frequently they serve them best by being patient educators and advocates at the same time.

Research Role

How does a profession develop and expand its knowledge base? How does it decide which techniques and procedures are obsolete and which are successful? The obvious answer is through research. The difficulty with this answer is that until the last decade no one knew for sure who should do this research.

In the past, professional organizations defined a scope of practice without articulating a research base. Theoretically, then, a professional's body of knowledge appeared to be stagnant. Knowledge was in fact expanding, of course, but researchers came from outside the individual health professions. Much research was conducted by biomedical engineers, experimental scientists, chemists, and physician researchers. These researchers then passed their findings on to the practicing or clinical health professionals.

As health professionals began to evolve a stronger identity and to gain control of their own programs via changes in accreditation laws, they became committed to conducting **their own research**. This desire indicates a recognition of themselves as the experts. It speaks of a renewed commitment to the consumer population. And it demands professional competency in research skills.

This commitment to research has had a profound impact on both the health professionals themselves and on educational enterprises. Previously, most allied health professionals were considered entry level practitioners with associate or bachelor of science degrees. In some professions doctorates were not available even to teaching faculty. The emphasis on research has increased the educational demands on the professional. Possessing research credentials has become a trend for the modern allied health and nursing professional.

Professional organizations have encouraged this trend in two ways. First, they have committed resources — grant monies, publications, conference time — to support research. Second, they have demanded that more advanced degrees be obtained by entry level practitioners and have thus increased the pressure for preparation upon teaching faculty. For example, a master's degree may soon be demanded before one can become a dietitian or a physical therapist.

Professional Development Role

The role of the professional organization with respect to professional development is very broad. As noted under research, a decision such as placing high professional value on conducting research has a far-reaching effect on all professionals. The academic base, future members, current members, and the health care system are all influenced by such a shift in role and responsibilities.

Standards of Practice and Credentialing. In the second section of Chapter 12 we emphasized the role of the professional organization in developing standards of practice and the legislation of credentialing. We must emphasize again that the standards of practice, including the scope and boundaries of practice, are primarily defined by the professional association through legislative influences and by creating a value for a code of ethics. Having such a code is a primary way for members to maintain a specified standard.

Continuing Education. Professional development beyond initial or entry level academic preparation needs to be ensured. As noted in Chapter 12, chief among the flaws in licensure is a potential weakness in competency for professionals who have been away from the classroom too long. Professional associations attempt to ensure continued competency by offering continuing education programs. Members who attend regional or national conventions always have an opportunity to attend continuing education programs given by or sponsored by the professional association. Generally they focus on the latest patient problems, technologies, methods, or research relevant to that profession.

Journals published by an association represent another means of disseminating knowledge that will best continue the education of its members.

Some professional associations offer continuing education credits to programs they sanction. Such programs may conceivably be offered anywhere at any time so long as they are taught at an acceptable standard. As mentioned in Chapter 12, some professions tie continuing education credits to maintaining licensure or certification.

Although the caliber of continuing education programs is sometimes challenged, there can be little doubt that they provide a much needed service to many health care professionals. They are an integral part of professional activity. Ensuring continued professional competence may someday rely on a system of clinical auditors; professional associations will undoubtedly take key responsibility for developing such a system.

Faculty Development.   Professional associations set a standard for professionals and their teachers to attain. The associations then promote and support those activities that lead to the further development of faculty. These supports include funding research, publishing research articles, and sponsoring workshops, seminars, and continuing education programs.

Advocacy Role

A central theme of all professional organizations is advocacy for the profession. As we have noted, one dividend of association membership is identification with other prestigious individuals. The value of this link is significant. Who among us would join an organization whose members had a negative reputation? Promoting the image of the profession is vital to the survival of any professional association.

Recruitment and Job Placement.   Recruiting new members to the profession is essential to success. One of the reasons for promoting the image of the profession is to gain new members. If members of a profession are attractive to student groups and if their work looks meaningful and benefits society as well as themselves, then new people will be attracted to the field.

Part of this attraction relies on what kind of educational preparation a profession requires. Some people are attracted to a profession because the educational preparation is rigorous; others turn away for the same reason. It is therefore important to the professional association that academic programs reflect the true nature of the field. In that way, those who are compatible with the required work will be attracted to the profession.

In general, a professional organization such as the American Society of Allied Health Professions (ASAHP) is concerned with broad-based recruitment in all allied health fields. ASAHP's chief concerns are the **image** of the allied health professions, **service** to the health care community, and **access** to professional membership. A value held by most members of the allied health professions is that professional associations must include at least representative membership from minority populations. Recruiting members from both genders and from all ethnic, cultural, and socio-economic backgrounds is essential. This focus of recruitment carries with it a responsibility to help those recruited gain access to higher education and to find jobs.

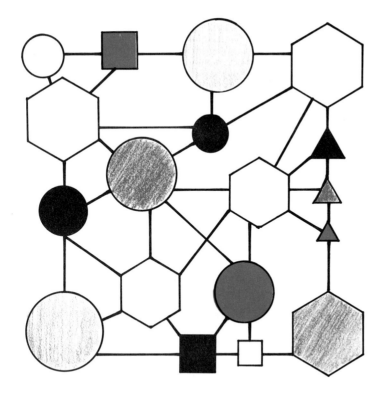

Indeed, all new recruits to a field are wise to examine the job opportunities. As a further commitment to advocacy of the profession, professional organizations stay current on the employment needs of their field. Many provide formal placement services and advertise job openings. The informal network of the professional association is also an advantageous way for new health professionals to learn about job opportunities. This fact may be a key reason that many future health professionals become **student members** of their professional associations. Students who attend professional meetings make the kinds of contacts that may lead to jobs.

Service. The image of providing service is universal for health professionals. Although there are individuals who say they became health professionals purely for the money or the prestige, most student health professionals say they wanted to help people (Adams 1981). Any health professional group that fails to advocate altruism and commitment to the consumer commits a grevious error.

If the image of the health professional is to remain honorable, it must always reflect the service commitment. For this reason the strongest professional advocacy focuses on the needs of society.

Health professional organizations typically act as advocates for the needs of the special populations they serve most. For example, physical therapists often volunteer their time to Special Olympics or Easter Seal Programs, ophthalmologists are associated with campaigns for good eye care, pediatricians are associated with prenatal clinics, and nurses are associated with a multitude of special needs such as diabetes and blood pressure screenings.

The Reimbursement Mechanism and Its Link with Professional Organizations

How health care is paid for in the United States is always a lively topic for discussion. One reason is the high cost of care. In 1985 health care costs were approximately $425 billion or 10.7 percent of the gross national product.* The proportion of the individual family's income dollar and the costs to employers for health care benefits have outstripped other costs.

Historically, free enterprise and competition have functioned in health care as well as in other segments of society. But, because the federal government is the largest payer for health services and because the federal treasury can no longer support deficit spending, attempts have been made to reduce the cost of health care. Until recently, however, competition among providers of care has not had an impact on costs. Because consumers have not traditionally challenged the cost of care, there has been little incentive from the private sector to contain costs.

Third party payment, which means payment by an individual or agency other than the recipient of care, began in the 1930's with the establishment of Blue Cross and Blue Shield. Because of the financial conditions of that period (the Depression), many persons could not pay for health services. Health care providers had difficulty getting paid for services rendered. Insurance programs met the needs of both recipients and providers.

> The section of this chapter on "The Reimbursement Mechanism and Its Link with Professional Organizations" was written by Glenda D. Price, Dean, School of Allied Health Professions, University of Connecticut, Storrs. Dr. Price has served as president of the American Society for Medical Technology and the National Certification Agency for Medical Laboratory Professions and the National Committee for Health Certifying Agencies.

*Statistical Abstracts, U.S. Department of Commerce, 107th edition, published in 1987. (Latest available figures are for 1985.)

During World War II and in the postwar era, employers began to provide health insurance coverage as a benefit of employment. Insurance programs were attractive to employers because the premiums were tax deductible as a business expense. They were attractive to employees because health care services were available without the necessity of accounting for the money as taxable income. Many individuals who had jobs thus had access to quality health care as a benefit of their employment. Those who were unemployed and had no other sources of income found it difficult to receive health care services.

With the advent of the Medicare and Medicaid programs in 1965, health care in this country became thought of as a right of all citizens. No longer was quality care restricted to those who could afford to pay. The government guaranteed access to care to everyone. As a result of this changing philosophy, costs soared as individuals took advantage of their right and used the health care delivery system.

Reimbursement Models

Fee-for-Service.   With fee-for-service, the practitioner or institution is paid directly for providing a health service. Consistent with their professional credentials, individual professionals have the freedom to determine their own rates, the conditions under which they practice, the number and type of patients/clients they serve, and the scope of their practice.

The fee-for-service system has created great imbalances in access to health care services and is subject to multiple abuses. Because of the high costs involved, many people have limited or no access to health care. Third party reimbursement allows for varying levels of care depending on the extent of coverage, but in most instances there are real limits beyond which there is no reimbursement.

Prepayment Systems.   Prepayment systems are based on the idea that a prepaid per-person managed care process will guarantee access to high quality services at a known cost. A predetermined, prepaid amount for a selected group of recipients is designated for a specific provider to provide a wide range of services. Clients pay a set fee and receive subsequent care at no or a minimal additional charge at the time service is rendered.

Prepayment systems have the advantage of a predictable cost, a health care provider who is obligated to provide service, and continual access to care by the recipient group.

The health maintenance organization (HMO) is the typical model for prepayment systems. Generally an employer contracts with an HMO to provide service to its employees at a per-person rate for the company. The employee and covered dependents then have access to a full range of health care as contracted. The employee is certain of who will provide his or her care and knows what specific additional charges will be levied.

Because this payment system is based on how many persons use it, the HMO has an incentive to keep its clientele healthy. Healthy persons require less medical service, which keeps costs to the HMO to a minimum. Health promotion and disease prevention programs are, therefore, frequently an additional benefit to the insured.

Another model for prepayment systems is the individual practice association (IPA). The IPA creates a network of physicians with widely diverse and dispersed offices. The physicians use a range of hospitals and ancillary services, but they are linked through an administrative organization to provide service to a recipient population on a prepaid per-person basis.

The IPA has all the advantages of an HMO plus the added benefit of allowing the insured to select from a wide choice of physicians and establish traditional rapport with a single physician.

The preferred provider organization (PPO) is the newest of the payment systems. This model assumes some of the characteristics of the prepayment systems yet allows for fee-for-service reimbursement. The PPO consists of a group of providers who agree to a standard fee schedule yet retain total authority in determining which services they will offer and which clients they will accept. No per-person arrangement is involved. The providers agree to the prenegotiated fee schedule in exchange for referrals from the employer or insurance carrier.

The concept of utilization management or managed care is inherent in the PPO system. The medical necessity for the care is determined first so that a conscious decision can be made about the efficiency and effectiveness of each procedure. Utilization of services is managed by the health care providers with all attempts made to ensure the highest quality of care and reflect the most economical processes. The recipient benefits from contact with a provider of his/her choice and a system designed to standardize costs.

Issues for Practitioners

No matter what the mechanism, the ability of various health care providers to receive direct third party reimbursement for their services is an issue for professional associations. **Individual practitioners who receive direct payment have greater control over their professional affairs** than do those who cannot receive direct reimbursement. Most patients choose their health care provider based on the ability to be reimbursed for service.

Independence. Throughout history, physicians and dentists have received a fee for service and have been reimbursed by all insurance programs. Recently, however, nonphysician providers have asserted that their services should be eligible for direct payment rather than payment through an institution or another provider such as a physician or dentist. For example, optometrists, psychologists, and podiatrists have successfully argued that they should be available as providers of service to the patient. They now receive direct reimbursement because they provide similar service as that provided by a physician. The underlying issue is the independence of practice.

Given the numerous tests, treatments, modalities, concepts, and principles related to health care today, it is no longer possible for any one professional to know all that might be needed to successfully diagnose and treat a patient. Because multiple practitioners are involved in the care of each client, the specialized expertise that each brings to the situation should be recognized and reimbursed.

The degree of independent judgment that each professional is able to exercise during the evaluation and treatment process is generally the factor that determines their ability to receive third party reimbursement. Licensure status is another major factor.

Many allied health professionals believe that they can provide services at a lower cost to the recipient and that their services are equal to or of higher quality than services that can be provided by certain professionals who are eligible for third party reimbursement. Unfortunately, to date, too few studies that demonstrate the cost effectiveness and efficacy of the care provided by these practitioners have been conducted. The freedom necessary to function in an indepen-

dent manner is many times impeded by state licensure laws. These laws inhibit those who do not possess a license from providing certain services.

The ability to receive third party reimbursement has been viewed as one of the prerequisites of independent practice. Many professional groups, therefore, have focused attention on the decison makers involved in the process of reimbursement. This enhances the probability that their members might receive direct reimbursement. Third party reimbursement signals a provider with the confidence of the insurers.

Compensation Level. Besides the perception of independence, health care practitioners are concerned with the amount of compensation provided under some reimbursement systems. The prepaid per person systems generally do not allow for a practitioner or group to increase their compensation easily without increasing the number of clients enrolled in the program. Individuals with chronic or severe conditions benefit from such programs, but the health care provider receives no additional income for extensive services provided to such individuals.

While methods of capitation vary, for the most part, prepaid systems provide a guaranteed level of income for the practitioner or group participating in the program. A known level of income provides a basis for professionals to concentrate on efficient, effective care for each client. They need not pay much attention to soliciting additional patients and competing with other practitioners.

Role of Professional Organizations

Professional associations undertake advocacy and political activities with respect to reimbursement issues in other arenas. The well-organized and well-financed AMA initially voiced strong opposition to the Medicare and Medicaid programs. Subsequent progress in developing reimbursement mechanisms came from within the health care establishment and its organized professional groups as well as for the public sector.

Examples of activities in which associations have participated include:

- Lobbying for reimbursement of a service rather than reimbursement of the provider of the service.
- Influencing the decision to include specific services in insurance programs.
- Undertaking legislative initiatives to include reimbursable services within the scope of practice of licensed prac-

titioners.

- Promoting the reimbursement of health promotion and disease prevention services.
- Functioning as an administrative structure for a loosely associated group of practitioners.
- Gathering and disseminating information on the advantages and disadvantages of various reimbursement systems.
- Fighting for licensure status for their members.

To the degree that their members are affected professional associations become involved in initiating, implementing, promulgating, and supporting reimbursement mechanisms. The association role of fostering the welfare of its members is demonstrated no where better than in this arena.

Chapter Summary

The roles of the professional organization are to (1) influence and survey public policy, (2) promote research endeavors within its own field, (3) seek to continue the development of its members by setting standards of practice and credentialing, continuing education, and faculty development, and (4) promote the profession through recruitment, access, and job placement and maintain the image of the professional as a service provider.

Reimbursement for the services of health care professionals falls into two major categories: fee-for-service and prepayment. Although the fee-for-service approach is a time-honored mechanism, it has not been universally applicable to all practitioners. Further, it has the disadvantage of eliminating individuals who cannot afford to pay for health care.

Prepayment per person systems enhance the probability of access to care for larger numbers of the population and provide a guaranteed income to providers. Fee schedules that are fixed by a group of practitioners are another approach to reimbursement that improves access to care.

Professional associations include reimbursement issues in their advocacy and political activities. Additionally, they provide information to their members and to the public on the advantages and disadvantages of various reimbursement systems.

Access: a way, means, or right to approach

Advocate: a person who works on behalf of another, the act of working for another

Altruism: done for the good of others

Ancillary: additional, helping, auxiliary

Collective: gathered into a whole; characteristic of individuals acting together for a common good

Disseminating: passing out (information), making something known to others

Fee-for-service: direct payment to provider of a service. Money may come from the recipient's pocket or a third-party payer but is paid out for each service rendered (may decrease access)

Prepayment system: predetermined amount paid in *advance* to health care provider (either individual or institution) to cover a specific group's health care needs for a specified length of time (may increase access)

Third-party payment: reimbursement by someone or by an agency on behalf of another; when an insurance company pays for an individual's (policyholder's) care, it is a third-party payer

1. What are the advantages for the health care provider to membership in a professional organization?
2. What does the professional organization contribute to society?
3. How does the professional organization influence the political system? How does it influence health care costs?
4. Assume you are a health care professional who belongs to, and is very active in, a professional association. Your dues and time investment payoff in many advancements for your profession. How do you feel about other members of your profession receiving benefits you have worked for when they refuse to join the professional association?
5. How do insurance companies manage to pay for health care and still make a profit?
6. Compare and contrast the value of a fee-for-service system versus a prepaid system.
7. Describe any potential you see for a *decrease* in the *quality* of health care when offered by a prepaid provider.
8. How do you think the method of reimbursement may affect the style and quality of care rendered by a health professional?

Additional Reading

Adams, C. H. 1981. "Responsible Counseling for Prospective Allied Health Students." *The Guidance Clinic.* Parker Publishing Co.: New York, pp. 4-8.

Hershey, N. 1987. "Policy Issues Relevant to Independent Practice of the Health Professions." Paper presented at the Independent Practice Conference, Washington, D.C., June.

Price, G. D. and C. Del Polito. 1988. "The Role of Professional Associations in Allied Health Education." In *Allied Health Education*, N. Farber and E. McTernon, Eds., Charles C. Thomas: Springfield, IL.

Ramsey, J., et al. 1982. "Physicians and Nurse Practitioners: Do They Provide Equivalent Health Care?" *American Journal of Public Health*, pp. 721-55.

Starr, P. 1982. *The Social Transformation of American Medicine.* New York: Basic Books.

Index

E

F

G

O

P